THE ENGLISH THEATRICAL AVANT-GARDE, 1900–1925

The English Theatrical Avant-Garde, 1900–1925 unearths an extensive range of hitherto forgotten or ignored theatre practices. In doing so it reveals some of the well-known figures of the early twentieth-century English theatre in a strikingly new light. It fluently describes an intensity of innovation and experiment that together made the Edwardian theatre rather more radical, and rather more queer, than we've ever thought.

Where the majority of writing on the early twentieth-century theatrical avant-garde is concerned with European movements and experiments, English activity of the period is often seen as parochial and conservative – mainly realism and issues-based drama. This book presents a new model of how avant-gardes might work; a model based not on masculine individualism but on communal inclusion. In describing this fascinating material, the author introduces us to many new figures and shows familiar ones in different ways: there's Florence Farr, independent woman; Bob Trevelyan, radical pacifist and music drama pioneer; Granville Barker doing fairy plays while de-dramatising drama; Laurence Housman, socialist, homosexual, scripting St Francis; and the oddly modern J.M. Barrie. Together they made theatre practices rich in their diversity but consistent in their attempt to be new, producing a theatrical avant-garde unlike any other.

This is a vital and indispensable new study for scholars and students of early twentieth-century theatre in England and beyond.

Simon Shepherd is a Fellow of the British Academy and Professor Emeritus of Theatre at the Royal Central School of Speech and Drama. He has published on the cultural history of theatre, performance theory and formal analysis of drama. His most recent books are *The Unknown Granville Barker* (2021) and *The Cambridge Introduction to Performance Theory* (2016).

THE ENGLISH THEATRICAL AVANT-GARDE, 1900–1925

Simon Shepherd

Routledge
Taylor & Francis Group
LONDON AND NEW YORK

Designed cover image: Karl Hagedorn, design for *Harbour*, 1921.
The Unnamed Book, 1924. Reproduced by permission of Sue Cowan and Nicholas Harris.

First published 2023
by Routledge
4 Park Square, Milton Park, Abingdon, Oxon OX14 4RN

and by Routledge
605 Third Avenue, New York, NY 10158

Routledge is an imprint of the Taylor & Francis Group, an informa business

© 2023 Simon Shepherd

The right of Simon Shepherd to be identified as author of this work has been asserted in accordance with sections 77 and 78 of the Copyright, Designs and Patents Act 1988.

All rights reserved. No part of this book may be reprinted or reproduced or utilised in any form or by any electronic, mechanical, or other means, now known or hereafter invented, including photocopying and recording, or in any information storage or retrieval system, without permission in writing from the publishers.

Trademark notice: Product or corporate names may be trademarks or registered trademarks, and are used only for identification and explanation without intent to infringe.

British Library Cataloguing-in-Publication Data
A catalogue record for this book is available from the British Library

ISBN: 9780367470890 (hbk)
ISBN: 9780367470852 (pbk)
ISBN: 9781003033295 (ebk)

DOI: 10.4324/9781003033295

Typeset in Bembo
by KnowledgeWorks Global Ltd.

PREFACE

If most of the theatre histories are to be believed, there is nothing in this book. There was, they suggest, next to no English theatrical avant-garde between 1900 and 1925. So we may as well stop here.

Unless we want to try lifting a few stones to peer at the life underneath. In the historical darkness, we begin to discern some creatures of wondrous shapes and iridescent colours. And who knows, maybe eventually an avant-garde mincing around on its many legs.

Under the first stone, in Chapter 1, we see how, soon into the new century, dominant conventions of realist stage representation are explored and implode. Chapter 2 describes the engagement with ideas of theatrical modernity, particularly those associated with Europe. In Chapter 3, the central group of verse dramatists, a coterie making explicit challenge to dominant practices, comes close to what is often understood as an avant-garde. But in Chapter 4, the concept of avant-garde is discovered to be shifting and baggy, and not always the sort of thing we thought we were looking for, especially when it comes to the English theatre. After being largely concerned with forms, ideas, particularly about sexuality, are the main concern of the last chapter, which describes how that quaint period piece the fantasy play might be seen as disruptively modern. The chapters are deliberately arranged in this order but they don't depend on it. The intention is to give a feel for some of the practices before we try to decide if they are avant-garde or not.

CONTENTS

List of Illustrations   *viii*
Acknowledgements   *x*

1   Experimental theatre   1

2   Modernities   28

3   Renovation of the stage   59

4   Advanced guards   102

5   Fantasy play   130

Index   *164*

ILLUSTRATIONS

2.1 Florence Farr as Phaedra in Thomas Sturge Moore's *Aphrodite against Artemis*, designed by Charles Ricketts, 1906. MS 982/G/3. Senate House Library, University of London. 56
2.2 Charles Ricketts, design for *Salome*, 1906. Victoria and Albert Museum, London. Reproduced by permission of Leonie Sturge Moore and Charmian O'Neil. 57
2.3 Norman Wilkinson, design for *Twelfth Night*: Orsino's Court, 'Come away, death', 1912. Granville Barker promptbook for Savoy Theatre, 1912. University of Michigan Library. 57
2.4 Charles Ricketts, design for *The Death of Tintagiles*, 1913. The Gordon Bottomley papers, Add MS 88957/6/45. The British Library. 58
2.5 Norman Wilkinson, design for *Iphigenia in Tauris*, 1912/1915. Scrapbooks. Yale University Library. 58
3.1 Lilian Reburn, mask designs for *The Loves of the Elements*, 1919. *The Unnamed Book*, 1924. 99
3.2 Claud Lovat Fraser, The Forest of Arden, design for *As You Like It*, 1919. Claud Lovat Fraser and Grace Crawford Lovat Fraser Collections, Bryn Mawr College Libraries. Reproduced by permission of Bryn Mawr College Libraries. 100
3.3 Claud Lovat Fraser, Rosalind's Cottage, design for *As You Like It*, 1919. Claud Lovat Fraser and Grace Crawford Lovat Fraser Collections, Bryn Mawr College Libraries. Reproduced by permission of Bryn Mawr College Libraries. 100

3.4 Paul Nash, design for *The Truth about the Russian Dancers*,
     1920. Gordon Bottomley papers, Add MS 88957/4/10.
     The British Library. 101
3.5 Karl Hagedorn, design for *Harbour*, 1921. *The Unnamed
     Book*, 1924. Reproduced by permission of Sue Cowan
     and Nicholas Harris. 101

ACKNOWLEDGEMENTS

All sorts of people have been helpful in various ways. Thanks are due to Jeff Cooper for discussions of Abercrombie's unpublished letters, Dennis Kennedy and Niall Slater for generously sharing their separate researches into Harley Granville Barker; Scirard Lancelyn Green for making available his father's collection of photographs; Janette Dillon and Brean Hammond for reading Chapter 1 (and alerting me to Vaughan Williams' Whitman); Christopher Morash for sharing, with huge scholarly generosity, his Yeats work before it was even published; Scott Palmer for putting me right on gas lighting; Jonathan Pitches for reading Chapter 4 and Mick Wallis for endless genealogical and newspaper searches together with an encyclopaedic knowledge of cultural networks of the period. For help with research expenses I'm grateful to Maria Delgado and Royal Central School of Speech and Drama. Archivists who put in time to search for material include Amy Cary at Raynor Memorial Libraries, Marquette University; Ian Douglas at Bedales; Marianne Hansen at Bryn Mawr College Libraries; Juli and Pablo Alvarez at University of Michigan Library; Jane Muskett at Chethams; Helen Roberts at University of Surrey; Ursula Romero at the Lilly Library, University of Indiana; Alec Smith at University of Pennsylvania Library; also staff in digital services at the British Library St Pancras who sped things through and the wonderfully helpful counter staff at British Library Boston Spa. Finally I must thank Steph Hines at Routledge for her efficiency and speed. Rights holders of material used are acknowledged below, with my thanks.

> Unpublished work by Harley Granville Barker is reproduced by permission of The Society of Authors as the Literary Representative of the Estate of Harley Granville Barker.
> Unpublished work from the archive of Gordon Bottomley is reproduced by permission of Scirard Lancelyn Green.

Unpublished work by Claud Lovat Fraser is reproduced by permission of Bryn Mawr College Libraries.

Unpublished work by Laurence Housman is reproduced by permission of Bryn Mawr College Libraries.

Unpublished work from the archive of Thomas Sturge Moore is reproduced by permission of Leonie Sturge Moore and Charmian O'Neil.

Unpublished work from the archive of Charles Ricketts is reproduced by permission of Leonie Sturge Moore and Charmian O'Neil.

A published design by Karl Hagedorn is reproduced by permission of Sue Cowan and Nicholas Harris.

All efforts have been made to identify and contact the rights holders of the copyrighted material used in this book. Any rights holders who believe that their material has been used without permission should please contact the publisher.

1
EXPERIMENTAL THEATRE

It begins in darkness. The stage is still and quiet. Leaves occasionally rustle. Suddenly a shrill, frightened scream. A woman runs on, panting. A man follows. 'I apologise', he says. She asks: 'Why is it so dark?' He says he's sorry for having kissed her. She replies: 'Thank you. Mind the steps down'. Gradually other people appear, all feeling their way in the dark. One carries an unlit candlestick and starts talking to the wrong person. The woman who first entered has in the darkness shrunk silently to the edge.

A conversation develops during which it becomes clear that when the woman screamed the man won a bet he had taken with the other men. Their talk then turns to the card game which had been interrupted by the scream. Silently the owner of the house has joined them on stage. Up to this point the first woman, Ann, has requested that the cause of her scream, the kiss, not be made public. Now, with five other people distributed in darkness across the stage, she abruptly declares: 'I was kissed'. What follows is 'a pause of some discomfort' (Barker 1967: 30–33). There is a brief embarrassed exchange about insult and apology and then another short pause. By now the light of dawn has increased enough to show all the faces plainly. We are looking at people in a faded formal garden sometime in the eighteenth century.

But in real time it is January 1902. We are sitting in the Royalty Theatre in London's Soho. Eleven years ago the theatre had been notorious because members of a group called the Independent Theatre, founded by J.T. Grein, used it to stage Ibsen's *Ghosts*, causing scandal and outrage among reviewers and some audiences. Today the players in front of us are members of the Stage Society. Founded in 1899, with an initial membership of 300, it differed from its predecessor in the range of work it performed. The Independent Theatre mainly did 'foreign successes […] faithfully translated'. As Schoonderwoerd says, 'the only thing it was really independent of was the commercial theatre' (1963: 116, 118).

2 Experimental theatre

The Stage Society by contrast was explicitly committed to being an 'Experimental Theatre'. Its plays were selected according to the Society's three basic principles: first, and most importantly, 'the search for new playwrights'; then 'the production of classical and contemporary foreign plays'; and, third, 'the production of plays for which the Censor has refused a licence' (Incorporated Stage Society 1909: 8). By January 1902 it had done 17 productions, both one-act and full-length. Of these the 'foreign' ones were by Hauptmann, Ibsen and Maeterlinck, and Euripides as translated by Gilbert Murray. The inaugural production on 26 November 1899 was Bernard Shaw's *You Never Can Tell*, a play not in itself particularly experimental but its author had a certain amount of notoriety, and was thus recognisable, from having been associated with the Independent Theatre. Today, however, in January 1902, we are watching a play by a new dramatist, the actor Granville Barker (1877–1946). He has directed it himself and it is called *The Marrying of Ann Leete*.

Anxious pauses

As members of an 'Experimental' theatre society, the audience around us have seen previous productions and maybe also the scandalous works by Ibsen. They are used to plays that bluntly tackle difficult social issues. This time, however, their expectations get a slight jolt. For years serious plays, however difficult or shocking, had begun with the curtain opening to reveal a furnished room or garden or some such, the features of which can be easily interpreted and socially categorised. Such a set draws the eye into its depth, enabling it to be imaginatively inhabited by a viewer. The recognisable geometry of a room's walls, window frames and fixed furnishings facilitate the viewers' secure positioning of themselves within that space. As *Ann Leete* opens the viewers are, by contrast, peering into darkness. The space can't be easily read. No sense can be made of the distribution of bodies on stage. It's difficult to get bearings in relation to it. When finally there's enough light to see the speakers, we realise they're not even in our world. They're from the eighteenth century. Young Mr Barker is playing games with our expectations. By simple manipulation of the scenography, he has wobbled the ease with which we habitually read and take visual possession of the setting in front of us. But that, as we shall see, was only the start of the problems.

First, however, we must move to another theatre in the same part of London. We have to go there at this point because the aim of this opening chapter is to explore the emergence just after 1900 of new ways of using, and indeed upsetting, the dominant form of social realism. The exploration will initially be hung on three specific instances in which dramatists play with the forms and circumstances available to them in order to move on from where theatre – and ideas – had been previously.

So we now find ourselves in the Duke of York's at Piccadilly Circus. It is late in the same year, 1902, but this is not a club performance. It's a commercial show mounted by the American entrepreneur Charles Frohman (1856–1915). The dramatist, J.M. Barrie (1860–1937), is by no means a newcomer. He has already written four plays and a fifth opened with great success about six weeks before. At the start of the new play, a butler is showing a young gentleman into a very comfortably furnished wealthy room. It's a special day, the monthly event when the master of the house, an aristocrat of Radical leanings, has his family entertain to tea their servants, on supposedly equal terms. It is clear that the butler disapproves of both the event and its intentions.

The guest that he shows in, Ernest, has been asked to give a short speech, so he proceeds to try out various positions and postures. Peering over the back of a very high chair, in dumb show he addresses a gathering. The butler helpfully gives him a stool to stand on, and leaves. Ernest's immediate response is angrily to throw the stool aside, but changing his mind picks it up again. As he does two young women enter. They ask why he is holding a stool. He explains that he was practising holding a tea-tray and thus, when another sister comes in, he promptly offers her the stool as if he were carrying tea. All three women droop with boredom and laziness. He, however, would like to impress them, so at the right moment he produces an epigram: 'Agatha, I'm not young enough to know everything'. Agatha doesn't understand, nor do her sisters. Catherine suggests he try it out on the young clergyman who has just entered. But he doesn't understand it either. So Lady Mary suggests Ernest repeat it very very slowly. The clergyman then says he's made a mistake, saying 'young' instead of 'old'. In desperation Ernest turns to the butler: 'It is an anxious moment', says the stage direction, 'but a smile is at length extorted from Crichton as with a corkscrew'. 'Thank you, sir', says the butler, and leaves (Barrie 1948: 345–48).

This is the opening of *The Admirable Crichton*. The immediate setting of the beautiful wealthy house is familiar enough although the occasion – the 'Radical' entertaining of servants as equals – is more unusual. Mockery of such an event allows the audience to place itself safely somewhere different from such class aberrations. But whatever their Radicalism all members of the family seem a good-for-nothing lot, pretentious, rich and idle. This is the audience for Ernest's failure at epigrams. Hitherto, in a main strand of recent drama, an audience watching this social class or indeed the one beneath it might have expected to be entertained by the brilliance of conversation. Understanding and laughing with that brilliance permits an audience as it were to inhabit the same milieu as is depicted on stage. Here, however, the epigram is painfully laboured. It is misunderstood, repeated, slowed down, more or less taken apart. Holbrook Jackson, writing in 1913, saw epigrams as a by now out-of-date feature of the 1890s (1988: 172–76). And the specific ancestry of the epigram is of course flagged in the character's name. Wilde's *Importance of Being Earnest* had been a sensation seven years before. This was not missed by the cleverest of contemporary Edwardian critics, Percy Howe (1886–1944), who saw in Ernest the 'symbol' of Barrie's 'reaction from the drama of verbal decoration' and that Barrie's use of him here 'saved us' from 'a long course of discipleship' to such drama (Howe 1913: 124). But it's not just the demolition of the epigram that unsettles a hitherto comfortable relationship between stage and audience.

Most plays that begin in a furnished room either discover people already there or just entering to it. In each case, they use the facilities of the room as is customary for those facilities. They sit in the chairs, turn on lights, pour drinks, poke the fire, kick the dog. When we watch Ernest's dumb-show by contrast we are looking at the room not as a place which we might in fantasy inhabit but as a site of clowning, external to us. Ernest's efforts to peer over the chair show him in an awkward relationship to the furnishings. This awkwardness becomes comically estranged when the footstool is put to use as a tray. It is perverted from its supposedly natural function and starts to lead a theatrical life of its own, still a practical object, but not in the proper way. This is the prelude to and context for Barrie's demolition of the epigram.

The injured epigram's final point of rest is with the butler. Crichton is meticulous in his duties and tight-lipped as to his own opinions. The smile that is extracted from him is highly ambivalent. It hovers between getting the joke, dutifully rewarding Ernest and cynically humouring the whole bunch of them. In the anxiety of the pause there's the merest suggestion of their dependence on his approbation. Act 2 will demonstrate the extent of that dependence but for the moment it is glanced, then gone. Barrie's management of the degrees of embarrassment, his secure balancing of discomfort and comedy, his capacity, above all, to suggest several things at once, led to the play being immensely successful.

From here we step ahead just over four years and return to the Stage Society performing the third of our opening examples. This time it is late in the play. A party is gathered in a country house in Leicestershire. It is after dinner, tension is in the air. The jewellery glitters sharply. Early in the play we have learnt that the son of the house, Geoffrey, has fallen in love with a girl he met in London. She is not of his class, and the relationship has caused consternation among his mother's friends. But his mother's way of handling the situation is to show no opposition. Instead she has invited to stay not only the girl, Ethel, but her mother, Mrs Borridge. This causes embarrassment even to Geoffrey, in that Mrs Borridge is so capaciously of the wrong class, wrong taste, wrong bearing. Geoffrey's mother's plan to invite the Borridges to stay for a week, with all due appearance of helpfulness and sociability, effectively dislodges them from their native territory thereby not only exposing them to the conditions of upper-class provincial life but also demonstrating that exposure to Geoffrey. Over the week Ethel becomes increasingly annoyed with being patronised and humiliated, while her mother, luxuriating in her new environment, rather enjoys herself. This all winds to a climax at the party given for the neighbouring toffs, which is where we now find them. As after-dinner entertainment, Geoffrey's childhood friend Mabel – a girl of remorselessly suitable class – is invited to sing a song at the piano. She elects to sing Schubert, in German to boot. Her mother listens with 'seraphic appreciation', most of the other guests listen attentively, Ethel ignores it and Mrs Borridge, discovering it to be both in German and long, falls asleep. When Mabel has finished, the Rector invites Ethel to sing. She demurs at first, then takes a seat at the piano. After a slight pause in which she glances at Geoffrey and Mabel, she launches into a song the chorus of which goes: 'Stop that, Joey! Stow it, Joe!/Stop that ticklin'' when I tell yer toe./ You're too free to suit a girl like me,/Just you stop that ticklin' or I'll slap yer!' As she builds to the second chorus, with a look specifically at Mabel's snobbish mother, she invites everyone to join in and herself sings fortissimo. When she finishes her mother leaps to her feet to applaud. She then become conscious of the 'horrified silence' around her. She sits down, and there follows 'an awful pause' (Hankin 1923: 67–70).

By contrast with the pauses of discomfort or anxiety in the previous two plays, this is a more strident effect. The conservative upper order sits icily, freezing out the improper event. The only person apart from Mrs Borridge who seems to enjoy it is Major Warrington. He is the brother of Mabel's mother, but shares none of her snobbery. His cultural distance from the others is marked when he moves to stand behind the piano 'facing audience, and looking much amused' as Ethel's song proceeds (Hankin 1923: 68). In the last chorus, he joins in by beating time, she 'slaps him cordially on the cheek', and as she finishes he declares his approval. His may be a minority response but the script insists that he not only enjoy himself but also do so by facing the disapproving silence of the other members of his social class.

The stage that carries this image is that of the Imperial Theatre in Westminster, hired for the occasion by the Stage Society, the members of which surround us. Despite being interested in 'experimental' theatre, they are similar to those sitting in the Duke of York's in that both audiences are largely composed of the rapidly expanded professional class (Perkin 2002), along with some gentry and aristocrats, in the richest capital city in Europe. While these professionals may have mingled with the class above them, they had their own income and power base. In the year following this third play, 1908, H.H. Asquith, a lawyer by training, became Prime Minister leading a Liberal administration. Among his friends were Granville Barker and his wife. Asquith's daughter-in-law Cynthia, a child of the Earl of Wemyss, later became secretary to J.M. Barrie. These sorts of networks, substantially dominated by educated professionals, were woven through the metropolitan theatre audience. And it's that audience which now watches the image of affronted provincial squirearchy.

The play that provides this image is *The Cassilis Engagement*. Its author, St. John Hankin (1869–1909), was a committed and vocal supporter of the Stage Society. In an essay published a couple of months before his play opened he likened the Stage Society to Berlin's Freie Bühne. Like the Freie Bühne, he says, it will be an engine that will finally destroy the institution of theatre censorship. Certainly the founders of the Society were eligible for such a role: Janet Achurch and her husband Charles Charrington had acted in *The Doll's House* in 1889, in a theatre leased by Charrington for that purpose (Ince 2010); Walter Crane, a socialist from the Arts and Crafts movement; Grant Richards, who published

Shaw among many others; William Sharp, inventor of the author Fiona Macleod; and Frederick Whelen, like Charrington, a Fabian and activist in local politics. Joining their Society, Hankin, who previously made his name writing parodies, not only displayed his own political seriousness by publishing his essay but also provided the Society with a rare statement of position.

Censorship, he argued, needs destroying because it has made the British stage trivial. It bans any play that deals seriously with religious or moral issues but is content to allow comedies revolving around adultery. As a consequence theatre managers only offer frivolous entertainments which then alienate audiences who want to be more intellectually engaged. For them, consequently, theatre is not worth attending. Thus the British theatre can only be transformed into a serious art-form by abolishing the Censor. And the way to do that is to follow the Freie Bühne all the way and, instead of hiring a set of largely inappropriate halls and theatres, to purchase a dedicated building which will become an Art Theatre.

Hankin hastens to add that the serious intellectual theatre will not be without its laughter. Indeed the relationship between Art Theatre and popular entertainment will be a complex one, as *The Cassilis Engagement* begins to suggest. For in that scene where Ethel sings her song from the halls, the dramaturgy and its performance make the engagement with the action rather difficult. The dramaturgy ensures that the various members of the provincial hierarchy come across as stuffy and dowdy in their moral rectitude, what Hankin calls 'a sort of Puritanism of the intellect […] not always distinguishable from Priggishness' (1906: 1057). The dissident member of that class, Warrington, whose amused look is balanced against theirs, is at the same time ineffectual. When Ethel suggests he should take her away to Paris, he takes fright at the indecency of the prospect. And neither Ethel herself nor, especially, her mother is a character who is comfortably sympathetic, if at all. But here the casting of these parts becomes interesting. Mrs Borridge was played by Clare Greet, who had been touring the provinces with the Shakespeare Company of Ben Greet (no relation). The voice of the Shakespeare actress may lend its weight to the as it were uncultured mother. Her inappropriate daughter Ethel meanwhile was played by probably the most famous actress in the cast. This was Maudi Darrell (1882–1910), a 'Gaiety Girl' who recently had success in the musical comedy *The Beauty of Bath* and whose image circulated on postcards. Maudi presumably really did know how to deliver a song from the halls, giving proper emphasis to the abjuration to Joey to stop his ticklin. And if indeed she delivered the admonition to Joey with anything like the gusto that Hankin's script requires, then the performance may well have offered both pleasure and cultural authenticity as against those repressed, priggish provincials.

This incorporation of a popular culture form, and its singer, into the work of an artistically serious company is an aesthetic strategy that has a plausible parallel in the work of contemporary painters such as Picasso, reaching back to Manet. In his account of them Thomas Crow points to their 'subversive equations between high and low' and to their 'appropriation of devalued or marginal materials', with the latter being seen as deliberate 'tactics of provocation' (1985: 255, 234). This discussion of visual art is important because it introduces a couple of terms that have hitherto been absent from our analysis of theatre. Those equations of high and low are typically done, Crow says, by 'Modernism'. And the provocative appropriation of the marginal is habitual in the 'avant-garde'. Not often connected with the plays we've just been looking at, these terms will be re-appearing regularly as we move on.

Provisional endings

For English theatre audiences – or, rather, those who presumed to speak for them, the reviewers – Hankin's experiments were perplexing. They were unsatisfactory or even difficult insofar as, while well written, the characters lacked human 'warmth' and the comic happy endings were not happy. Even clever critics were flummoxed. Desmond MacCarthy said Hankin's third play, *The Charity that Began at Home*, is not so good because 'At the close of the play you are left in doubt as to which characters are meant to be in the right and which in the wrong' (1907: 23). In *Cassilis,* Max Beerbohm wanted Mrs Borridge cut because the fun of the contrast between her and Mrs Cassilis is snobbish. This doesn't matter if the spirit is 'kindly', 'But when the spirit is a dry, sardonic one, the snobbishness jars, and the fun is spoilt' (1970: 278). Indeed kindliness was in short supply. There's next to nobody in that after-dinner scene who substantially engages our sympathy, let alone identification. None of the characters is likeable. The ending of their comedy is engineered by Geoffrey's charming, manipulative and duplicitous mother, who gets entirely her own way. Her triumph is founded upon the successful breaking apart of two young lovers. Of another ending, writing a decade or so later John Drinkwater, himself a dramatist of somewhat sentimental sort, criticised Hankin's refusal to allow romantic union at the end of *Return of the Prodigal*: 'It is the prerogative of passion to take no account of institutions or social expediency. [...] it was Hankin's limitation as an artist that he could not see life detached from such institutions and expediencies' (1917: 246). He omitted to ask whether the omission to subscribe to a detached, if not six-bedroomed, life might have a purpose of its own.

When he published *The Cassilis Engagement*, with two other plays, Hankin titled the volume *Three Plays with Happy Endings*. By way of preface, he wrote an essay on such endings. Taking each of his plays in turn he demonstrates that their endings are entirely appropriate. For instance, had he let Geoffrey marry Ethel it would have ended in the divorce court. Geoffrey's mother 'realised that the stirrings of young blood and the attractions of a pretty face are not an all-sufficient basis for a union that is to last a lifetime'. A critic who does not rejoice that the termination of the engagement was a happy ending for all concerned is a critic who cannot grasp that Hankin's play is 'a piece of real life' rather than 'the plot of a comedy'. In saying this, Hankin was being slightly disingenuous, in that most of his play works very like a comedy. This means that when he springs the trap of the ending it is felt with extra force. Rather than invalidating his point about ideological entrainment, it rams it home. That needs doing, Hankin thinks, because when they enter a theatre dramatic critics 'seem to leave all sense of reality outside and judge what they see there by some purely artificial standard which they would never dream of applying to the fortunes of themselves and their friends'. Years later, Bertolt Brecht would similarly reprove audiences who hung up their brains with their hats. The end result, says Hankin (1909: xiii–xiv), is that such critics 'have reduced our drama to the last stage of intellectual decrepitude'.

When Hankin talks about judging by 'some purely artificial standard' he is in effect describing comedy as an ideological mechanism that encourages audiences to subscribe to false ideas about how human relationships work. But his argument reaches further than the ideology of dramatic form. The concept of an ending, happy or not, is, Hankin argues, itself mistaken: 'All "endings" in fact are purely arbitrary, and my play "endings" are no more arbitrary than anyone else's. There is a sense, of course, in which nothing in life ever "ends" – just as there is a sense in which nothing in life ever begins'. From here Hankin articulates a view that might be recognised by the Maeterlinck who wrote *Death*. 'We began ages before our individual birth' says Hankin 'and shall continue ages after our individual death. We exist forever in our causes and results'. This sense of deep biological continuity cannot be faced without ideological containment: 'for practical purposes we find it convenient to assume that things do begin and do end at some particular point, and we divide our lives more or less arbitrarily into a series of episodes' (Hankin 1909: viii). That ideological process of arbitrary and artificial division is assisted by drama, which necessarily deals in episodes and endings.

To make ideological intervention, then, requires unsettling how drama is assumed to work. This is particularly pressing in the case of social realism, a form that offers itself as normal practice, bound by the logic of dutiful mimesis. An audience is perhaps most vulnerable to being unsettled where it has been set up to expect the operation of a predictable form, even an audience that has an appetite for 'experimental' theatre. When Barker's *Ann Leete* began in darkness it was signalling that this was both realism and yet not quite comfortable realism. But Barker had labelled it a comedy and given it a narrative that at the outset looks barely experimental, indeed sets up the traditional polarities of romantic comedy. Ann, the young, socially trapped aristocratic woman makes a successful bid for freedom from her father's house and insists on choosing the man she herself wants to marry, the family gardener Abud. But the slightly troubling way that Barker handles this narrative grows to a point of maximum discomfort in the final scene, which takes us further than the comic closure where girl gets boy – or, depending on taste, girl or cat or antelope.

Barker's two young lovers, wet from the rain, arrive onto a dark stage with the sound of a door being unlocked, the door as it were into the new world, from darkness to light as the romantic symbolism would have it. But the light is a flickering candle lit by Abud. The setting is new to us, and in extreme contrast to the spacious crowded country-house interior of the preceding scene. The lovers may now be on their own in a new world, but it's darker and more enclosed. As Abud shows her its various details, Ann, cold and weary, makes minimal response. 'Well.. this is an experiment' she says. He replies, with reverence, 'God help us both'. 'Amen. Some people are so careful of their lives. If we fail miserably we'll hold our tongues.. won't we?' He replies: 'I don't know.. I can't speak of this' (Barker 1967: 85–87).

As Hankin would say, the marriage ending of comedy is just the start of another narrative. Between drama's arbitrarily imposed end-points there's a deep continuity. Barker's romantic comedy has us face the new beginning's connection with what preceded. When Ann shows her ring to Abud he angrily tells her not to remind him of the 'difference' between them: 'Now I'm your better'. 'My master' says Ann '.. The door's locked'. He worries he has angered her; she promises him never to make a fool of him; his hand, resting on the table, shakes. Ann's defiance of the patriarchal will is not, here, the vehicle for a late nineteenth-century heroic New Woman narrative. The eighteenth-century setting is carefully chosen. Looking to her future Ann says: 'My white hands must redden. No more dainty appetite.. no more pretty books'. 'Have you learned to scrub?' he asks (Barker 1967: 87).

This writing is not only cautious, intimate exploration of love within a material history of class distinction. It also destroys the stage fantasy of constant linguistic competence. As that most astute of Barker analysts, Dennis Kennedy, notes, 'Barker's frequent employment of the ellipsis' (with its characteristic two dots) leads to sudden changes of tone and pauses reminiscent of 'Beckett and Pinter' (2008: 14). Which makes a difficult watch for any realist play, let alone the final scene of a comedy. When Abud goes to kiss and put his arms round her, she refuses. *'Almost by force he kisses her. Afterwards she clenches her hand and seems to suffer.* Have I hurt you? *She gives him her hand with a strange little smile.* I forgive you'. At the opening of the play she was kissed and screamed. That kiss was part of a bet among the men, and was followed by a discussion of their card game. At the end of the play that heritage of being a woman in a man's world seems to be there still, marked now in the nervousness about any form of physical contact, indeed any physical expression of love: 'Think of me.. not as a wife.. but as a mother of your children.. if it's to be so. Treat me so'. The nearest this comedy gets to closure is this: 'I was afraid to live.. and now.. I am content' (Barker 1967: 88).

Some of the consternation this produced was articulated by the reviews. *The Illustrated Sporting and Dramatic News* said the play was a 'mysterious and mystifying jumble' (1902: 821), though perhaps the reviewer here was out of the comfort zone of golf. Arthur Bingham Walkley (1855–1926), relatively new in his grand career at *The Times*, said the audience remained in ignorance of the play's meaning. While there was 'cleverness' in it 'there is no trace of constructive talent, no skill in building up the framework of a drama, no coherency, no clearness' (quoted in Purdom 1955: 15–16). For realists and symbolists alike it was difficult. For the committed realist William Archer (1856–1924) 'the characters depicted, and the reasons for their sayings and doings, remained utterly enigmatic' (in Kennedy 2008: 16). The champion of Symbolism and new art, Arthur Symons, felt the characters 'talk with bewildering abruptness'. It was clearly new, but uncomfortably so: 'The last scene is an admirable episode, a new thing on the stage', he judged, 'but it is an episode, not a conclusion, much less a solution' (1928: 28, 30). He too seems to have wanted dramatic form to have diligently carried out its job of providing tidy endings. That 'experimental' audience didn't get what they expected. To Allan Wade, who later became Barker's secretary, they were 'puzzled and a little resentful [...] it was no "social drama" in the sense they were accustomed to use those words: it exposed no shocking state of affairs and preached no gospel of reform' (1983: 5–6).

But consternation is not always a reliable symptom that experiment is taking place. The work might, straightforwardly, be rubbish. The reverse is also true. Because a work is not unpopular, it doesn't mean there's no experiment. The classic case here is that of Barrie, the most technically accomplished dramatist of his generation, perhaps of the century, and yet also, at the same time, quite alarmingly popular. One of his strengths was the finesse of the negotiation between sustaining dominant expectations and their demolition. This work can be illustrated from the play we have already met, *Crichton*.

A party of indolent aristocrats on a leisure trip at sea get wrecked on an uncivilised island. For two years an entirely different hierarchy is established, with the most capable person, the butler Crichton, as 'king' at the top. In the final act they return. Crichton resumes his role as butler and the aristocrats slide back into their appropriated places, like sewage in a jelly mould. Aware of Crichton's presence they 'furtively', to use Barrie's word, proceed to deny and lie about the previous events. But this is put under some disquieting pressure when they are visited by the formidable Lady Brocklehurst, whose son is destined for Lady Mary. Lady Brocklehurst, a forensically proper mother, wants to know what really happened on the island. Convinced, rightly, that the other aristocrats are fudging and lying, she interrogates Crichton.

Crichton, we're aware, is a firm believer in social hierarchy and disapproves strongly of Lord Loam's 'Radical' attitude to his servants. On the island he establishes a strict hierarchy, with himself at the top, based on people's capacity for productive work. Inherited rank, we understand, will not feed them in this situation. Lord Loam later says that the experience teaches him to abandon liberalism and become a Tory. For the audience who watch the group on the island, no such clear lesson can be drawn. They may, as part of the narrative, see that nature always requires a hierarchy, and indeed that Toryism is thus, at base – if base be the word – natural, but Barrie organises it that simultaneously the whole thing feels like pastiche. Lady Mary's account of her hunting expedition sounds like the language of a boys' adventure novel. At the end of Act 2 as Crichton sits over a cooking pot while the aristocrats creep nearer, Barrie requires that a red light shine on his face, much like an effect of melodrama or pantomime. Back in London, pastiche vanishes as does the island's inverted hierarchy and society returns to a system of discrimination based on inherited rank and wealth. Because this is the prevailing order in London, Crichton accepts it. His commitment to it is as fierce as that of Lady Brocklehurst, with whom he is placed in structural balance in the final act, as against the rest of the company who are shifty, deceitful and idle. In establishing a recognition between Lady Brocklehurst and the butler the play springs its trap.

Crichton doesn't need to lie to assure Lady Brocklehurst that there has been order on the island. Of course it was an order in which aristocrats learnt new skills and enjoyed productive work, which makes it very different from the order of which Lady Brocklehurst approves. But the island order cannot be an alternative to that in London, because, once he is in London, Crichton submits to the established order. For the audience the island order is not available as a – shall we say 'realistic' – alternative because Barrie has written it as pastiche, a fantasy of a way of living that can never be actualised. The human potential discovered and celebrated in that fantasy, the audience joy in watching the actors' bodies released into new sorts of physical expressivity, are closed down when the party returns to London. Within the diegesis Crichton embraces the Lady Brocklehurst order because he is a committed believer in hierarchy. But the play's staging arrangements have its audience pause over his transformation back to butler role. Standing opposite Lady Brocklehurst in the Loams' house, while he may be her intellectual equal, with a similar commitment to the value of order, it is an order in which her energy and power may be expressed unconstrained while his must be suppressed. And they must be suppressed not because anyone explicitly shuts him down but because he himself believes in an order in which he must be shut down. To put it somewhat banally, in Crichton we see a man whose own chosen ideological commitment leads him to live in a way which attenuates his full potency as a human being. This produces an ending, and indeed a play, which were felt to be not wholly satisfactory. The reviews, as Beerbohm noted, called it 'an "entertainment", a "charade", a "caprice", anything but a play' (1969: 595). Barrie was a playwright who didn't write Plays.

But it gets worse. Here we come to the really radical part of Barrie's unsettling of realist conventions. In many works an open-ended narrative is in effect closed in the last instance insofar as the whole work is finished and complete. It will be open-ended in precisely the same tidy way every time you return to it. But that is not the case with Barrie, and I use the present tense advisedly, for the openness still remains. In his essay on endings Hankin had demonstrated the arbitrary nature of dramatic form by promising at some future date to provide extra final scenes for each of the plays in his volume. Sadly he killed himself before carrying out the plan, if he ever was going to do it. But Barrie had already got some way there. Ian Jack (1991) claims to know of nearly twenty variant endings for *Crichton*. For example the butler had special lines for different war-time and post-war revivals. For a single performance in New York in 1931, after the curtain fell, an actor stepped forward to read a letter from Barrie which provided a 'happy ending'. The reading was disturbed by the sound of a splash, at which point the cast discussed among themselves who it might be. It turns out, says the letter, to be Lady Mary who has swum to join Crichton on the island where they had spent acts 2 and 3 (Jack 1991: 126, 128), the play thereby ending happily – until the next variation.

These frequent changes make it impossible to claim that there is any one single authoritative version of a complete text. While his rival Shaw insisted adamantly that his texts could never be changed, Barrie supplied new lines or cues for performance that came and went as occasion required. Sometimes they arrived for just one performance. So it is to printed versions that we look for finalised texts. But Barrie carefully distinguished between the performing text in the theatre and the text printed for readers. They are different objects doing different jobs of work. In the printed texts, for example, the stage directions were greatly extended and often addressed to the reader as reader. Yet even the printed texts are not safe from uncertainty. The supposedly 'Definitive' edition of the plays doesn't include a number of them.

For want of anything more secure, I have quoted where possible from the Definitive edition, though accepting that what it defines may have only partial relationship to what was staged. This gap between printed and performed is not just illustrated by but also constituent of the nature of *Peter Pan*. Barrie thought of it as a continuous performance, flowing on from one season to another, adjusting itself through variations. Within that flow any printed copy is only an artificially arrested moment. This working practice, with its persistently unfinalised texts, created a more radically open-ended drama, one in which the notion of a clear division between performed fiction and real life gets very murky. When at that New York *Crichton* they read out a letter from Barrie he was putting a version of himself almost on stage. Decades before he had done it more literally in the final show of a season of *Peter Pan* when, at the curtain call, he appeared, a short man all in black, between Peter and Wendy, staging a deliberately dark version of himself as author. The possibility of such novelties became one of the pleasures from repeated watching of *Peter Pan*. Not only was the performance of the play itself potentially open-ended but it gained in interest by its relationship with a different sort of performance, that of Barrie the author. In these circumstances we have to acknowledge that a performance of *Peter Pan* or indeed *Crichton* spills off the stage into the real-life processes whereby it was created… and that those very processes are in turn activities of performance, staging Barrie's persona, his relationship to the theatre, the play's historic relationship to audiences. At this point we have to say that the provisional ending has begun to blur the supposed boundary between dramatic fiction and dramatised life.

That boundary was staged by Barrie the year after *Peter Pan*'s first performances. In *Alice-Sit-by-the-Fire* (1905) the 17-year-old Amy has been looking after the house and her siblings, awaiting her parents' return from India. And she has in the last week started going to the theatre with her friend Ginevra to watch 'serious' plays. These have taught them both about Life. After the parents have returned the adolescents overhear Amy's mother Alice making an arrangement to see a male friend. Experienced in serious theatre they firmly grab hold of the wrong end of the stick and resolve to confront the man and rescue Alice. Hilarious complications follow. Obviously these are a parody of, and an attack on, the narrative conventions and values of the Society play. More interesting (though less funny) is the role of Alice. She goes along with her daughter's misapprehension in order to allow herself to be 'rescued' by her. She does this because on arrival back from India she was upset, and jealous, that all three children preferred their father to her. In maintaining her daughter's theatrical delusion Alice performs a part that will regain Amy's love. Within the fiction of the play, then, there are three orders of human behaviour: the 'normal' everyday life of Amy's father (perhaps the only one in this position), the learnt theatrical behaviour of the adolescents, and Alice's real-life performance.

The importance of this fiction is that it tells us that experimental dramatists were not simply attacking the artifice and values of a previous mode of drama but they were also modelling new understandings of performance. As Howe astutely observed at the time (1913: 125): 'How many constant playgoers' watched the play 'in the belief that it was the real article […] until that final fall of the curtain shocked them, perhaps, into a reconsideration of the dramatic values on their way home?' The two major dramatists leading such reconsideration were the ones we are concerned with here, Barker and Barrie. Although they approached their work in different ways, they were close friends and their work overlapped. We shall follow each of them further in order to see how far they pushed social realism towards its implosion.

The undramatised play

Barker's first solo play, as we've noted, was regarded by reviewers as a 'jumble', incoherent. There was a similar negative response to *The Madras House* in 1910. Done in tandem with Shaw's *Misalliance* in it reviewers thought Barker was trying to write a Shavian play. But, as Kennedy (2008) shows, Shaw picked up the ideas from Barker, though not the dramatic ability. Shaw had become notorious for his plays of 'ideas', 'discussion plays' that largely consisted of 'talk'. Indeed, *Misalliance* doesn't really need to be on a stage to make its somewhat tedious effects. Even someone sympathetic to his political project, Holbrook Jackson, conceded that Shaw 'has added nothing to stage-craft, nor to the art of playwriting […] In structure, the plays differ very little from the ordinary play' (1909: 162). Barker, by contrast, was interested in developing new sorts of stage speech, new structures. A serious theatre intellectual, William Archer, was clear about the difference of the two plays. *Misalliance*, he said, had no place in the 'evolution' of the drama but 'was the personal prank of a brilliant, self-willed intellect'. In *Madras House* Barker's 'technique was undeniably new. He did not tell a definite story with a beginning, middle and end, but he wandered around, as it were, in a fortuitously inter-related group of personages, studying various aspects of the character and destiny of modern womankind' (Archer 1910: 741–42).

That sense of wandering around was created by the different settings, with different situations and often different characters, for each act. Acts 1 and 3 are visually full, busy, complexly articulated; Act 2 begins with four characters sitting tensely in an ugly waiting-room; Act 4 is a 'charming' drawing-room with three people. It's emptying itself. For most critics the novelty was too much. *The Illustrated Sporting and Dramatic News* found the whole play undramatic, concluding that as a playwright Barker didn't have 'a plot to elaborate, with characters to render comprehensible, or even with a didactic motive to work out'. The play consists only of conversation, 'sometimes well-written [...] but never leading anywhere in particular' (1910: 86). The pioneer of 'Independent' theatre, J.T. Grein, hated it (Kennedy 2008: 110).

Three years earlier Desmond MacCarthy (1877–1952), perceptive historian of the Court Theatre, said 'The tendency of modern dramatic art is now to make the characters and the emotional and moral significance of the situations the most important elements, and to reduce the plot to a minimum' (1907: 18). Indeed at around that time Hankin was opening up the gap between real life and comedy plotting. Barrie similarly showed in *Alice* the gap between Life and life. Disapproval of such things stentorian in its range and authority came from W.L. George in 1913. George (1882–1926) had begun his publishing career writing about the social conditions and possibilities in new settlements such as Port Sunlight (1909), so he regarded himself as someone who knew about that creature that was as rare as the Bengal tiger, and about as fierce, the common man. His summary of the charges made by the intelligent 'common man' against the 'intellectual drama' is that 'it gives them no plots [...] its climaxes do not thrill them [...] its characters are soulless machines [...] it smothers interest under a heavy, enveloping shroud of words'. He continues: 'We' – this is George and the Bengal tiger – 'want reality – reality in ideas, reality in situations, reality in persons; we do not want anything that is not reality. And, as nothing is so unreal as intellectual realism, the common man has rejected the intellectual drama'. Shaw, Barker and their followers are simply '*épateurs de* [sic] *bourgeois*' (1913: 571–72, 573). For such bourgeois George had just embarked on the somewhat uncommon employment of being a novelist.

But his analysis was continued by a rather more robustly bourgeois figure, the doyen of New York theatre criticism, John Corbin (1870–1959). To this sort of modern drama he gave a name. Using his review of Edward Knoblock's *Tiger! Tiger!* in November 1918 he took the opportunity to comment in general on developments in dramatic writing: 'There has of late been a tendency among our most literary playwrights [...] to make a virtue of getting away from typical drama, with its insistence upon a generalised theme and a balanced struggle of wills, and toward the merely novelistic representation of character, a transcript of life uncontrolled and unformed by any dominant motive. With the legitimacy of this undramatized play we have not now to deal. Of its interest for audiences [*who in New York were possibly unlikely to be the Bengal tiger*] one can only say that in the conventicle art theatres of the Continent it seems to have considerable vogue. On the English-speaking stage, where it is mainly represented by the plays of Granville Barker, it has never achieved more than a highly critical success' (Corbin 1918).

Other reviewers' complaints about incoherence, lack of skill in dramatic framework, no plot elaboration, conversations going nowhere reappear in Corbin's formula of 'a transcript of life uncontrolled and unformed'. They were right. Barker's project was precisely to unform and reform. While *Ann Leete* made the romantic comedy ending creak and strain and wither, *Madras House*, within its seemingly realistic texture, abandons any overarching plot. The separate acts work as free-standing units, sitting in contrast with one another. Part of the dramatic effect depends on this juxtaposition of its parts. For the play doesn't chart the fates of individuals but encourages reflection on the workings of a particular sort of economic and gendered order. It is perhaps significant for the general argument of my book that Corbin thinks that the natural home of the undramatised play, of which Granville Barker is the leading exponent, is the 'conventicle art theatres' of mainland Europe. With a quiver of distaste we have to realise that such a thing is neither commercial nor English.

But there was one contemporary analyst who placed Barker very much more accurately and indeed very much more interestingly. Percy Howe, whose insights on Barrie we've already noted, worked in publishing and wrote about drama regularly – and more perceptively than most of his contemporaries. He also thought deeply about the practice of criticism and became a specialist on Hazlitt. Thus his writing about drama began to shape the protocols of a specialist dramatic analysis as opposed to journalistic reviewing. In his book *Criticism* ([1915]) he analysed the various sorts of writing about plays, mostly dismissing them as inadequate and celebrating only the work of Max Beerbohm (1872–1956) as a true critic. He proposed not only more criticism but 'also, to see the function of criticism more clearly and generally separated from that of creative production' (Howe [1915]: 57). In this proposition we can observe that, even as dramatists were remodelling dramatic form, alongside them a new, separate, analytic practice was being developed. Howe himself offers an example of such analysis in his essay on Barker, which became part of his remarkable book *Dramatic Portraits*. Howe observed: 'His plays make it clear that the creation of character, which is the business of the dramatist, need not stop short at the creation of individual character only, but may go on to the creation of what one may call the corporate character of a group. A play by Granville Barker is, in fact, a series of dramatisations of these group emotions'. He then compares this to Chekhov who, he thinks, pushes it further: but 'the unity of *The Madras House* is just as much a matter of an impalpable presiding influence [...] as is the unity of *The Cherry Orchard*. There is every reason to believe that Mr Barker has arrived at this subtle dramatic technique entirely for himself'. Chekhov is then combined with another Russian parallel: 'The dining-room at Chislehurst [*the scene of* Waste's *Act 1*] pleases as a number by M. Fokine's Ballet pleases: it is the perfection of individual freedom within the perfection of unifying control' (Howe 1913:

194–95, 198: the original essay has 'de Diaghilew's ballet'). In these insights Howe as critic was extraordinarily close to Barker's own private description of his method. Writing to Laurence Housman in November 1928 he said 'my plays are scores – very elaborately orchestrated – and correspondingly hard to read'. If Housman is a Schubert, Barker says, he is Richard Strauss (Bryn Mawr 24.11.28).

Despite Howe's general enthusiasm for Barker, whom he judged as solely responsible for the technical improvement of contemporary English drama, like almost all other critics he had problems with the final act of *Madras House*. To an extent the difficulty comes from associating Barker with his dramatic creation Philip, positioned, wrongly, as *raisonneur*. But mainly it's caused I think by this Act's refusal to perform a satisfactory tying up of threads. It is given over to characters reflecting, inconclusively, on their circumstances and structured, carefully, to give the sense of the play stumbling to a close. It consists of two very rough halves, with a dwindling number of characters: Philip, his wife and parents in the first; in the second Philip and Jessica his wife alone. Philip's mother is ideologically trapped and abused by the father; the father is a self-centred persistent womaniser, happily and successfully complacent. We hear Jessica and Philip's conversation in the shadow of the parents. Philip's complete rejection of all that his father stands for, his embrace of public-spirited ideals, is pursued in a way that constrains Jessica. For her he is sometimes like an 'intellectual' version of his father. In part it's an image of a man struggling to be different, and having to face the difference, again, of women; and in part it's an image of his, their, entrapment in the parental legacy of abuse. As carefully orchestrated as the rest of the play, this is an image of the inability to arrive at closure. In that sense it was indeed just 'talk', but talk handled very differently from plays of ideas.

Five years on from this, in January 1915, a newspaper interviewer in the United States reported Barker as saying that a play 'is anything that can be made effective upon the stage of a theatre by human agency' (in Shepherd 2021: 4). In other words, a play is not defined by its contents – its dramaturgy or verbal interactions, for example – but by the way it is framed, by its being made to work on a stage. He had experienced the effects of such framing nearly six months earlier when he participated in a project dreamt up by his friend Barrie.

Barrie had invited about a hundred and fifty people to attend what he called a 'Cinema Supper' on 3 July 1914 at the Savoy Theatre. These guests included the Prime Minister and his wife, several aristocrats, Edward Elgar and his wife, Bernard Shaw, and some leading theatre managers, among many others. The first act, as it was billed, was a banquet at many small tables set on the stage. This was to be followed, as Mackail tells it (1941: 268), by '*Frank Tinney's Revue* [...] and a whole series of all-star sketches' by Barrie. And 'all-star' it literally was. Indeed the cream of the London theatre is listed. So the stage was cleared and the company settled into the auditorium. At which point Shaw stood up, and here we let G.K. Chesterton take over the story: 'Bernard Shaw harangued them in a furious speech, with savage gesticulations denouncing Barker and Barrie and finally drawing an enormous sword. The other three of us [*William Archer, Lord Howard de Walden and Chesterton*] rose at this signal, also brandishing swords, and stormed the stage, going out through the back scenery' (1936: 240).

Chesterton says they were given no instructions before the event. The only people really in the know were Barrie and Barker, the former of whom was nowhere to be seen. Barker meanwhile was in charge of the most outrageous part of the evening. Men with cameras had been stationed throughout the space to film the entire event. Elgar noticed, but many didn't. They were, as Chesterton noted, 'showing marked relaxation from the cares of State' and throwing bread about (1936: 239). Unsurprisingly a letter of complaint later turned up from 10 Downing Street, with the Prime Minister saying he thought he'd been invited to a private party.

The resulting film, according to a newspaper report, was to be used at a second event later in the year. On this occasion there would be four separate plays, all by Barrie, each complete in itself but each with characters in the manner of a different dramatist – Bennett, Galsworthy, Masefield, Shaw. The ruse is that the characters of one author wander into the play of another. Extracts from the film made on the previous occasion were to be shown between the plays. 'I believe there is a thrilling moment' said the Guardian journalist previewing the event 'when Mr. Shaw is seen to read a telegram on the screen. He discovers that a Masefield character has come into his play and is committing murder' (Manchester Guardian 1914).

The second event didn't take place. War had been declared. Whether it was ever intended to take place is unclear, but the day after the Cinema Supper (according to Mackail) Barrie went off to Essex to make a film of Chesterton and the others doing a cowboy adventure, with Barker again on the camera and directing. Chesterton didn't understand the point of either film, though he reports Shaw as saying that nobody knew what the joke was, which was the joke. For us, however, being academic, and therefore not concerned with jokes, we can soberly note several features of both the Supper and the plan. The planned event, real or not, suggests Barrie's interest in exploring dramatic form, about which we'll discover more. He was also interested, beyond his playwright contemporaries, in film as medium and genre. And above all, he was interested in the interrelation of forms and media. Included in this interrelation, and specifically obvious at the Supper, is the blurring of everyday life and performance. This was not confined to filming the behaviour of the guests but extended, perhaps even more riskily, to scripting an as it were spontaneous and unrehearsed intervention by Shaw and the others. The risk was potentially enhanced by swords being brandished among inebriated people. The plan for a second event, if real, imagined a relationship in which two events were mutually dependent for their completion. The second one relied on material generated at the first, and the first achieved closure in the second. As with other Barrie productions, this one was difficult to pigeon-hole. The Guardian reporter, perhaps pecked by the pigeon, lamely resorted to calling the Supper an 'entertainment'. Nowadays, we might say that it did the aesthetic work that we expect from a 'performance' event.

Included in it of course there were also Barker's interests. The guests at the planned second event would have watched their filmed selves acting, albeit unconsciously, as links between four plays. The everyday behaviour at the Cinema Supper, including presumably, among that class, the bread-throwing, became performed behaviour once it was filmed, by being framed as such. This would be especially clear if the film were used as part of a subsequent revue. Barker, we know, thought that everyday behaviour, once framed, could become a play. But a year later he went further than this. He told a lecture audience at Harvard in December 1915 that 'We all of us act. We acted in our cradles. Go into any nursery and you will see the children acting, playing at soldiers or policemen. It is a sort of instinct. As we grow up we dramatize our lives. We are the principal characters and the rest of the world's business is to play up to us' (in Shepherd 2021: 7).

The implications of these insights and experiments became evident seven years later when he completed his first full-length play since 1910, *The Secret Life*. This play caused difficulties even for those who knew Barker best, and indeed for theatre-makers since. It is not because it is a bad play. It is arguably one of his finest, but the dramaturgy and scripting are difficult, dense, complex. The nearest *The Secret Life* gets to a story-line is the question as to whether its two central figures will re-establish the relationship they each walked away from 18 years ago. Joan has lost her two sons in the war and has since lost her home in a fire. She is, literally and metaphorically, 'burnt out'. Before the war Evan abandoned a potentially high-flying career in politics because of disillusion. Through much of the play he is under pressure to return, but remains outside: 'One fine day I find that the world I'm living in is nothing like the idea of the world I've been living by. It comes quite casually … conversion to disbelief'. Joan summarises their relationship, in a form of confessional to the elderly Mr Kittredge who is sitting by her death-bed in New England: 'We loved the unattainable in each other, so we said … and were content to part. When there was no more need for parting we found that it was true. A faith was born to us … a dead faith … to my shame' (Barker 1923: 124, 140). This is followed by an intensifying of the agony from her brain tumour, and the old man has to squeeze her hand, very hard.

But it's not just Evan and Joan who have a sense of defeat and disillusion and scepticism. It affects many of the older generation. And, among the young, Oliver, invalided out of the war, wants there to be another war – this is 1922 – so that things can really change. The young fellow soldiers whom he had hoped would bring an end to the 'muddle' are now dead. Those responsible for the muddle, the older generation, politically powerful, rich, titled, still live on. This chimes with the 'modernist' take on the post-war world as described by Armstrong (2008: 19), showing 'a lost past; a traumatic present; a blighted future'. But Barker makes almost all of them talk about their lives and emotions with precision, reflection, some bursts of emotion and then restraint and 'common sense'. They may be spiritually bankrupt but they know what they are. As Joan puts it, 'this terrible constant consciousness of being … of purposeless being' (Barker 1923: 109).

And that consciousness, while it may not make them sympathetic, does make them both complicated and unignorable.

It's not, however, its characterisation which makes the play difficult. Instead of offering a clear narrative to follow it works by atmospheres, rhythms, contrasts. Writing about the play to a bemused Desmond MacCarthy in October 1923 Barker suggests: 'if one visualises as distinct from reading, if one imagines the thing in being, as a shifting picutre [sic], not a story told, I do think it is as plain as a pikestaff' (Lilly: 21 October 1923). This makes succinct analysis difficult, without lengthy quotation. But take, for example, the scene in Act 2 where a group sit in the house's interior first-floor gallery. They begin to talk of death, with Evan proposing that we're trapped by our minds, 'cumbered with things we won't let die'. He suggests that if he returns to government Oliver should have him assassinated. At which point their hostess's daughter Dolly shouts through the open window to Oliver below, who offers that it isn't decided yet but Evan may choose his lamp-post just in case. Dolly then goes off down the gallery, stopping briefly to refuse Evan's offer to take a bet on the toss of a coin. She vanishes. Evan remarks: 'The life of the mind is a prison in which we go melancholy mad'. Then Dolly shouts from offstage, accepting the bet. While the coin is tossed, Mr Kittredge conjectures, with an echo of Whitman, about 'that faculty which we call the soul by which we may escape into uncharted regions'. Evan shouts 'Heads' and Dolly is joyous. And Mr Kittredge continues: 'But the rulers of men seldom seek them'. And the conversation moves towards failures in government (Barker 1923: 77–78).

This is neither the elaboration of an argument nor the exploration of character. The remarks about the value of the mind and soul, about subjectivity and government, and their interconnection, are thoughtful, depressed and sceptical. But they're only a part of a whole unit structured around a contrast of youth and age. While the older ones talk together, Dolly has more freedom, speaking out through the window to Oliver, young and outside, and walking and shouting the length of the gallery. That energy breaks into the discourse of the elders, but it doesn't stop the train of thought. And while the elders meditate so articulately and feelingly, the energetic Dolly shows herself capable of neither. The poles of the contrast are locked into one another, each valuable and neither preferred to the other.

This is a fairly simple, albeit dialectical, version of the play's method. The end of the first scene shows its metaphoric and emotional, poetic, effectiveness. There remain on stage the politician Serocold sitting at the piano strumming and singing snatches from *Tristan und Isolde* and two women leaning on the parapet looking into the night. One of the women is Evan's sister Eleanor, the other is Joan. Eleanor tries to cheer up Joan by saying that her husband will be home from Egypt next year and they'll have fun 're-building'. She herself is locked into the project of editing her brother's multi-volume historical work. Serocold comments that, by contrast, politicians may be philistines but they get things done. Joan, looking at the sky, remarks half to herself that now she must pray to the moon, 'as one burnt-out lady to another'. Serocold sings from Wagner 'Give forgetting' 'in deinen schoss' (Barker 1923: 14–15). Joan stares out to sea, alone now. Against her sense of loss, Eleanor has purpose but both of them are caught into roles constructed for them. The man has a confident sense of his own efficacy. Joan, wearing white, is visually aligned with the moonlight, but for her it means not romance but emptiness. That image is enhanced by Wagner's music of love and oblivion. The music, though, is played by the 'philistine' politician, for whom it recalls university days with his two male friends. It remains at the same time passionately serious. He opened the play singing the Liebestod, resisting his friends' cynicism, taking the part of Isolde.

In their tensions these images condense the dialectical relationship of cynicism and longing that runs through the play. And to that relationship the Wagner opera is crucial. It was associated for Barker with the early days of his relationship with Helen Huntington (1867–1950). She reports how in spring 1915 he had an idea for a play based on it. The text as it finally emerged opens with the closing bars of the opera. And its penultimate scene has its main male character, Isolde-like, setting off across the sea to join the dying Joan. That mission, and its pointlessness – for we know Joan is dead – hangs over the final scene. But the scene itself gives us Oliver, Kittredge's grand-daughter Susan and a new character, Lord Clumbermere. He is a wealthy businessman who originally made his money selling ink. Raised as a Baptist he still thinks of himself as spiritually minded, with a greed for thought, faith and honour. When Oliver asks him if he understands why people want to blow up his factories, he says he does, but 'Subtracting evil doesn't leave good'. After he's left, Susan and Oliver argue about whether Evan should return, and the play ends with Oliver telling her he's afraid of her as she sits, says Barker, confident 'in an honest mind and her unclouded youth' (Barker 1923: 150–54, 160). While the inhabitants of his *Tristan* story stepped away from their love 18 years ago and have been dying ever since, they are but an episode in a bigger history that ends, in post-war England, with a complex thoughtful industrialist and two young people, the most confident of whom is a young girl from New England.

When Barker explained the play to MacCarthy he drew attention to its comments about spiritual death and accommodations to current morality. He concedes, in the face of the puzzled reaction, that it may have been 'A piece of bravado, no doubt, to write a play about people's souls for a theatre which mainly calls for physical action and "new" scenery' (Lilly: 21 October 1923). For us that deliberate deviation from the expected norms of the medium, the staging of fragmented conversation and disrupted narrative, together with the focus on those dead souls, suggests a plausible parallel to another work that emerged in 1922, T.S. Eliot's *The Wasteland*. Eliot's poem works as a set of fragments, characterising the deadliness of contemporary culture. In both its social critique and formal experiment *Wasteland* has come to exemplify a particular sort of modern, specifically early 1920s, artwork. But whereas this sort of thing is now expected of Eliot, it may come as some surprise to find something similar from Granville Barker. But Barker himself regarded it as a modernising intervention modelling a new form of drama. Writing several years later to Desmond MacCarthy from Paris, he said: 'I wrote it almost deliberately as a challenge to actors. It is the drama of being instead of doing'. He then refers to the last of his Clark lectures where he expounded his new theory of a 'drama of being' (Lilly: 15 May 1931). Corbin was possibly right to suggest that Barker's experiments with the undramatised play really did belong, spiritually if not physically, in that incubator of new modern drama, the conventicle art theatres of Europe.

If *Secret Life* is an 'undramatized' play, its roots reach back 20 years. In *Ann Leete* and then *Cassilis* with an 'experimental' theatre society, and even with *Crichton* on the commercial stage, we have seen various challenges to assumptions about how plays work. These challenges were not accompanied by polemical manifestoes, although Hankin's account of his 'happy endings' gets close to that. Certainly they were not staged as explicit aggression against audiences. Nonetheless what was going on was in various respects unsettling. The formal experiments were placing audiences in unfamiliar territory. This may explain why, looking back from 1913, Holbrook Jackson thought that drama of the 1890s had changed nothing. For him, as for those around him, the real break came after 1900.

The play of forms

While Barker, as an 'art theatre' director and dramatist, may be a predictable part of that change, less so is Barrie. Although a few scholars have tried to argue for his work's experimentalism (Bold and Nash 2014), the general understanding persists that he was a conventional commercial dramatist specialising in sentiment. But we have seen that he was capable of the Cinema Supper and all its slippage between real life and performance. Barrie was one of those artists for whom the binary opposition between commercial and experimental doesn't work, much like, say, Jeff Koons or David Bowie. And his relationship with the commercial theatre was itself highly ambivalent. The play which followed *Crichton* was *Little Mary*, which proposed among other things that aristocrats eat too much. Its jokes about the closeness between celebrity actors and the aristocratic élite seem to indicate Barrie's awareness of the commercial theatre's function as a class machine. And the supernumeraries of that machine, the critics, disliked it. Nevertheless audiences filled the theatre night after night. To reconcile this mismatch between what audiences liked and what reviewers said they should like, there emerged a critical consensus that Barrie had a special status that allowed him to get away with what would have been condemned in others (Beerbohm 1970: 152). When Shaw noted 'Barrie is now first and the rest nowhere as a popular playwright' (Pearson 1950: 228–29) we need to attach very precise meaning to 'popular'. Barrie, as licensed fool, made work that reveals the fracture-line in assumed cultural hegemony. Or, put another way, it revealed the irrelevance of professional opinion to the experiences of happy punters. The licensed fool was, as usual, a skilful manager of pleasure. Barrie knew what dramatic forms could do, and could make them do it, while ignoring the proprieties attached to those forms. It was this complex relationship with form, taste and pleasure that eventually led to one of the most extraordinary dramatic works of the early twenties ....

It resulted from an approach to experimentation which was very different from Barker's. Barker was interested in the architecture and function of stage interactions, in the operation of picture rather than story, in the dialectical image. Barrie sustained the sense of story and more straightforward interactions, but this was done within texts that were interested both in the conventions of form and the potentials of different media. We have already seen his cultivation of the distinction between printed play and performed script, his quotation of Society play and melodrama, his interest in filmed alongside live performance. For him a play was a visual entity that pressurised physical limits. His requirements for *Crichton* were so complex that the stage carpenters went on strike on opening night. His distinctive interest in film showed a grasp of, and jokes with, Hollywood conventions (as in the cowboy movie). The embrace of both the forms and technology of new media challenged the material constraints of theatre, driven by scepticism about fads for the new.

While in Barker's case that scepticism is seen in the quotation marks in his phrase '"new" scenery', Barrie made a whole play from it, his hilarious one-acter, *Punch: A Little Tragedy* (1906). In it Punch with his puppets is booed off the stage. He is upset and says he would be prepared to compromise, by, for example, inserting a moral where necessary. He will do what it takes to dress up his drama as serious, in order to please an audience. But O'Caries enters, as a figure for the public, to tell him that once he was popular but now no longer. There is a New Man, who formerly was liked only by the cognoscenti but is now liked by the public, though they don't know why. Punch beats O'Caries and kills him with his stick. The New Man comes in and Punch tries to get rid of him too, but finds his blows have no effect. He and Judy admit defeat.

Obviously this is a satire about changing theatre fashions and their triviality. Punch is prepared to create the trappings of serious drama if that will sell. The New Man, whose name was changed at the last minute to Superpunch, is, says Barrie's direction, made up to look like the actor who played Tanner in *Man and Superman*, in other words as Granville Barker who was made up for the part to look like Shaw. Superpunch, now enjoying the success of the commercial theatre, says that it's odd to think that Ibsen was once considered 'advanced'. Punch, preparing to leave, offers his puppets to Superpunch, who refuses them on the basis that his is a drama of ideas not 'action'.

Punch and Judy are outraged to learn that the New Man's drama is not 'action'. And we too will miss it. For Barrie, noting that Punch never had much use for legs, requests that the performer's legs are continually floppy, producing much slapstick. In moments of extreme haste Punch's legs get tangled up. This feature is combined with his readiness to beat people with his stick. He kills O'Caries with all the bashing and yells of the puppet routine. When theatre porters come and collect the body as if it were an everyday occurrence, Judy looks serious but Punch can barely suppress giggles. When these erupt his wife joins in, and the two laugh hysterically about O'Caries' murder. That laughter, wild and amoral, combined with the physical clowning, suggests what is lost to the stage when Punch vanishes from it. Or, rather, what is temporarily brought onto it by Barrie's *jeu*. Most reviewers sniffed disapprovingly at the 'infantile' piece, which may have had 'charm' but no 'taste', with *The Observer* complaining about a 'breach of good manners' (Hugo 1990: 60). But that tasteless breach effectively sidesteps anxieties about being fashionable and 'new', doesn't ask for approval or disapproval within current terms, and offers instead a different way of being on stage, a form of physical performance that releases wild laughter not bound by established proprieties.

A few years after this performance Punch's contemporary, the Russian director Vsevolod Meyerhold recommended that 'to make a dramatist out of a storyteller who writes for the stage, it would be a good idea to make him write a few pantomimes. The pantomime is a good antidote against excessive misuse of words'. We can pause and hear Punch's outrage at Superpunch's drama of ideas. Meyerhold continues with his recommendations as to how to reform the theatre by contrasting two examples of puppet performance. One director wants the puppets to be life-like, so replaces them with real people. The other director realises that the appeal of puppets is based precisely on them being unlife-like: 'The puppet did not want to become an exact replica of man, because the world of the puppet is a wonderland of make-believe, and the man which it impersonates is a make-believe man'. These sorts of performance belong to modes of entertainment banished from the theatre, modes which use 'mask, gesture and movement'. Together they are associated with the 'fairground booth'. It's the introduction of the principles of this mode of performing of which, says Meyerhold, theatre reformers dream (1978: 124, 129, 134).

This could be a commentary on Barrie's play, six years after it. Barrie, not one for commentaries, states the aesthetic position by dramatic means and in doing so suggests something that Bakhtin, quite apart from Meyerhold, might have recognised. Humans work as puppets, the bearded Superpunch is a simulacrum of a simulacrum. We not only recognise the distance of this performance from a form of drama that is trying to be purposeful, serious and New, but we are also collapsed into a state of play amenable neither to taste nor to morality, beyond manners and belly-laugh hilarious.

Key to the show is a form of physical performance outside that normally done on the dramatic stage. As such it's similar to the experiments with film. Barrie pursued the opportunities offered by both, following the Savoy event, for example, with a musical comedy burlesque, *Rosy Rapture* (1915), requiring a film sequence. His interest in physical modes began much earlier. For example *Pantaloon* in 1905 included two characters who were completely silent, speaking only in mime and dance. This was then taken forward, and made more elaborate, in the 1919 *Truth about the Russian Dancers*.

The Russian ballet had been all the rage in London before the war though by 1918, following the Bolshevik revolution, there was increased coolness towards Russia. Barrie himself, as Sobolev (2016: 24) points out, was not a great fan of the ballet, but was persuaded by the prima ballerina Lydia Lopokova to write a play for her. When she suddenly left Britain Barrie approached another leading Russian dancer already known to him, Tamara Karsavina. The idea was that Karsavina's role, called Karissima, should communicate only through dance. This required close collaboration, so that Barrie could explore the possibilities of a medium more formalised than the physical regimes he had used hitherto. What emerged was something rather more than an amalgam of ballet and stage drama.

As we sit in the London Coliseum on 15 March 1920 the curtain goes up on Vere Castle. Lady Vere is sewing when her brother-in-law Bill enters in a foul temper and golfing clothes, accusing their guest of cheating. Lady Vere observes that the guest, a Russian dancer called Karissima, already seems to have had an effect on the decorations of the house. Which draws to our attention Paul Nash's sub-Cubist designs for a set which, says Barrie, must have, as is proper to the Russian ballet, 'a touch of the bizarre' about it. Furthermore, Lady V has gathered from her son that the Russian ballet only speak with their toes and, while 'clever London audiences' understand immediately, she wishes that she could be kissed good night rather than have the dancer stand on one foot with the other leg in the air. When Karissima appears, in a Russian ballet version of golf attire, she is asked to demonstrate how she putted the ball into the hole. The demonstration, says Barrie, should be 'a thing of beauty [...] a glorified version of the ordinary procedure', during which she pats the ball into the hole with her hand. Helpfully Lady V tries to teach Karissima to walk on the soles of her feet because 'it's rather expected in this country'. Her son then enters and asks permission to marry Karissima, which horrifies his mother. He points out that Karissima is willing to die if they can't marry. To which his mother: 'It seems unkind, but, Roger, I *would* prefer that' (Barrie 1962: 13, 14, 16, 18, 19). After Karissima does a tragic dance, Lady V gives way. Wedding bells promptly ring, the ballet chorus enters, on toes, then a clergyman, on soles. The hitch in the ceremony is that Karissima can't speak her replies, so the clergyman breaks down the vows into small units to which she dances responses.

This is rather more than a burlesque of the Russian ballet. It makes space for laughter against those, outside 'London', who don't understand the ballet, but above all it works to estrange the assumed norms of English habitus and behaviour, from playing golf to the wedding ceremony. On the way it takes pot-shots at English racism and violent snobbery. But at the wedding ceremony this binary between Englishness and ballet is complicated with the entrance of the Maestro, an 'excitable little man', 'foreign, with a black beard', 'with ballet movements of a restrained order' (Barrie 1962: 22). He interrupts the ceremony. 'Sensation' requests Barrie's stage direction, drawing directly on a classic melodrama technique of tableau. Then Maestro takes his seat, the ceremony ends to wedding bells, the couple leave. The stage darkens, the clock strikes midnight, there's thunder and lightning. Maestro enters dressed as a necromancer. We're now fully in melodrama. Roger enters to ask whether they can have a child and announces that Bill has been trying, by various trusted melodrama means, to kill Karissima. Maestro eventually agrees they can have a child and sets about making one with chisel and putty. Meanwhile Bill is spying through a window. Maestro, feeling a draught, but with his mind on other things, slams the window shut, thereby guillotining Bill. Later when he comes across Bill's head he tidily pops it in the waste basket. When Bill finally re-appears he is a reformed character, although his head is on slightly crooked.

In a one-act piece, Barrie has the actors perform in the modes of Society drama, melodrama, farce and Russian ballet, and he draws attention to the interfaces between these modes, the dancer learning to walk as a 'Society' woman, the melodrama necromancer with ballet movements. These proliferating physical regimes are accompanied by a time-scheme that slows down, in the wedding ceremony, and then rapidly speeds up, suddenly striking midnight. Karissima, about twenty minutes after being married, gives birth. But, as Maestro says, with the baby entering as a young member of the company, an old one has to leave. Karissima, the new mum, promptly dies. Her corpse is solemnly carried on. She then gets up and does a final tragic dance and goes back to the bier but 'as if expecting an encore' (Barrie 1962: 30).

There is brutality in the sequence, especially with the immediate death after childbirth, but at the same time there's laughter, triggered not only by the burlesque of modes of performing but also by a more profound assault on the respect for and coherence of the body. Barrie reaches back to Punch's slapstick murder of O'Caries when he has Maestro unintentionally guillotine Bill. And when, further, he creates a separate narrative for Bill's head. This is motivated neither by political jokes nor jokes about theatrical form. It is a sort of gratuitously cruel and hilarious physical clowning.

This 1920 play is, then, a collage of different physical regimes, including Russian ballet, done in a sub-Cubist setting to a full musical score by Arnold Bax which quotes Russianness, and exoticism, and musical comedy. The London audience was encouraged to celebrate their knowledge of various theatrical forms and how they work, to enjoy games with theatrical presentation. And – two years after a brutal war in which Barrie himself lost one of his beloved Llewellyn-Davies boys – that London audience was also encouraged to laugh at the jokey destruction of the human body. What we're observing here can be described as a work where 'the historical succession of techniques and styles has been transformed into a simultaneity of the radically disparate'. With its dance, music, design, all conscious of themselves, it seems that, in its making, 'the totality of artistic means becomes available as means'. These phrases, borrowed from Peter Bürger (2007: 63, 18), take us somewhere new. For he argues that all these features are specifically characteristic of, only made possible by, 'the historical avant-garde movements'.

This, then, is the point to which we have arrived in tracing the variety of ways in which a tiny group of two or three dramatists pressurised the conventions of realist social drama until they imploded. New dramatic languages came into being, whether it was Barker with his orchestrated non-narrative, post-Chekhov, stage or Barrie, with his games with convention, form and expectation. The world in which they were doing this was highly conscious of European experiments and, above all, what it was to be 'modern', to which we next turn.

But first, in case you were wondering, the secret about Russian dancers as revealed by Maestro is that they were made out of putty.

References

Unpublished

Bryn Mawr: Bryn Mawr College Libraries, Laurence Housman papers, Box 2, folders 3.1–2.
Lilly: Lilly Library, University of Indiana, MacCarthy MSS, Box 1.

Published

Archer, William 1910 'The Theatrical Situation' *The Fortnightly Review* volume 88: 736–49
Armstrong, Tim 2008 *Modernism: A Cultural History* Cambridge: Polity
Barker, H. Granville 1923 *The Secret Life: A Play in three Acts* London: Chatto & Windus
Barker, H. Granville 1967 *The Marrying of Ann Leete* in *The Collected Plays*, volume 1 London: Sidgwick & Jackson
Barrie, J.M. 1948 *The Plays of J.M. Barrie [The Definitive Edition]*, ed. A.E. Wilson London: Hodder and Stoughton
Barrie, J.M. 1962 *The Truth about the Russian Dancers,* with an Introduction by Tamara Karsavina *Dance Perspectives*, volume 14.
Barrie, J.M. 1990 *Punch: A Little Tragedy in One Act* in Hugo.
Beerbohm, Max 1969. *More Theatres 1898–1903* London: Rupert Hart-Davis
Beerbohm, Max 1970. *Last Theatres 1904–1910*, introduced by Rupert Hart-Davis London: Rupert Hart-Davis.
Bold, Valentina and Nash, Andrew (eds) 2014 *Gateway to the Modern: Resituating J.M. Barrie* Glasgow: Scottish Literature International
Bürger, Peter 2007 *Theory of the Avant-garde*, translated by Michael Shaw Minneapolis: University of Minnesota Press
Chesterton, G.K. 1936 *The Autobiography of G.K. Chesterton* New York: Sheed & Ward
Clark, T.J. 1985 'Clement Greenberg's Theory of Art' in Francis Frascina (ed.) *Pollock and After: The Critical Debate* London: Paul Chapman Publishing: 47–63
Corbin, John 1918 'The Undramatized Play' *New York Times* 17 November
Crow, Thomas 1985 'Modernism and Mass Culture in the Visual Arts' in Francis Frascina (ed.) *Pollock and After: The Critical Debate* London: Paul Chapman Publishing: 233–66.
Drinkwater, John 1917 *Prose Papers* London: Elkin Mathews
George, W.L. 1909 *Labour and Housing at Port Sunlight* London: Alston Divers
George, W.L. 1913 'Drama for the Common Man' *The Fortnightly Review* volume 94: 568–78

Hankin, St. John 1906 'Puritanism and the English Stage' *The Fortnightly Review* volume 80: 1055–64
Hankin, St. John 1907 'A Note on Happy Endings' *Three Plays with Happy Endings* London: Samuel French
Hankin, St. John 1907 'How to Run an Art Theatre for London' *The Fortnightly Review* volume 82: 814–18
Hankin, St. John 1923 *The Cassilis Engagement* in *The Plays of St. John Hankin*, introduced by John Drinkwater, volume 2 London: Martin Secker
Howe, P.P. 1913 *Dramatic Portraits* London: Martin Secker
Howe, P.P. [1915] *Criticism* New York: George H. Doran Company
Hugo, Leon H. 1990 '*Punch*: J.M. Barrie's Gentle Swipe at "Supershaw"' in Stanley Weintraub and Fred D. Crawford (eds) *Shaw: The Annual of Bernard Shaw Studies*, volume 10 Pennsylvania State University Park: The Pennsylvania State University Press: 60–72
Illustrated Sporting and Dramatic News, The 1902 1 February
Illustrated Sporting and Dramatic News, The 1910 19 March
Ince, Bernard 2010 'An Early Pioneer of the New Drama: Charles Charrington, Actor-Manager and Fabian Socialist' *Theatre Notebook* volume 64, number 3: 130–59
Incorporated Stage Society, The 1909 *Ten Years 1899–1909* London: The Chiswick Press
Jack, R.D.S. 1991 *The Road to the Never Land: A Reassessment of J M Barrie's Dramatic Art* Aberdeen: Aberdeen University Press
Jackson, Holbrook 1909 *Bernard Shaw* London: Grant Richards
Jackson, Holbrook 1988 *The Eighteen Nineties: A Review of Art and Ideas at the Close of the Nineteenth Century* London: The Cresset Library
Kennedy, Dennis 2008 *Granville Barker and the Dream of Theatre* Cambridge: Cambridge University Press
MacCarthy, Desmond 1907 *The Court Theatre* London: A.H. Bullen
Mackail, Denis 1941 *The Story of J.M.B.: A Biography* London: Peter Davies
Maeterlinck, Maurice 1911 *Death*, translated by Alexander Teixeira de Mattos London: Methuen
Manchester Guardian 1914 'Sir J.M. Barrie's Noted Guests' *Manchester Guardian* 10 July
Meyerhold, Vsevolod 1978 'The Fairground Booth' in Edward Braun (ed.) *Meyerhold on Theatre* London: Eyre Methuen
Pearson, Hesketh 1950 *Bernard Shaw* London: St James's Library/Collins
Perkin, Harold 2002 *The Rise of Professional Society: England since 1880* London: Routledge
Purdom, C.B. 1955 *Harley Granville Barker: Man of the Theatre, Dramatist and Scholar* London: Rockliff
Schoonderwoerd, N. 1963 *J.T. Grein Ambassador of the Theatre 1862–1935: A Study in Anglo-Continental Theatrical Relations* Assen: van Gorcum & Comp
Shaw, G. Bernard 1984 *Misalliance and The Fascinating Foundling* Harmondsworth: Penguin Books
Shepherd, Simon (ed.) 2021 *The Unknown Granville Barker: Letters to Helen and Other Texts 1915–18* London: Society for Theatre Research
Sobolev, Olga 2016 'J M Barrie and the ballets russes' *International Journal of Comparative Literature & Translation Studies* volume 4, number 1: 23–30
Symons, Arthur 1928 *Plays, Acting and Music: A Book of Theory* London: Jonathan Cape
Wade, Allan 1983 *Memories of the London Theatre 1900–1914* London: Society for Theatre Research

2
MODERNITIES

In 1913, Horace Samuel published a book called *Modernities*. It offered accounts of individuals who were 'reasonably characteristic of that modern movement of the last and present century which started with the French Revolution' (Samuel 1913a: vi). Beginning with Stendhal, it included Nietzsche and ended with Futurism. Samuel (1883–1950) was one of a number of authors mapping what appeared to be significant modern developments. Such developments were not necessarily driven by particular individuals. Sometimes they were felt as changes in attitudes and practices.

The intention in what follows is to see how the English stage self-consciously engaged itself with the various facets of what it regarded as modernity. Note that this is something more specific than simply being generally 'experimental'. Some writers more than others might be labelled 'modern', and in Samuel's book, as with several others, these were European rather than English. So the project of consciously 'modernising' the English theatre led to the importing of ideas and artworks specifically from Europe. The notorious example of such an import was that of Ibsen. Indeed it was so notorious that in subsequent decades the arrival of Ibsen's plays in England has been regarded as an historical watershed, the moment at which the English stage had modernity thrust upon it. We're potentially dealing with two topics then – the stage's engagement with modernity and the received story about that engagement.

There are two key figures in that received story. Alongside Ibsen there is Edward Gordon Craig. Craig met hostility from English theatre managements and so after some productions around 1900–1902 he took himself and his ideas off to Europe. Craig, like Ibsen, is thus regarded as another modern European with whom the English stage had to learn to catch up. Each of them inevitably appears in this chapter. But once we focus on the ways the English stage consciously tried to modernise, rather than following the story of how it supposedly did so, the positions of Ibsen and Craig start sliding.

That focus will fall into roughly two parts. The first deals with 'modern' playwrights, the second with new scenographies. In that second part we encounter a specifically English project that drew on Craig but took its own direction towards modernised staging. It followed a very different direction from European work, but came eventually to stand alongside it, rather than being subsumed by it, in the great exhibition of 1922.

Ibsen and the bearded drama

Four of Samuel's ten chapters are on dramatists: Strindberg, Wedekind, Schnitzler, Verhaeren. Note immediately the absence of the name that almost all histories, and most Edwardian contemporaries, say was central to modernising the stage: Ibsen. His absence reminds us that by 1913 the Ibsen sensation of the early nineties was a long time ago. Ibsen had become absorbed and accommodated in various ways. It's with that process we need to begin.

When *Ghosts* was staged in London in 1891, it had all the sensational impact of the shockingly new. By doing it as a 'club' performance Grein's Independent Theatre avoided state censorship, but not the vituperative frothing of supposedly morally offended reviewers. The result was an animated discussion of Ibsen in the public sphere. But interest started earlier. *Doll's House* was staged in 1889 and in 1890 the left-wing Fabian Society included Ibsen in a course of lectures on modern thinkers. One of their number, the critic Bernard Shaw, offered to give the lecture. This 'exposition' was then printed as *The Quintessence of Ibsenism* (1891). When it was reprinted 22 years later in an enlarged version Ibsen had become a canonical figure.

The Ibsen scandal more or less fizzled out by the close of the 1890s. The process began once the *Ghosts* excitement died down. There was slightly less fuss about *Hedda Gabler*, done just over a month after *Ghosts*. Then immediately *Hedda* finished a new show opened. Called *Ibsen's Ghost* it starred the comedian J.L. Toole in his own theatre and was a burlesque of three Ibsen plays including *Hedda*. It was followed three days after its opening by Robert Buchanan's *The Gifted Lady*, another rather longer, and much less funny, burlesque and by Mrs Hugh Bell's parody *Jerry-Builder Solness*. While the first two were the only ones on the commercial stage, in the journal *Punch* the young St. John Hankin (1901) had written a series of suggested new endings for famous plays. One of these was Ibsen's *The Lady from the Sea*, now re-named *The Lady on the Sea*, because the heroine, instead of turning against the seaman who came to claim her from the past, now goes off to join him at sea. She stands on the deck of an English steamer feeling thoroughly sea-sick. The seaman is not at all pleased to see her and resolves to return her to her husband, but since she has neither luggage nor money, she will have to work her passage home as a stewardess.

If burlesques of Ibsen were somewhat limited in London, in Berlin and Munich, with highly educated and often left-wing audiences, they were a minor industry. Beginning in the late 1880s, they frequently appeared in satirical journals such as *Kladderadatsch*, *Lustige Blätter* and *Ulk*. But there was another outlet which Berlin and Munich had, and London largely lacked, namely an established cabaret culture. Among the stage burlesques of Ibsen were those by Rudolph Brenauer, who was associated with Max Reinhardt's parody theatre Noise and Smoke, and Hanns Gumppenberg, who wrote for Munich's Eleven Executioners cabaret (Roßbach 2005). In London, the people doing the burlesques had different sets of associations. Hankin, as we know, not only went on to write plays but also to campaign against state censorship. And the play that initiated London's Ibsen parodies, *Ibsen's Ghost*, was the first play by a man who hitherto had written journalism and novels, J.M. Barrie.

Ibsen's Ghost picks up at the end of *Hedda*, and combines with it *Doll's House*, *Ghosts* and a fashionable mime-musical *L'Enfant Prodigue*. During its performance, Toole transformed into Ibsen, replete with beard. Humour is made out of all elements of Ibsen's dramatic work – the characters, famous incidents (such as Hedda burning manuscripts), philosophical concerns such as the effects of heredity (to which is attributed the sudden extinguishing of the gas), dramaturgic techniques such as flashback, use of repeated phrases in dialogue (such things as 'Fancy that!' and 'Put vineleaves in your hair'). Separated from the narrative contexts that give them justification, these elements, seen in a new light, are revealed as the stage apparatus of melodrama. At one point the dialogue drifts quite naturally towards incorporating a version of that legendary line 'never called me mother'. It's burlesque working as detailed textual critique, and shows Barrie's fine analytic sharpness.

It also shows his delight in the metadramatic. There were two different translations of Ibsen at this period, by Archer and by Gosse. Barrie ensures that the textual instability itself becomes staged:

> Tia (*aside*): so well, that is your cue —
> Peter (*aside*): No, 'other women' is my cue. I am using Gosse's version, you know.
> Tia: I am using Archer's. Say something.
> Peter: All right. Ghosts.
>
> (Barrie 1975: 31)

Later when Delia is about to enter, and when the play will lurch into *Doll's House*, Peter wonders whether she uses Gosse or Archer. He's so obsessed that it muddles itself up with a key narrative word: 'Gosse – I mean Ghosts'. In one wonderful moment, the metadrama is propelled beyond text into performance: 'Tia, weep no more or if you must weep and wring your hands, because that is your idea of the character, let it be for me' (Barrie 1975: 39, 33).

By this point we're a long way from the Ibsen furore. While it exploits a satiric opportunity, *Ibsen's Ghost* is just as interested in the ways Ibsen's drama works.

This provides a foundation on which Barrie can explore his own characteristic interests in textual instability and complex, ironised modes of watching. Ibsen is being mutated into Barrie. Three plays later he did it again, but this time in a serious play called *The Wedding Guest* (1900), a story of the sins of the past returning in the present. On the eve of his wedding Paul meets the woman whom he made pregnant several years ago. In his characterisation of Kate Ommaney Barrie has her lapse between everyday behaviour and an obsessive irrational preoccupation in which she loses her bearings in the present (Barrie 1948). That fast change between psychological states, indeed identities, is a precursor to Barrie's later interest in both subjectivity and the effects of form. One reviewer thought it made melodrama of the 'Ibsenite problem play' (in Jack 1991: 63), another that the problem had been made insoluble: 'The impossibility of a conclusion […] becomes very glaring before the footlights' (ZYX 1900: 862). Barrie's friend Granville Barker, a decade later, suggested it showed 'Barrie's growing interest in his new art by the experiment he makes as to how far pathology is justified in the theatre. He uses madness, and very pathologically too. It was a daring thing to do' (Barker 1910: 14). This is not melodramatic degradation but the conversion of Ibsen's return of the past into a new sort of dramaturgic vehicle.

It was not Barrie alone who was interested in Ibsen's technique and its possibilities. The Stage Society justified their production of *Lady Inger of Ostråt* by explaining that in this very early work the workmanship is 'in many ways curiously naïve and old-fashioned', but for those interested 'to see from what humble beginnings that flawless technique sprang' the play has an interest (Incorporated Stage Society 1909: 67). This engagement with Ibsen as technician, rather than dramatist of progressive ideas, contrasts rather sharply with Bernard Shaw's 'defence' of Ibsen, *The Quintessence*. The original 1891 version offered a reading of the plays as interconnected attacks on ideals and idealism. In 1913 Shaw added the more recent plays together with analyses of what constituted Ibsen's novelty and technical pre-eminence. Although by now Ibsen was acknowledged a great dramatist people still did not understand, said Shaw, the arguments made by the new post-Ibsen drama.

What made Ibsen new, Shaw suggested, was his insistence, as against idealism, on the truth of reality. That insistence was made forceful by Ibsen's technical innovation, 'discussion' between characters, usually at the end of the play. The use of the discussion technique made Ibsen more serious than Shakespeare. But, however artistically discussion is handled, this on its own, said Shaw, will not guarantee that a play stands the test of time. Indeed artistic elaborations, and especially anything conspicuously theatrical, will compromise the authority with which a play speaks of reality. The power of the play, and its ability to remain potent over time, derive solely from the relevance of its discussions to the reality of the audience's world. Those who properly appreciate Ibsen are people who have the ability to reflect. These are not the sort of people who are taken in by merely theatrical effects, not the sort of people who, says Shaw, laugh frivolously like 'Africans'.

By means of this argument Ibsen is recruited as one of Fabian socialism's experts, the people who, by strictly rational, if not scientific, discussion will lead us towards an understanding that lays the basis for a better society. Of course such experts only address those who are educated enough to understand them. These clearly do not include Africans or members of that class which Shaw referred to as 'tinkers' and 'riff-raff'. One of the problems of riff-raff is that they are apt to take pleasure in theatre, unlike the determinedly grim composure of that pre-eminent Fabian Beatrice Webb. This is why a social expert such as Ibsen has to have his drama hygienically segregated from the contagion of theatricality. The process was described by Huntly Carter (1912: 36) as Ibsen being 'butchered to make a Fabian holiday'.

But there was perhaps another, less dignified, motive to this appropriation. It was demonstrated with devastating force by Percy Howe. He argued that the first edition of *Quintessence* was 'an exposition of just so much in Ibsen as suited Mr. Shaw's purposes' and with the 1913 edition 'he played just the same trick on him. He triumphantly found embedded in his subject [...] not this time his own opinions [...] but the aesthetic principle on which he had written his own plays'. Howe shows that Shaw's claim about 'discussion' being a 'technical novelty' is spurious, and, more seriously, that he so completely misunderstood Ibsen's dramaturgy, or indeed any dramaturgy, that he was doing the exact opposite of Ibsen. His rival Barrie, we should note, had spotted that Ibsen's work is powered by techniques of atmosphere, repetition, climax and reversal. These effects are used because Ibsen, as Howe says, embedded the general in the particular, while for Shaw 'Society' is 'the principal protagonist'. His focus is not on the drama, but on the 'message'. Shaw naturally disliked this analysis but the correctness of Howe's judgement was further underlined by a work which post-dated his book, *Heartbreak House* (1919). Shaw claimed that he had been influenced by Chekhov's mode of writing, and some modern academics have been sufficiently seduced by this claim to argue that *Heartbreak House* demonstrates Shaw's contribution to the shaping of a new dramaturgy. But, as with Ibsen, what the play actually demonstrates is that Shaw had little understanding of his source material, just as he didn't understand Barker or Barrie whom he tried to copy. Chekhov's carefully orchestrated stage, with its over-lapping conversations, its pauses and non-sequiturs, the rhythm of movement across grouped bodies, all of it is replaced by a series of over-elaborated conversations following one another in sequence, like circus elephants trapped in glitter. The properly Chekhovian English dramatist was Granville Barker, as Howe knew. His *Secret Life*, developed while Shaw was writing *Heartbreak House*, offers a lesson in how to build on Chekhovian dramaturgy. But Shaw was impervious to such lessons. Of his persistent mode Howe observes, correctly I think, that the jokes and redundant effects, to which we might add the highly oratorical and loudly gestured performance style, are mere proscenium-window dressing, with none of Ibsen's purpose. Discussion is not made any more pleasurable by being shouted. At base, Howe argues, Shaw's definition of drama as 'discussion' was a convenience necessitated by the fact that he was a 'natural hand at discussion' and not much else. In short, it has to be said, that Shaw 'is no kind of a dramatist at all'. In his desire to get his work into the theatre, he had concentrated his efforts on elaborating anecdote, because that's what he thought dramatists did, but once he got there 'he paid very little further attention to anecdote but went on delivering his philosophic goods in the thinnest and lightest of fictional disguises. That is the explanation of why Mr. Shaw has not advanced one single step upon *Arms and the Man* in any direction that has anything at all to do with the mastery of the theatre' (Howe 1915: 77–78, 98, 118, 111, 117). And this, I shall add, is why he figures so marginally in this book.

Howe was not alone in his analysis. Huntly Carter (??–1942) argued that Ibsen's proper influence in England had been 'ruined' by 'his English interpreters'. Shaw's treatment of Ibsen was part of a 'policy' to 'capture the public' (1912: 36, 37). This analysis comes from somewhere different from Howe. Carter at this period associated himself with the group of self-declared artistic radicals connected with the *Egoist* magazine. For him what was at stake in the Shaw-Ibsen story was the maintenance in place of an unhealthy dominant idea of drama and on the back of that the promotion of a personal career. In 'The Re-Incarnations of Mr. Bernard Shaw', from September 1914, he reviewed the *New Statesman*'s supplement on Modern Theatre. As well as accusing Archer and Shaw of murdering 'the spiritual Ibsen', he points out that the Fabian *New Statesman* was a 'Shaw-ridden journal' and that Shaw's name was everywhere in the supplement. The so-called 'Modern Theatre' celebrated here was actually 'a form of drama rotting on the manure-heap of barren intellect and actuality' (1914: 337–38). Carter's rhetoric has all the customary register of *The* – or an – *Egoist*. But his argument echoes one made nearly a decade before by someone apparently very different.

In Barrie's *Punch* (1906) Superpunch, the Shaw figure, says: 'Queer now to think that Ibsen was once considered advanced'. Superpunch has taken over as the fashionable representative of the new, and unlike Ibsen's this new 'bearded' drama is only interested in ideas. Judy calls it bearded drama because Punch has explained, in one of the most wonderful speeches in the play, that Superpunch's distinguishing feature is that he has a beard: 'Everything in drama has changed, Ju, since the coming of the beard. It came originally, I've heard tell, from Norway, and had a roughish time, but quickly it spread all over the drama – like the first rabbit in Australia' (Barrie 1990: 71, 70). In extension of Barrie's metaphor we might summarise by saying that in effectively assimilating Ibsen to himself, Shaw created not so much a Shavian as perhaps a shaven Ibsen.

Shaw's positioning of Ibsen, and thus of himself, have had long-lasting effect on theatre historiography. Crudely speaking, it establishes Ibsen as the single originating force of change in English drama, with Shaw positioned as the only significant dramatist between 1900 and the 1920s. To demonstrate this proposition, let's take a couple of texts written several decades apart.

Raymond Williams' influential study *Drama from Ibsen to Brecht* has the project of exploring relationships between individual creativity and shared conventions, what Williams called 'structure of feeling'. Within this project he selects for analysis only two English dramatists before 1930 – Shaw and Lawrence. Lawrence is there because he was, unusually, writing plays of working-class life. These were, not unusually, unperformed. Indeed his is a somewhat marginal case. His individual handling of stage convention is very much less thoughtful, rich and radical than any of the more well-known dramatists we have noted in the preceding chapter. But those dramatists are excluded and in their place we're given only Shaw. Now Williams is thoroughly alert to Shaw's tricks, showing that *Quintessence* deliberately misrepresents Ibsen and that Shaw dramaturgically relied on melodrama and other devices lifted from the very theatre he attacked. He is also clear that Shaw was a committed self-publicist. Even so he says that Shaw was 'self-evidently' a 'Modern' and that *Quintessence* was one of 'the forces' which produced the 'new drama' (1973: 276). But it's not clear what is so evident about these assertions. We know that contemporary critics had already, decades before, made these same points about Shaw, and for Carter, Howe, Jackson and Samuel, Shaw was definitely neither new nor Modern. That Shaw, despite this, takes pride of place in Williams' book seems to me testimony to the efficacy of the self-produced Shaw myth. That efficacy persists into a much more recent account, Ben Levitas' 'Theatre of Modernity'. The essay has the obviously huge task of describing all the theatrical activity of that unhelpfully baggy thing called 'modernity', and it's done with a lot of good detail. The detail thins out, however, for England. Here we meet only the immovable bearded dramatist, because Shaw's combination of theatrical and social activism, explaining 'the principles of progressive drama' in *Quintessence* and battling the Censor, was, says Levitas, the 'hallmark of theatrical innovation'. It led to plays where 'prolix expansiveness [...] systematically overwhelmed narrative with polemic' (2016: 354). Of this, a clearer-sighted contemporary such as Howe would say it was not only not usefully innovative but it also made for deadly drama. But Howe was merely concerned with good art. It's the production of self-image which tends to have the greater impact on the history of this – or any – period. That history changes, however, when we listen to those who were there.

'Modern' dramatists

To demonstrate the ineptitude of Shaw's dramaturgy, Howe compared it to that of Maurice Maeterlinck (1862–1949). From his base in Belgium, Maeterlinck was associated with the most recently exciting art movement emanating from Paris, Symbolism. When his plays reached England theatre-makers discovered a different way of using the stage and Maeterlinck became the subject of sustained critical commentary. Nearly four decades later, giving an account of the new poetic drama of the period Granville Barker dated it from Maeterlinck (1937: 10). If Ibsen presented one sort of European stimulus to modernisation, Maeterlinck was another. We need therefore to know what was on offer and why it was so different. We shall then look at the other European dramatist who was regarded as significantly modern, Schnitzler.

It is 29 April 1900. We are watching an English version of Maeterlinck's *The Death of Tintagiles* directed by Granville Barker for the Stage Society at the Globe theatre. We have reached the closing moments of Act 3. In front of us is a castle room, with three doors. In it there are two young women and an old man. One of the young women has an unconscious little boy in her arms. The castle belongs to their grandmother who is never seen. The boy, Tintagiles, has been summoned to the castle, probably to be killed. We hear a key turning in a lock. The three ready themselves. There's silence, then the largest of the doors begins to open. They try to stop it, but it continues to open although nobody can be heard or seen behind it. A 'cold and calm light penetrates into the room'. The child awakes, emits 'a long cry of deliverance', embraces his sister and the door immediately closes. In the next act, three veiled servants enter the room while its inhabitants sleep. Their mission is to abduct Tintagiles from the others: 'Come quickly; they have begun to move…' 'Their hearts and their eyelids are throbbing together…' 'Yes; I caught a glimpse of the elder girl's blue eyes…' 'She looked at us but did not see us…' 'If one touches one of them, the other two tremble…' 'They are trying hard, but they cannot stir…' 'The elder sister wishes to scream, but she cannot…' 'Come quickly; they seem to know…' (Maeterlinck 1899: 111, 115–16).

The handling of both scene and script is radically different from realist stage conventions. Realist rooms have conventions of usage based on their habitual function. They offer information about those who inhabit them. Here the scene apparently moves of its own accord and cannot be controlled by humans. The movement and light resist simple explanation and the mystery has the status of threat. As important as what we can see on stage is a sense of what is happening off it. The group with the child, and implicitly us, through our sympathy, are vulnerable to the intentions of unseen, unexplained presences. The speech on stage is similarly strange. The servants' lines function as a form of chorus, narrating what is seen rather than expressing individual character. The syntax and balance of the lines are carefully repetitive. This as much as the mysterious setting would become a famous hallmark of Materlinck's theatrical method. In a series of plays the dramaturgy withholds reference points and mechanisms whereby sense can be made of what is going on. The conventional ordering principles of spoken language are suspended. Rather than giving a sense of forward movement, the scripted dialogue enacts stasis. Structured as repetition of incomplete syntactic units, it feels as if characters control neither their means of expression nor their environment but are instead themselves controlled.

This sort of scripting grew out of the Symbolist project and went beyond it. The challenge for Symbolist theatre was to use its irreducibly material elements to stage what is beneath the surface of the everyday, to pay witness to the dreamt, the inexplicable, that which is cognitively beyond. In what Maeterlinck called 'second degree dialogue' there's a sense behind the fractured utterance and silences of the always present. Language users are revealed as functions of a language system beyond their individual selves. To create a 'displacement of the habitual angle of vision' (in McGuinness 2000: 249) Maeterlinck made the material elements of the stage function in ways that inhibited customary modes of recognition and explanation, using their very materiality against themselves. The heavier that castle door is, the more it carries a sense of mysterious threat. Voices that repeat words are hypnotic not because they reject sound but because they organise it in particular ways. As McGuinness accurately observes, 'This theatre of "suggestion" [...] is the result of an altogether more *concrete* manipulation of practical theatrical resources' than Symbolists would allow (2000: 248–49).

Not the least of those resources is the actor. We saw how in the servants' scene their speeches did not express character but created instead a vocal elaboration of the picture of the sleepers. Those sleepers get their effect by being silent. Here what is required of the actor is not primarily the work of characterisation. Indeed when it was published *Tintagiles* was in a volume subtitled *Three Little Plays for Marionettes*. In Symbolist theatre, the presence of the living actor has the potential always to thwart the evocation of otherworldliness, its physical energy distracting from the aloof composure of the image. Maeterlinck's solution was to construct a dramaturgy which insisted on physical stillness and the mutual dependence of voices caught up into repetitive sound. These effects required a collective discipline which had no place for the star actor's self-production. The staged image of human beings entrained into the laws of a language system beyond them was thus both a philosophical statement and a mode of doing acting. And we should note here in passing that Maeterlinck's marionette mode anticipated by several years Gordon Craig's invention of the Übermarionette, in an essay from 1907, as a vehicle for attacking both realist aesthetics and commercial theatre.

It was though a minority experiment. Social realism remained largely intact on stage, like a granite tea pot, and there were few copies of Maeterlinck's dramaturgy. Most of his plays were translated by A. Teixeira de Mattos and Alfred Sutro. The first didn't seem to write plays and the second continued to produce clunky, very granity, indeed very potty, realism. The only translator whose own plays approached the feel of the originals was Laurence Alma-Tadema (1865–1940), daughter of the artist. Her *Unseen Helmsman* (1897), a dialogue between two women, makes much of silence, restricted gestures such as touching, an offstage space in which children sleep, an external storm, and a sense of unseen presence. Likewise her *Childe Vyet* uses flickering light and obscure shadows. But Maeterlinck's major impact came with the later emergence of the new verse dramatists. One of the finest of them, Gordon Bottomley, said Maeterlinck was an early influence, learning from him the potency of the one-act play (*Tintagiles* is technically five acts, but all very short). The form facilitated concentration on a simplified action. So too Maeterlinck's experiments with broken syntax and repeated phrases pointed the way towards theatrical uses of verse. Barker, himself a moderniser, was perhaps right about the foundational influence of Maeterlinck.

Another European moderniser he championed was Arthur Schnitzler (1862–1931). While this interest in European work was shared by others in the Stage Society, in general they showed a preference for social realism. In the Society's first ten years, the most performed European dramatist after Ibsen was Brieux. There were also a couple of plays by the Dutch dramatist Herman Heijermans, who, like Brieux, wrote a form of campaigning realism. Beyond that there were Hauptman, Sudermann and several Russians. Barker, by contrast, explored more widely. He returned to Maeterlinck in 1904 in the early months at the Court; he did a new production of *Tintagiles* with music by the progressive young Vaughan Williams and scenography by Charles Ricketts in 1913; and post-war directed *The Betrothal*. With Lillah McCarthy he made plans to stage *Le Cloître* by Maeterlinck's compatriot Verhaeren in January 1915 and in December 1916 was reading Mayakovsky. But the interest was not only in dramatists. He travelled to Berlin in 1910 to look at the work of Reinhardt and to Moscow in 1914 to watch Stanislavski. What he was looking at was both the management of scenography and ways of doing acting. Indeed it was in part scenography that attracted him to Maeterlinck: 'I have always taken an intense interest in "opposite windows". Maeterlinck hit upon one of his really poetic ideas in Intérieur', where characters watch a family through the windows of their house (in Shepherd 2021: 187). The appearance of Schnitzler in this range of interests was even more innovative. His work had not been done before in England.

For those who knew the culture of Vienna and the Austro-Hungarian empire, he presented a figure very different from the Symbolist, and by now quite literary, Maeterlinck. Publication of his *Leutnant Gustl* in December 1900 had caused offence because of its anti-militarism. It led to Schnitzler losing his commission as a reserve officer, but he returned to the topic in *Der einsame Weg* in 1903 (Roberts 1989). His politics figure less in his impact on the English stage, however, than did his mode of writing. In the opinion of that champion of European Modernity, Horace Samuel, Schnitzler was 'one of the most modern of all modern dramatists'. This impression was produced by the combination of topic and treatment. Schnitzler writes about 'the complications of sociological sex' but does so without the 'drastic harshness' often found in modern problem plays. His 'essential characteristics' are 'the light touch, the psychological penetration, and the ironic wistfulness' (1913b: v–vi).

Those features were apparently less in evidence in Barker's first Schnitzler production, at the Court, in 1905. The play was *In the Hospital* (more literally translated as *Last Masks*, part of the *Lebendige Stunden* cycle). For one reviewer, its distinctive feature was 'brutality'. Consisting largely of conversation between two dying men, there was merely a 'thread of plot' with the emphasis on the dying (*St. James's Gazette* 1905: 12). What made it seem brutal was that, in the absence of much plot, the audience had to focus on the conversation and its circumstances, to experience it in the moment. That same, arguably brutal, control of the focus underpinned the longer and more famous work which Barker mounted in March 1911, *Anatol*. This is a sequence of apparently free-standing units, one of which Barker had tried out the previous month. They show Anatol in conversation with Max, frequently about his serial infidelities with women. The interest, in part, comes from Anatol's rehearsal of his habitual cynicism and sexism, double standards and classic masculine self-pity. The settings are very simple, almost unnecessary, with most of the work being done by the acting. What was required was understatement, playing that was almost inseparable from civil conversation. These were hallmarks of Barker's own style. And indeed he had closely identified himself with the production. He produced the show and played Anatol. But he was also playing his own script, based on a literal translation done for him by his close friend and doctor, Christopher Wheeler (1868–1947). The pair were to co-operate again on Schnitzler's *Das Märchen*, produced by Maurice Elvey in January 1912 (Morgan 1961: 310) among the new European works done by his Adelphi Play Society. The script of *Anatol* well exemplifies Barker's touch. It sharpened, as it were, the simplicity and fluidity, indeed the lightness, of the lines. Barker, almost melding himself with Schnitzler, spotted that in Schnitzler's dramaturgy the lighter the tone the more difficult is its combination with the cynicism and sexual exploitation of which it speaks. In a sense the very lightness and easefulness trap the audience into a perhaps brutally difficult focus.

This though was not the last word in Schnitzler's 'modern' handling of acting and sex. A couple of years later his play *The Green Cockatoo* was done in a double bill with *Comtesse Mitzi* by the Stage Society at the Aldwych Theatre on 9 and 10 March 1913. The translation of *Cockatoo* was attributed to Christopher Wheeler's wife Penelope (1868–1950), one of the period's sharply intelligent actresses, who worked with both Barker's company and the new poetic drama. In the same year Horace Samuel published his own translation of *Cockatoo* together with a perceptive introduction. *Cockatoo*, more than any, signals Schnitzler's 'ultra' modernity. It is set in a bar during the French Revolution. But it is no ordinary bar. The Host, Prosper, used to run a theatre company, and now puts them to use enacting the criminal clientele of his bar. Their bar-talk about their shocking crimes together with their disrespectful, if not aggressive, behaviour towards other drinkers provides a selling-point for the venue. Its customers are mainly aristocrats who get a pleasure from slumming among the underclass. It's a scenario which, we might note, Genet used later in *The Balcony*.

Schnitzler's model here was that relatively new thing, French cabaret. When he wrote his play in 1899, there was no cabaret in Vienna, but one of his associates in the so-called Young Vienna movement, Felix Salten, was taken with bohemianism, and would later, in spring 1901, start a cabaret, based on what he had seen in Berlin, where Wolzogen opened the first cabaret in mid-January 1901. Like other Germans, and presumably Austrians, Wolzogen had experienced French cabaret from Yvette Guilbert's tours in the 1890s and in Paris itself during the World's Fair in 1899. Wolzogen's importation of French cabaret had a cultural purpose signalled in his name for it, Überbrettl, where 'Brettl' means 'little boards' – where smallness and intimacy contrast with Schiller's name for the theatrical stage, Bretter/boards – and the prefix 'Über' evokes the Nietzschean perspective that rises above bourgeois limitation (Grange 2021). While Schnitzler clearly could not have seen an Überbrettl when he wrote his play, he had inferred the unsettling work that cabaret performance could do.

For it dissolves the dividing line between aesthetic performance and everyday life. The performers inhabit a persona and let that dictate the way they treat their audience. When the 17-year-old Albin is brought to the bar by Francois, whom Prosper treats as Albin's lover, he has to be told repeatedly that the behaviour he is offended by is all just performance. But this relationship between the performed and the apparently unperformed becomes much more interesting when Séverine arrives with her husband the Marquis and the poet Rollin. While her husband is embarrassed by the familiar manner of one of the bar women, Séverine becomes interested in her. The Marquis explains to Francois that his wife is good at adapting herself to every situation and Rollin observes that 'she gossips with those creatures as though she were one of them'. Except she is also 'Something quite different'. The difficulty is to know where the difference lies, so to speak. 'Reality passes into play – play into reality'. When later the bar women compete for a diamond garter, Séverine asks Rollin if he wants to let her join in, as a sexual excitement for him. And then she insists on hearing Henri's story of how he killed his wife, a story that even Prosper thinks may be true. At the end she shouts 'Bravo', to which Rollin replies: 'The moment you call out "bravo!" you make it all acting again – and the pleasant shudder is past' (Schnitzler 1913: 41–52). It's not simply that the distinction between acting and reality is indeterminate, with all its implications for real-life roles, but that this very indeterminacy is the source of pleasure.

While Maeterlinck had influence on the emergence of verse drama with its atmospherics and rhythms, Schnitzler had a different effect on acting. His requirement for a mode of performance close to everyday behaviour seemed to travel from *Anatol* to Barker's Savoy Shakespeares, which were acted with a speed and lightness that some found shocking. One of the important points about these different approaches to acting was, quite apart from their non-realism, the fact of their co-existence as alternatives. The readiness to embrace variety in performance mode was promoted, more or less as a programme for renewal, in an essay titled 'Renovation of the Theatre' which appeared in 1902. Written by the poet and dramatist Thomas Sturge Moore (1870–1944), it repeats Symbolist attacks on the bankruptcy of realism and proposes instead three alternative models which would renew theatre. Each is exemplified by one or more performers. The first is Yvette Guilbert – Moore was clearly one of those who had seen cabaret – with her inhabiting of personas for the duration of a song. Then there are the Japanese whose acting is 'as earnest as children's play'. Third is a pair of Spanish dancers in which the girl, egged on by the crowd, reaches 'such a pitch of intensity […] that she would often faint before the applause'. In all three models the relationship with script is fluid. The Japanese may be most reliant on it, but in their case it is treated in the manner of serious play. Indeed that concept may unite them all. Guilbert inhabits a persona for a song, but has already constructed a performance of herself as cabaret artist. For the Spanish dancers the script is the structure of the dance, being pressed upon by audience expectations. Much as Guilbert inhabited personas for a song, the female dancer is taken over by the dance, yet 'the restraint and economy of movement' are 'maintained even in the whirlwind of an assumed passion' (Moore 1902: 107–8). All these are models which in their different ways blur the boundaries between what Schnitzler's Rollin called 'reality' and 'play'. And all point forward to later discussions about everyday acting and the nature of play. But their importance here also derives from the point where we started: they are various equally possible models.

This gives an insight into how they did Edwardian Modernity. The project of the Stage Society, as with Barker's Court, was to mount a range of different sorts of play. The borrowings from Europe were part of this project, part of it not so much because any individual text brought Modernity to England but because, in the explosion of styles that followed the Ibsen moment, in the wilful demolition of forms, to be modern was to do variety, so to speak. If we are looking for one simple way to describe the ethos of the modernisers of this period in English theatre it is that they were resisting the dominance of a single dramatic model to which all plays should conform. The modernisers were united by an embrace of eclecticism and diversity.

This becomes more apparent, and polemically so, in the work of those who were specifically engaged with the visual organisation of the stage, the scenographers.

Decorative suggestion

In most theatre histories, there's only one name that needs mentioning in the context of English scenography at this period, Edward Gordon Craig. But he has to have a marginal place in the story of English scenography's modernising of itself. He was indeed a tireless campaigner for a new sort of theatre, a great designer, a highly articulate polemicist and about as good as Shaw at his own self-production (which, given his views of Shaw, is a comparison he might resent). But by his own account he didn't – and couldn't – modernise English theatre because the English, perhaps alone in Europe – hey ho – resisted his ideas. So after some highly influential early productions for the Purcell Operatic Society, which he co-founded with composer Martin Shaw, and Laurence Housman's *Bethlehem* at the Imperial Institute in December 1902 (Craig 1957: 242–43), he departed from England to find more receptive theatres in Germany and Russia. Thereafter, from his position in Europe, mainly Italy, he continued to polemicise for a different sort of theatre. His views, well enough known to us now, reached England, together with his designs and illustrations, in print publications. For these, there was an enthusiastic audience among the progressives. Lord Howard de Walden (1880–1946) offered the money to establish a training school, which was founded in Italy having been thwarted in England, and Barker, reviewing his work in 1922, said that it offered an unmissable 'lesson in the plastic aspect of drama' (1922b). But in terms of theatre practice, after 1903, as Craig himself said (1957: 245), he didn't work in England.

The effect of concentrating on Craig is to obscure from view the English designer who was regarded by contemporaries as the actual central figure,

Charles Ricketts (1866–1931). An artist, illustrator, collector and publisher, he had his feet in the 1890s. He and his partner Charles Shannon were friends of Oscar Wilde and particularly admired the work of Rossetti (Darracott 1980). But so too he kept pace with the aesthetic developments around him, even though he hated some of them, such as post-impressionism. He had strong views on the state of the theatre, encouraged new work for the stage and promoted an approach to design influenced by Wagner and Appia. These ideas, articulated in various places, were brought together in his essay on 'Stage Decoration'. This appeared in *The Fortnightly Review* in 1912 and was slightly re-written for his 1913 *Pages on Art*, where the concluding praise of German theatrical advances was, perhaps tactfully, deleted.

Like Craig – and most designers – Ricketts begins with the disorganised nature of contemporary play production, which he saw as intensified by 'lavish and quite speculative habits of expenditure'. The first person to address the problems of the theatre and to create conditions for higher quality design, he says, was Richard Wagner. Wagner modelled a different sort of auditorium allowing for a new relationship to the stage. But while in such practical matters his contribution has been unsurpassed, his 'pictorial taste' was less good, his settings 'merely a further elaboration of the sham-real scenery of all opera houses of his time, at once literal, complex, and trivial'. The properly progressive response to Wagner's new theatre – and to his operas – came from Adolphe Appia. His theories, summarised by Ricketts, amounted to 'a discarding of all attempts at realism, to which he would add an expressive use of ever-changing light, accompanying and interpreting the action like the presence of the music itself. He would reduce natural forms to silhouettes of a broad and imaginative treatment'. These 'abstract forms' have 'a beauty of their own, which is imaginative in temper' (1912: 1080, 1085, 1086).

From here, Ricketts moves to the example of the Russian ballet, which had created a huge impact in London in 1911, largely because of its designs by Bakst. These, says Ricketts, were the result of 'a decorative and personal treatment' very different from Appia's abstraction and not amenable to the lighting pioneered by him or Craig. Where this example is heading is towards a re-statement of a proposition with which Ricketts began, namely that 'there is no golden rule governing all contingencies […] that there are as many possible styles of theatre decoration as there are plays' (1912: 1086, 1087). This is very like a proposition we encountered slightly earlier, that what is wrong is a single rule and what is right is variety and eclecticism.

But Ricketts didn't leave it there. Although he was writing about 'Stage' decoration in general, he had a particular stage in view, the one closest to his heart, 'poetic' theatre. In this there was currently little interest, but that could be remedied by the creation in England of a Bayreuth-type theatre (which indeed Boughton and Buckley (1911) had just proposed), and of a 'compact and convinced audience' such as is only found in 'music-halls and football finals'. These examples lead Ricketts to re-state and modify his opening proposition. There is no single formula, 'yet "concentration," which I have praised above "simplicity," is a rule or guiding principle, and "simplicity" and economy are means towards that emphasis of poetic essentials which the production of the poetic drama requires' (1912: 1090). Questions of aesthetics finally, however, give way to the matter of organisation. The choice of any aesthetic convention has to be made by the right person, given sole artistic control of the theatre. That call for a new artistic overseer had also been made by Craig, indeed some people, not least of them Craig himself, saw Craig as a candidate for the role. But on this name Ricketts remained tight-lipped, and more so in his second version, which deleted a reference linking Craig to Appia.

The reason for this might be clarified by a piece written five years before. Published in *The Athenaeum* it is about Ricketts and the new poetic drama. Although it is signed 'S', it expresses Ricketts' ideas and he may have been involved. Certainly it was seen before publication by his close friend Sturge Moore. The piece is headed 'Colour on the Stage', analysis of which, it says, has been neglected. As remedy it discusses recent and immediately upcoming productions by the Literary Theatre Society 'under the artistic direction of Mr. Ricketts'. This group has 'devoted itself to the exposition of the new departure in stage decoration based on harmony and economy'. Harmony is important because 'colour-harmony' can express the 'dominating atmosphere' of a play and within that set up a distinction between the chorus, dressed 'in the key of the harmony', and the principals who 'symbolize their character in dress'. The article concludes by hoping that the design example set by the Literary Theatre Society 'may have something of the effect on the English stage that Mr. Gordon Craig, who is working on the same lines, has achieved in Germany' (S 1907: 332). Not only absent from the English scene, Craig was also unnecessary to it, because a new theatre company was leading the way in England. And driving the visual innovation of that company was the designer Charles Ricketts, whose account of Stage Decoration five years later didn't need to give a major place to Craig because Ricketts was already in that place.

And certainly it was his ideas, rather more than Craig's, that were disseminating through the English design world. Those ideas are summarised in general terms in a single sentence from the article on 'Colour': 'In its productions it has aimed at a harmonious setting by which essentials only are brought into prominence, while the scene is a background suggesting the situation rather than realizing it' (S 1907: 332). That emphasis on suggestion reappears in a lecture given at the University of Leeds in 1915 by the painter and designer Albert Rutherston (1881–1953; in 1916 he anglicised his name from Rothenstein). He begins in a familiar place: the theatre is in need of reorganisation, which requires the oversight of a designer to bring together all elements of production. From here he makes an equally familiar attack on the 'dreary realism' which uses the theatre as a pulpit, the only exceptions being the work of Synge, Yeats, Masefield, Barker. Note that Shaw, a leading pulpiteer, is of course not on the list, although Albert's brother, the artist William Rothenstein, felt that even Shaw's dull dialogue as done at the Court Theatre could have been scenographically rescued: 'irony should be shown in scenes as it was in dialogue'; even realistic plays could be given 'point and meaning' by design (Rothenstein 1934: 203). Albert was more polemically anti-realist: '"realistic methods" fail to carry conviction and do not express any sense of reality'. If realism has to be staged it must be governed by the one foundational principle which applies to all theatre design. This is 'the relation between a living and moving thing, the actor, to his background' [sic]. Each of the two elements here is 'indispensable to the other [...] playing, as it were, into each other's hands'. In this basic relationship, the requirement is not for imitation but for 'decorative suggestion' (Rutherston 1919: 9, 14–16).

In that last phrase both words are key. 'Suggestion', as Ricketts used it above, is connected to the poet-dramatists' aim to clear the stage of clutter and busyness in order to open the space for imagination. 'Decoration' is positioned for us by Yeats. He makes an antithesis between 'Naturalistic scene-painting', a 'trade' that simply copies nature, as against 'Decorative scene-painting' which is inseparable from the movements and the clothes (1989: 100). Together suggestion and decoration offered an alternative to a realism understood as dead materiality that constrains movement of both imagination and body. Describing in 1916 'the great revolution in scenic art' a review of Thomas Beecham's company said that realism and naturalism had been replaced by 'imaginative expression and power of decorative suggestion'. In particular, 'the most important fundamental principle laid down by the new school is in regard to the relation of the moving figures on the stage to their background' (C.G.A. 1916).

The approach of this new school of English design was shaped by the distant influence of Craig operating in a context where Ricketts was a powerful voice. In 1915, in his Leeds lecture, Rutherston promoted Craig as the greatest genius of the time, rather than Bakst, for example, whose work for the Russian ballet, admired by Ricketts, he dismissed (1919: 24) as 'plagiarism and sensational vulgarity'. Against Ricketts' emphasis on the importance of colour, Rutherston argues that form and proportion take precedence. To illustrate his argument he describes the design principles of the Shakespeare productions done by Granville Barker at the Savoy theatre in 1912. The first production, *The Winter's Tale*, caused uproar among realists and Shakespeare traditionalists. But the art historian and critic Paul Konody (1872–1933) hailed it as Shakespeare done on Craig's lines, an example of 'modern stage' reform. In the row that followed, if Barker were to lose, he said, 'the birth of the art of theatre may be delayed for ten or twenty years' (1912). By the second production, *Twelfth Night*, there was nearly unanimous enthusiasm.

These supposed Craigian productions used a double stage with a front curtain and a built scene. Everything was based on 'the design and plan that was demanded by the play', which to us may seem obvious enough. But less so in a world where design was intended to show off spectacular gimmicks or foreground the star actor. The curtain was 'suggestive only of the time, place, and mood', while the built scene gave 'the charm of light and shade, line, form, and colour, which resulted from that [*the plan*] and the mimes in front, and that alone'.

Here again are the key elements of suggestion, perhaps deriving from Ricketts, and the interactive relationship between actor and scene, deriving more from Craig. And there's an emphatic distance from mimetic realism: 'The whole art and charm of the Theatre is its artificiality' (Rutherston 1919: 21, 19, 18). We should note, in passing, that remark about the self-declared artifice of art would have rather neatly fitted what, about seventy years later, Peter Bürger said was a defining stance of the avant-garde.

Rutherston's co-designer on *The Winter's Tale* was Norman Wilkinson of Four Oaks (1883–1934; he insisted on that formula to distinguish himself from the other Norman Wilkinson, a marine painter, naval officer and designer of camouflage). Wilkinson (of FO) had recently done Barker's productions of *The Sentimentalists*, *The Madras House* and *Iphigenia*. He described his and Rutherston's approach as 'simple and direct treatment, free from style and period' (quoted in Rutherston 1919: 19). That somewhat slippery notion of being 'free from style' becomes easier to pin down if viewed retrospectively from an interview given by Wilkinson about two decades later. Discussing a production of *Romeo and Juliet* in 1933, he said that most of the production would be played on the front stage behind which was a façade containing an inset stage and balcony. In plan and elevation it was consciously Elizabethan though the detailing would look like the contemporary Stratford auditorium. There would be no trick lighting effects. 'The unlimited resources of the theatre will be utilised to show how straightforward and how simple we can be' (in H.G. 1933).

But it was not quite that simple. When he made his basically Elizabethan stage look like a continuation of the contemporary Stratford auditorium Wilkinson created a stage that did straightforward imitation, but what it was imitating was the theatre the audience were sitting in. It was the theatre, with all the art and simple charm of artificiality, pretending to be the theatre. That scenographic joking emerged from a process that had moved itself away from mere 'decorative suggestion' in order to reflect upon and play games with its art of design. It had started a couple of decades earlier.

Post-impressionists

Wilkinson was rather good at scenic jokes. His design for Barker's 1911 production of Schnitzler's *Anatol* hung post-impressionist paintings on the main character's walls. London had somewhat scandalously encountered post-impressionism at Roger Fry's exhibition at the Grafton Gallery in late 1910. So when such paintings turned up on Barker's stage the next year they underlined the fact that Schnitzler was a very 'modern' dramatist, and that Barker was a modern director. Furthermore they suggested that painters have a role to play in providing decoration for a stage. Wilkinson, like Ricketts, Rutherston, Craig, was also an artist. None of them were scene painters. Although the set for *Anatol* might have been realist, having walls on which pictures could be hung, those pictures set up a quizzical relationship with what supported them. This was a feature of Wilkinson's style. He foregrounded his design by incorporating quotation of visual artefacts. For Barker's production of *Iphigenia in Tauris*, done in March 1912 (and revived to tour New England universities in 1915), he did research on ancient Greek pottery designs and colouring. In front of a temple portal, with huge red columns, Iphigenia was in brick red, the chorus in black robes lined in blue silk, with orange skirts. The costumes were covered in elaborate pattern, as it were quoting two-dimensional friezes on vases that moved and re-grouped against a geometric setting, refunctioning Attic art into a new scenographic rhythm. By September, when Barker's *Winter's Tale* opened, with designs by Wilkinson and Rutherston, the critic A. B. Walkley, looking for a term which would catch the moment, labelled it 'Post-Impressionist Shakespeare' (in Kennedy 2008: 123).

Now 'post-impressionism' covers a multitude of possibilities, almost as bad as post-modernism, because it was a label invented by Fry (1866–1934) as an umbrella term for the sort of new work he wanted to exhibit. He explained the paintings' shared characteristics in a lecture given at the close of the first exhibition. They had their effects, he said, not through representation of an external world but through formal pictorial qualities: 'There is no immediately obvious reason why the artist should represent actual things at all, why he should not have a music of line and colour. […] We may get, in fact, from a mere pattern, if it be really noble in design and vital in execution, intense aesthetic pleasure'. The reason a pattern can give pleasure is because 'Particular rhythms of line and particular harmonies of colour have their spiritual correspondences, and tend to arouse now one set of feelings, now another'. In this formulation, Fry used what was to become a key term in both visual art and poetic drama: 'Rhythm is the fundamental and vital quality of painting, as of all the arts – representation is secondary to that, and must never encroach on the more ultimate and fundamental demands of rhythm' (Fry 1911: 862, 863). As Tillyard (1988: 98) notes, even those who hated the post-impressionist exhibition, such as the poet Laurence Binyon, shared this same pre-occupation with the effects of rhythm, as we shall see in the next chapter.

The general fluidity of definition of post-impressionism is apparent in Desmond MacCarthy's insistence that the costumes of Barker's *Winter's Tale* lacked the 'synthesis' and 'simplicity' of post-impressionist paintings (in Kennedy 2008: 134), while on the other hand Walkley could be seen as right in thinking that the scenography fitted precisely with what Fry said about the importance of 'linear design and pure colour as the main organs of expression' (1911: 865). Striking features of the disturbingly radical production were the colour palette of Rutherston's costumes – magenta, lemon yellow, emerald green – and the graphic patterning of Wilkinson's curtains. The effects of colour and linear design became even more strongly apparent in *Twelfth Night*, for which Wilkinson did the total design. In Orsino's court, the actors in their patterned costumes were almost visually absorbed into the patterning behind them, the moving three-dimensional body slipping into two-dimensional graphics. When the curtains were raised to reveal the set scene of Olivia's garden, the actual three-dimensional volume was apparently pulled towards flatness by the simplified picture-book perspective and the conspicuously geometric patterning of the trees. In both productions Rutherston and Wilkinson were playing with the conventions of pictorial representation, not concealing the artifice of the stage but celebrating its potency as a machine that makes pictures. Its whole charm, as Rutherston said, was both its capacity to suggest and its artificiality, like perhaps a Cézanne landscape.

That post-impressionist label is important here because it marks the deviation from the two poles that had structured the design world, Ricketts and Craig. Ricketts, as we've noted, was hostile to Craig. So too he made a public attack on Fry's post-impressionist exhibition. His designs, at base, tended to reach back to the visual language of the 1890s. In his scenography for the Literary Theatre Society production of *The Persians* in 1907, the stage was dimly lit with 'dusky reds, purples and black forms' (S 1907: 332). By contrast Rutherston and Wilkinson, declared followers of Craig, were committed to a brightened palette and simplified lines. But that's where, despite Konody's claim about *Winter's Tale*, Craigism stopped. Rather than the three-dimensional volumes, orchestrated shadows and atmospheric monumentality of the drawings in Craig's *Towards a New Theatre* (1913), Wilkinson and Rutherston emphasised colour, line and graphic pattern. For them the stage was a flat platform for actors, for whose work they had perhaps a higher opinion than did Craig. The 'background' against which actors moved was lit with bright light to foreground the intensity of colour as both movement and three-dimensional volumes repeatedly came into tension with patterned pictures.

These elements were picked up and developed by another designer, Claud Lovat Fraser (1890–1921). Of them all he felt closest to Craig, whom he had met in spring 1911, yet was visually perhaps most distant. Indeed Michael Sadler (1861–1943), writing in the flagship post-impressionist magazine *Rhythm*, suggested that Fraser was less of a Craig disciple than a post-impressionist. Fraser was at his best, he argued, when uninfluenced by Craig, for Craig's 'dehumanised art' gave no scope for Fraser's 'love of colour, and his belief in life'. When he painted Rotterdam houses with roofs in pink and blue, it was a deliberate brightening designed to express vivacity and energy (Sadler 1913: 477). In this respect Fraser should be linked not to Craig but to the French Fauves, or indeed to the followers of the man who trained him, Walter Sickert.

Fraser approached the theatre as a book-illustrator and artist who valued inks, line, gouache, bright colour, the eighteenth century (Drinkwater and Rutherston 1923: 27). Like Wilkinson, he began working for the Phoenix Society, an offshoot of the Stage Society founded in 1919. But unlike Wilkinson his first stage work, Playfair's *As You Like It* for the Stratford Shakespeare Festival in 1919, caused furore among its audiences, some of whom might have been fearful, suggested one reviewer, that they had 'fallen into a den of theatrical Bolsheviks' (C.E.M. [C.E. Montague] 1919). The main culprit in this hideous encounter, the Trot of Avon, was Fraser's design. It was, said one review, 'a jumble of styles' with the Forest of Arden 'three sickly trees on the edge of an open field', 'exciting and fresh'. Montague, him of the Bolshevik menace, noted it was 'of course unrealistic, severe, and abstract', producing an 'exciting, challenging vivacity'. But while many playgoers may have found it innovatory, 'it only goes behind a few modernisms back to something really old' (*Observer* 1919; C.E.M. 1919).

Among those 'modernisms' there was a short-hand word applied to innovative design that was rather more specific than 'post-impressionist'. Paul Shelving (1888–1968), scenographer for Barry Jackson at Birmingham, embraced principles very similar to Fraser's and was consequently labelled a 'futurist'. This he rejected: 'So far from being anything of the kind, I suppose I draw all my inspiration from the past. The fearless use of brilliant colour, simplified outlines, occasionally, where it seems appropriate, the introduction of a bright toy-like quality'. This use of colour and line belongs with a coherent approach to staging which all of these 'decorative' designers would recognise. Writing in 1927, Shelving said: 'What we try to do today is to accept the fact boldly that all scenery is a convention, and to simplify it wherever possible, having as our aim a background which throws up the actors and helps them to suggest the fiction of the play by a few characteristics rather than a wealth of detail. These simpler forms of scenery are capable of great beauty of colour and form and light, and are quickly handled in the changes' (Shelving 1927: 22). Colour, simplicity, suggestion, efficiency: they all go together.

To these regulars Fraser added his own innovation, the use of found materials. Playfair tells how for Milne's *Make-Believe* (1918) a regular scene painter did a desert island with sea around it, on which Fraser then 'super-imposed several odd bits of cloth'. He 'got his effects actually by *not* spending money' (Playfair 1925: 23, 32). When the realist stage used a fashion-house gown it established continuity with the world inhabited by a moneyed audience and ostended expenditure as spectacle. By contrast Fraser's found materials and picture-book designs were displaced from their natural homes, communicated not their cost but their playfulness. They were symptomatic of an approach that played games with what we look at. Friend of Craig he may have been, but this was not Craig's stage as a place for 'Belief and the power to worship' (1921: 65). Fraser's wrestling scene in *As You Like It* had a cloister at the front of the stage, forming what Playfair (1925: 51) calls a 'false or second proscenium'. Here in shadow stood the watching court. Upstage on a sunlit triangle the wrestling happened. While the lighting gave them emphasis, the false proscenium partially obscured them, so they came in and out of view, centred and de-centred.

But above all Fraser was famous for simplicity. For *As You Like It*, like Wilkinson, he had researched antique visual artefacts for costume and scene, this time sixteenth-century missals, but all were rendered in pure colour, with no half-tones, nothing dusky, nothing, as he would say, like 'mud'. His trees had emerald green leaves, with a palest blue backcloth, and sharp green stage at the front. The combination of bright colour with simplicity gave startlingly 'modern' effects. Reviewers said the trees of the forest were 'cubist' (Playfair

1925: 49) even though their loops were accurate copies of original missals. But even with this labelling Fraser played games. By contrast with Shelving's distaste, Fraser actually claimed to be a futurist. Being a regular in Harold Monro's Poetry Bookshop, which entertained Marinetti (Hibberd 2001), and as a collaborator with the Vorticist Gaudier-Brzeska, he certainly knew what he was claiming. But Playfair points out that he pronounced it 'futúrist'. The accent is important. It suggests both the association and its misapplication. While a futurist on Marinetti's model authenticated himself by denouncing contemporary culture, a futúrist seems instead to play games with authentication, replacing belligerence with joke. Fraser and his predecessors didn't need Marinetti's shouting. Those colours and lines themselves constituted a rhetorical challenge. To decorate was to modernise.

And it gained its force in doing so because of its association with one of the key developments in theatre production of the period.

Platforms

When Wilkinson outlined his mission for simplicity in 1933 his acknowledged influence was the method of William Poel (1852–1934) who taught that 'Shakespeare had to make his effects on his own audience by the magic of the spoken word, and that for a producer the method of simplicity is best'. Indeed 'any deviation from the Poel method of simplicity is silly, old-fashioned, and dull' (in H.G. 1933). Poel's method was based on research into the staging of the medieval and early-modern plays of England. In a theatre world dominated by the elaborately detailed settings of social drama, with its tea cups and antimacassars, and spectacular Shakespeare, with costume processions and live rabbits – a sort of Shakespacular – Poel's commitment to honouring what he perceived as the conventions of early-modern staging led to productions done on a more or less bare stage. But, as Beerbohm saw it, 'Mr Poel's aim in founding the Elizabethan Stage Society was archaeological rather than aesthetic. His aim was not so much to produce plays delightfully as to show how they were originally produced' (1969: 145). This use of the stage space seemed motivated by the project of recovery rather than offering a model for new aesthetic practices. As Craig put it, with typical firmness, the sixteenth century was not relevant to 'the living Theatre' (1921: 125).

Slightly after the first Poel experiments came productions that had their roots somewhere more ancient, Greek tragedy. This dramatic form received considerable attention in the opening years of the century, principally in the work of a group of anthropologists based in Cambridge. Their scholarship advanced the understanding of drama in general in that it revealed a viable dramatic form which was not driven by the aim of copying the image of everyday life but derived instead from communal dance and the *sacer ludus* (Murray 1977). One of these classical scholars, Gilbert Murray, had interests in making theatre and embarked on a series of translations of Euripides. Staged by his friend Granville

Barker the productions were not conceived as antiquarian revivals but shared the same aesthetic values as Barker's handling of more modern texts, with the emphasis on simplicity and contemporary accessibility. Since they didn't require detailed replication of a room or park, on his proscenium stage Barker used a simple backdrop with a schematic image. The discipline imposed by the proscenium opening was relaxed, following Reinhardt's example, by dispensing with the curtain and having entrances through the audience.

An even more radical relationship with audience was discovered in the encounter with Japanese Nō (about which more in Chapter 3). This ancient and valued form worked on a stage that was merely, as Yeats said, 'a platform surrounded on three sides by the audience' (1989: 230). But, like classical Greek tragedy, Nō was specific to a different culture. Its wider application to English drama was thus limited. Nonetheless a key design feature had already entered the scenographic vocabulary of the early experiments of Gordon Craig. His first production for the Purcell Operatic Society, *Dido and Aeneas*, was staged with a plain blue background and grey proscenium. For the subsequent production of Housman's *Bethlehem* the spectators were in a tent, with a larger curtained space for the players (1913: 57; 1957: 242).

In all four of these instances, the stage is not controlled by, and subservient to, a spatial logic governed by the habitual function of what is represented, such as a park or room. While in each different performance conventions obtain, these are not necessarily inherent in the arrangements of the material entity. At base, the theatrical stage was, to use Yeats' word, a 'platform'. Connected to these wider experiments with platform, there was, in a more limited way, exploration of the use of curtain. Traditionally curtains closed the hole in the proscenium and opened to reveal the fictional scene, but 'curtain scenes' – played in front of the curtain – had developed as a way of covering elaborate scene changes. Here the curtains become background, but understood as a transition from one scene to another. In Craig's Purcell shows the plain blue curtain background replaced a three-dimensional scene, not now as a transition but as an abstract space in its own right. As Symons said, 'a plain cloth, modulated by light, can stand for space or for limit [..] The eye loses itself among these severe, precise, and yet mysterious lines and surfaces' (1906: 352). A decade later, working for a director who hated wood and canvas fictional scenes, Wilkinson designed elaborately patterned curtains for Barker's Savoy Shakespeares. The following year, for Barker's second *Tintagiles*, Ricketts replaced Maeterlinck's mysterious medieval castle with heavy drapes that partly revealed impenetrable blackness. Later again Sturge Moore used the curtain as a staging of concealment. Thus, like the platform, the curtain came into use as a complex scenic device. Within a contemporary design discourse that was not only adamantly anti-realist but also, more positively, committed to economy, simplicity and 'suggestion', the foregrounding of the physical arrangements of the stage was both a polemical declaration and the basis for an aesthetic. This aesthetic was insistently different from the three-dimensional volumes proposed – but often not actually used – in Craig's drawings. His human figure may be positioned for great visual effect on a structure such as steps, but those steps in turn constrained what that human body could do. By contrast the decorated two-dimensional backdrop leaves the platform clear for the movement of the actor. The character and effects of that movement depend on the interaction of elements, the co-dependency between actor and scene.

In the repeated experiments with different sorts of non-realist platform, there is an aesthetic drive that runs in parallel to, and may partly be explained by, a longer-term development in visual art. As Clark describes it, avant-garde painting between 1860 and 1918 was interested in working with, and revealing, the basic material arrangements of the picture, its flatness. To this flatness, it gave a range of values. It could be 'an analogue of the "popular" – something therefore conceived as plain, workmanlike, and emphatic. Or it could signify "modernity"' (by suggesting the two dimensions of, for example, wall posters). Then again 'unbrokenness of surface could be seen [...] as standing for the truth of *seeing*'. Used more aggressively flatness 'appeared as a barrier to the ordinary bourgeois' wish to enter a picture and dream'. Flatness was thus in play between being a material fact of painting and a metaphor (Clark 1985: 57–58). The platform was similarly in play, and in three cases with similar values. Wilkinson was signalling modernity, Yeats felt in Craig's design for Purcell's *Dido and Aeneas* he was 'watching people wavering on the edge of infinity, somewhere at the Worlds End' (in Morash 2021: 123), and Fraser's early work debarred the bourgeois from their preferred romance of Shakespeare. In the fourth case, Poel's stagings were 'popular' in the sense that they evoked the heritage of a shared national culture. We have here then an apparently parallel project to what, in a different art-form, is labelled the avant-garde.

The great exhibition

In the year of Barker's first Savoy Shakespeares appeared a book called *The New Spirit in Drama and Art*. To assist English theatre's project of renewal the author, Huntly Carter, described various examples of new work he had seen in a range of European cities. His main focus was on the visual aspects of theatre, rather than, say, mode of acting, but encompassing the design of buildings alongside scenography. For Carter, both the experience of the stage setting and the positioning of the spectator in relation to it are crucial for a theatre that wants to put its watchers in touch with something beyond daily life. In general terms, the imitative apparatus of realist theatre has to be stripped away to be replaced by a new simplicity. This will in large part follow from a new visual attitude to the theatre.

That new approach, exemplified by the work of Craig, Reinhardt and the Russian ballet, aimed to make the stage 'more mystical', to 'foster mood'. Its method was an 'attempt to frame stage-pictures in rectangular frames' working to the principles of 'simplification, synthesis and suggestion' (Carter 1912: 226). Nearly a decade later in Kenneth MacGowan's *Theatre of Tomorrow* this non-realistic approach has fractured into 'two types of dramatic expression':

'the drama of reality lifted to a plane of sharp, clear, absolute expression' and 'the drama of imagination based upon the reality of spiritual truth but lifted to levels of sheer beauty'. Plays will be done in intimate playhouses and gigantic auditoria, for 'the new art of the theatre is curiously split upon the rock of the little theatre and the circus'. The 'little theatre' was familiar to MacGowan (1888–1963), an American who the following year took over management of the Provincetown Playhouse with his close friends Eugene O'Neill and the designer Robert Edmond Jones. His book naturally is grounded in American examples, but shares with Carter the argument that the new theatre was a product, not of the single influence of Craig, but of innovations that had sprung up at 'half a dozen points in Europe' (1923: 267–68, 14). Indeed Craig, with his atmospherics and spiritual emphasis, is only one pole of MacGowan's binary. The other, with its stage pictures and sharp, clear expression might include designers such as Rutherston and Wilkinson.

Neither name is mentioned by Carter or MacGowan. This omission is symptomatic of the general sense, well exemplified by Carter, that the English stage was not 'modern' because it didn't conspicuously follow any of the examples of European work he describes. That general sense has persisted in the way that theatre design history has been written. Put bluntly: European theatre was modern; English theatre didn't look like European theatre; English theatre wasn't modern.

For contemporaries these assumptions about English scenography's relationship with Europe, and therefore with Modernity, became available for scrutiny in the theatre design exhibition of 1922. This arrived in London from Amsterdam. Its significance was that it was both the first thing of its kind in England and an intervention in European practices. The idea for it came from the Dutch playwright and critic Franz Mijnssen and was taken up by the Kunst aan het Volk society which appointed an organising committee with the architect and set designer Hendrikus Theodorus Wijdeveld as secretary. Wijdeveld (1885–1987) edited a journal, *Wendingen* (Turnings) which published issues on dance and masks. In his own writing, he attacked both the commercial theatre industry and the minority challenges to it, which were compromised, he argued, by working in its buildings. When The International Theatre Exhibition opened at the Municipal Museum in Amsterdam in early 1922 Wijdeveld's design suggested that 'the whole of the exhibition could be read as a theoretical lecture' (Eversmann 2007: 76).

Craig was invited to open it. The choice signalled the status of the exhibition, which 'can be said to be the first major showing of set, costume and theatre designs of the international, avant-garde movement in the theatre' (Eversmann 2007: 67). Along with Appia Craig featured as one of the two visionaries who were transforming theatre practice. Norman Wilkinson was asked to coordinate the English submission but because of illness the job was done by Horace Shipp and Hermon Ould, editors of *Theatre Craft* journal. When Ould (1885–1951), a committed internationalist, saw it in Amsterdam he acknowledged that the 'practical application' in England of Craig's own ideas had been 'ineffectual'. The dynamic developments were happening in Germany, possibly America. Among the English only Paul Nash was heading somewhere new, in that, like European designers, he had understood that theatre is basically 'kinetic'. Indeed Nash's speculative model for Bottomley's *King Lear's Wife* was one of the hits of the show. Its visual vocabulary suggested the extent to which Nash had immersed himself, to the regret of Bottomley, in the new art he had seen in Paris. For the rest – such as Fraser, Rutherston, Wilkinson – they were 'craftsmen' working 'a vein of decorative expression which is now exhausted' (Ould 1922a).

What is interesting about this story of the exhibition is how the status of English design shifts. Craig, in his role as visionary and provocateur, issued a challenge to bring the exhibition to Britain. That was taken up by Cecil Smith of the Victoria and Albert museum who offered it as venue with funding being obtained from, among others, that great patron of the arts, and playwright, Thomas Lord Howard de Walden. The organisational skills of the new British Drama League were put to work and the exhibition duly arrived in London before going to Manchester and Bradford. When it opened the English design section, which in Amsterdam had been 'somewhat inadequate' (Whitworth 1922: 163), was now greatly extended, with work from many different designers and architects. Ould, after returning to the show, wrote a reflective piece about the emergence of new design in which English designers played a key part.

In 'New Tendencies in the Art of the Theatre' he argues that the International Exhibition was 'chiefly concerned' with the desire to escape from 'preoccupation with photographic realism'. After lamenting that the influential Craig was represented in England not by productions but by books, he charts England's own journey away from realism. It began with London's excitement over Reinhardt's wordless *Sumurun* from 1911. After this, he says, the Barker Shakespeares, 'in settings which flouted all the old conventions', created a stir. As he approvingly notes one of their designers, Rutherston, said that in theatre, just as in painting and sculpture, the 'mere copying of familiar objects' 'is a very poor affair indeed as an end in itself'. And Rutherston's setting for Shaw's *Androcles and the Lion*, composed only of hanging cloths in different colours, 'is likely to be regarded as a milestone in English theatre decoration'. Having used that key word he then argues that 'decoration' has 'served its turn by making us dissatisfied with unimaginative and unsuggestive staging of the realistic producer'. Now we have to open up to new developments, for 'the "expressionist" is already forcing his way in' (Ould 1922b: 51, 55, 56). Unfortunately, however, expressionism has little presence in England, apart from the work of the director Theodore Komisarjevsky and Paul Nash (who had little theatre experience). Nonetheless Ould was prophetic in that Terence Gray, producing, for example, the poet dramatist Gordon Bottomley at the Festival Theatre, Cambridge, in the mid-twenties, would be a major example of English expressionist work.

Ould's story could offer a lesson to subsequent histories. It puts Craig to one side, places Reinhardt more centrally as a European influence and gives significant place to Wilkinson and particularly Rutherston. It also foregrounds the key term 'decoration' and notes the work that it did. In this story, the English designers, while not looking like, or being dependent on, their European counterparts were nonetheless on their own journey away from realism towards 'Modernity'. As such they may be said to have had a legitimate place in what Eversmann calls the first major design showing of the 'avant-garde movement'.

That's not, however, what English contemporaries called it. Among the organisers its importance derived not only from its exhibits. In his after-dinner speech at the opening-night banquet, Granville Barker said that one of the most significant things about the exhibition was 'the housing of this show of the art of the theatre in the country's chief public museum of Fine art' (Barker 1922a). He then surveyed the national status of drama and its place within educational policy. Similar points were made, in more extended fashion, by Geoffrey Whitworth, the secretary of the British Drama League, in an article published in July of that year. It begins by emphasising 'the rare initiative of a Public Department in thus recognising the art of the stage as worthy of its patronage'. Such recognition is connected to the revival of interest in drama that occurred during the war and is seen in activities in towns and villages across the country. Drama has become 'a factor in national life which it is the public concern to cherish and to serve' (Whitworth 1922: 164–65). The importance of the arrival of the exhibition in London was nothing short of a demonstration of the extent of the revival of national interest, at all levels, in drama. As such it gave a new meaning to modernity. While Barker regarded consciously 'modern' writing and design as a bit of a fad, what he celebrated on that opening night was something that went well beyond aesthetics, the changed material circumstances of a new historical moment for English drama.

But for design at least it was an illusion. By the time he published *Design in the Theatre* in 1927, George Sheringham found there were very few theatre artists in work. Indeed, 'if it were not for the vision and educated taste of three or four men only, there would be no stage decoration in the professional theatres worth writing books about'. These men were Playfair with Fraser, Barker with Wilkinson and Rutherston, and Jackson with Shelving, plus Ricketts (1927: 1). So shocked was Sheringham that he wrote to Craig, who responded with a piece that Sheringham could publish. This consisted of a plan of action as to how designers could become an independent force in the theatre. They should, Craig said, form themselves into a group. To which end they should 'get a book of the rules of the Fascist Party, and [...] copy them in their rules which seem to you practical [...] especially those dealing in discipline' (in Sheringham 1927: 11). To that version of modernity none of them fortunately were inspired.

References

Alma-Tadema, Laurence 1905 *Four Plays* London: The Green Sheaf
Barker, H. Granville 1910 'J.M. Barrie as a Dramatist' *The Bookman* volume 39: 13–21

Barker, H. Granville 1922a 'DL. Dinner speech'. Unpublished. Victoria and Albert Museum, London THM 147/2
Barker, H. Granville 1922b 'The Theatre Exhibition in Manchester' *Manchester Guardian* 30 October
Barker, H. Granville 1937 *On Poetry in Drama* London: Sidgwick & Jackson
Barrie, J.M. 1948 *The Plays of J.M. Barrie [The Definitive Edition]*, ed. A.E. Wilson London: Hodder and Stoughton
Barrie, J.M. 1975 *Ibsen's Ghost*, ed. Penelope Griffin London: Cecil Woolf
Barrie, J.M. 1990 *Punch: A Little Tragedy in One Act* in Leon H. Hugo '*Punch*: J.M. Barrie's Gentle Swipe at "Supershaw"'in Stanley Weintraub and Fred D. Crawford (eds) *Shaw: The Annual of Bernard Shaw Studies*, volume 10 Pennsylvania State University Park: The Pennsylvania State University Press: 60–72
Beerbohm, Max 1969 *More Theatres 1898–1903* London: Rupert Hart-Davis
Boughton, Rutland and Buckley, Reginald R. 1911 *Music Drama of the Future: Uther and Igraine: Choral Drama, with Essays by the Collaborators* London: William Reeve
Carter, Huntly 1912 *The New Spirit in Drama and Art* London: Frank Palmer
Carter, Huntly 1914 'The Re-Incarnations of Mr. Bernard Shaw' *The Egoist* volume 1, number 17: 337–38
C.E.M. 1919 'Gaiety Theatre: "As You Like It"' *Manchester Guardian* 20 May
C.G.A. 1916 'Scenic Art at the New Theatre' *Manchester Guardian* 29 May
Clark, T.J. 1985 'Clement Greenberg's Theory of Art' in Francis Frascina (ed.) *Pollock and After: The Critical Debate* London: Paul Chapman Publishing: 47–63
Craig, E. Gordon 1913 *Towards a New Theatre* London: J.M. Dent & Sons
Craig, E. Gordon 1921 *The Theatre Advancing* London: Constable
Craig, E. Gordon 1957 *Index to the Story of My Days: Some Memoirs of Edward Gordon Craig* London: Hulton Press
Darracott, Joseph 1980 *The World of Charles Ricketts* London: Eyre Methuen
Drinkwater, John and Rutherston, Albert 1923 *Claud Lovat Fraser: A Memoir* London: William Heinemann
Eversmann, Peter G.F. 2007 'The International Theatre Exhibition of 1922 and the Critics' in Klaus Beekman and Jan De Vries (eds) *Avant-Garde and Criticism: Avant-Garde Critical Studies*, volume 21 Amsterdam: Rodopi
Fry, Roger 1911 'Post-Impressionism' *The Fortnightly Review* volume 89: 856–66
Grange, William 2021 *Cabaret* London: Bloomsbury
Hankin, St. John 1901 *Mr. Punch's Dramatic Sequels* London: Bradbury, Agnew & Co
H.G. 1933 'Stratford's New "Romeo": Norman Wilkinson's Plans' *The Observer* 18 June
Hibberd, Dominic 2001 *Harold Monro: Poet of the New Age* Basingstoke: Palgrave
Howe, P.P. 1915 *Bernard Shaw: A Critical Study* London: Martin Secker
Incorporated Stage Society 1909 *Ten Years 1899–1909* London: The Chiswick Press
Jack, R.D.S. 1991 *The Road to the Never Land: A Reassessment of J M Barrie's Dramatic Art* Aberdeen: Aberdeen University Press
Kennedy, Dennis 2008 *Granville Barker and the Dream of Theatre* Cambridge: Cambridge University Press
Konody, Paul 1912 'The Artist's Point of View' *The Observer* 29 September
Levitas, Ben 2016 'The Theatre of Modernity' in Vincent Sherry (ed.) *The Cambridge History of Modernism* Cambridge: Cambridge University Press
MacGowan, Kenneth 1923 *The Theatre of Tomorrow* London: T. Fisher Unwin
Maeterlinck, Maurice 1899 *The Death of Tintagiles*, translated by Alfred Sutro London: Duckworth & Co.

McGuinness, Patrick 2000 *Maurice Maeterlinck and the Making of Modern Theatre* Oxford: Oxford University Press
Moore, T. Sturge 1902 'The Renovation of the Theatre' *The Monthly Review* volume 7: 102–16
Morash, Christopher 2021 *Yeats on Theatre* Cambridge: Cambridge University Press
Morgan, Margery M. 1961 *A Drama of a Political Man: A Study in the Plays of Harley Granville Barker* London: Sidgwick & Jackson
Murray, Gilbert 1977 'Excursus on the Ritual Forms Preserved in Greek Tragedy' in Jane Harrison *Themis: A Study of the Social Origins of Greek Religion* London: Merlin Press
Observer, The 1919 'The Shakespeare Festival' 27 April
Ould, Hermon 1922a 'The Exhibition at Amsterdam' *Manchester Guardian* 30 January
Ould, Hermon 1922b 'New Tendencies in the Art of the Theatre' *The World's Work* volume 39: 49–58
Playfair, Nigel 1925 *The Story of the Lyric Theatre Hammersmith* London: Chatto & Windus
Ricketts, Charles 1912 'Stage Decoration' *The Fortnightly Review* volume 92: 1083–91
Ricketts, Charles 1913 *Pages on Art* London: Constable and Company
Roberts, Adrian Clive 1989 *Arthur Schnitzler and Politics* Riverside, CA: Ariadne Press
Roßbach, Nicola 2005 *Ibsen-Parodien in Der Frühen Moderne* Munich: Martin Meidenbauer
Rothenstein, William 1934 *Men and Memories: Recollections 1900–1922* London: Faber & Faber
Rutherston, Albert 1919 'Decoration in the Theatre' *Monthly Chapbook* volume 1, number 2
S 1907 'Colour on the Stage' *The Athenaeum* number 4142 (16 March): 331–32
Sadler, Michael 1913 'The Galleries: Lovat Fraser' *Rhythm* volume 2, number 14: 477–78
Samuel, Horace B. 1913a *Modernities* London: Kegan Paul, Trench, Trubner & Co
Samuel, Horace B. 1913b 'Introduction' in Schnitzler 1913
Schnitzler, Arthur 1911 *Anatol: A Sequence of Dialogues; Paraphrased for the English Stage by Granville Barker* New York: Mitchell Kennerley
Schnitzler, Arthur 1913 *The Green Cockatoo and Other Plays*, translated by Horace B. Samuel London: Gay & Hancock
Schnitzler, Arthur 1917 *Last Masks*, translated by Grace Isabel Colbron New York: Boni and Liveright
Shaw, G. Bernard 1957 *The Quintessence of Ibsenism* New York: Hill & Wang
Shaw, G. Bernard 1983 *Heartbreak House: A Fantasia in the Russian Manner on English Themes* Harmondsworth: Penguin Books
Shelving, Paul 1927 'Stage-Design' *Theatre World* January: 22
Shepherd, Simon (ed.) 2021 *The Unknown Granville Barker: Letters to Helen and Other Texts 1915-18* London: Society for Theatre Research
Sheringham, George 1927 *Design in the Theatre*, ed. Geoffrey Holme London: The Studio
St. James's Gazette 1905 'A Triple Bill at the Court' 1 March
Symons, Arthur 1906 *Studies in Seven Arts* London: Archibald Constable and Company
Tillyard, S.K. 1988 *The Impact of Modernism 1900–1920: Early Modernism and the Arts and Crafts Movement in Edwardian England* London: Routledge
Whitworth, Geoffrey 1922 'Hopes for the Theatre' *The Fortnightly Review* volume 112: 163–73
Williams, Raymond 1973 *Drama from Ibsen to Brecht* Harmondsworth: Penguin Books
Yeats, W.B. 1989 *Essays & Introductions* London: Macmillan
Z.Y.X. 1900 'Problems and Playwrights' *The Fortnightly Review* volume 68: 858–66

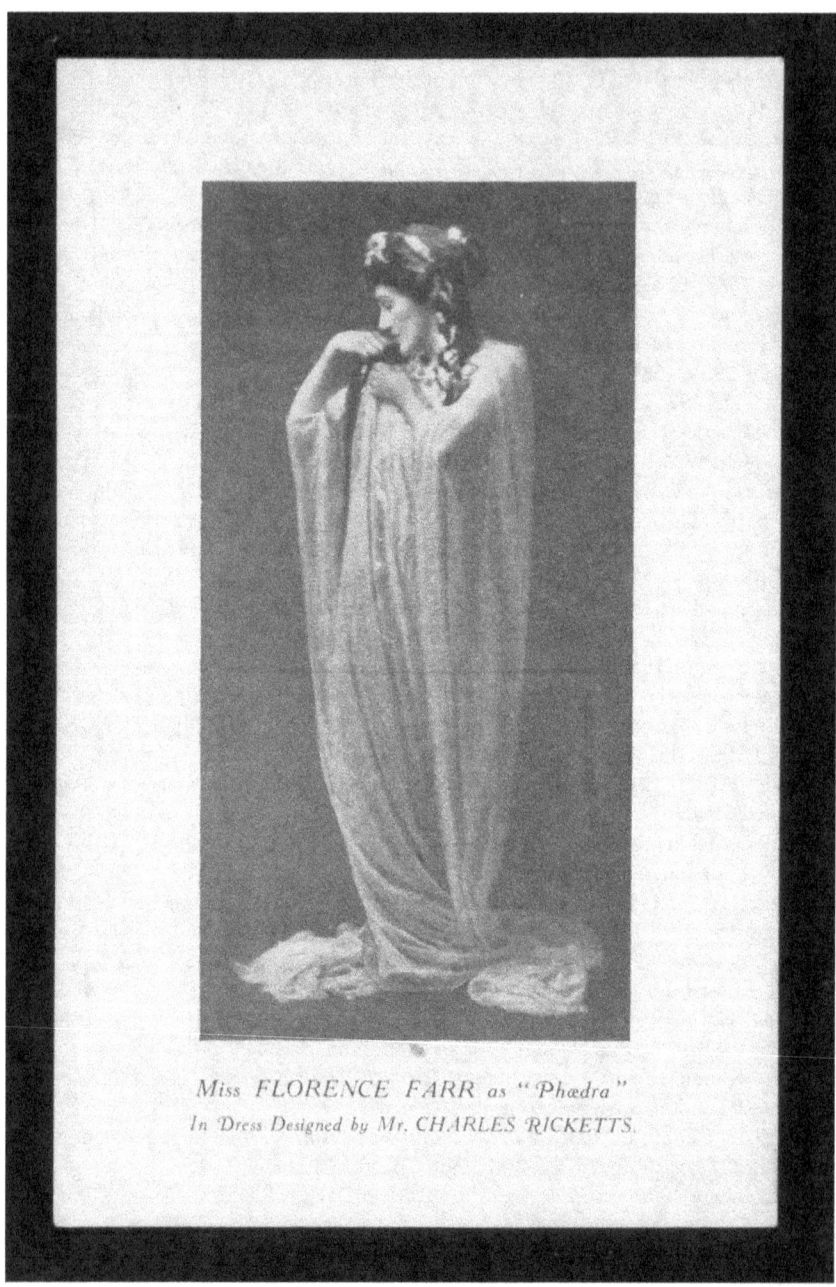

FIGURE 2.1 Florence Farr as Phaedra in Thomas Sturge Moore's *Aphrodite against Artemis*, designed by Charles Ricketts, 1906. MS 982/G/3. Senate House Library, University of London.

FIGURE 2.2 Charles Ricketts, design for *Salome*, 1906. Victoria and Albert Museum, London. Reproduced by permission of Leonie Sturge Moore and Charmian O'Neil.

FIGURE 2.3 Norman Wilkinson, design for *Twelfth Night*: Orsino's Court, 'Come away, death', 1912. Granville Barker promptbook for Savoy Theatre, 1912. University of Michigan Library.

58 Modernities

FIGURE 2.4 Charles Ricketts, design for *The Death of Tintagiles*, 1913. The Gordon Bottomley papers, Add MS 88957/6/45. The British Library.

FIGURE 2.5 Norman Wilkinson, design for *Iphigenia in Tauris*, 1912/1915. Scrapbooks. Yale University Library.

3
RENOVATION OF THE STAGE

It is Sunday evening, 1 April 1906. Sitting in the King's Hall, Covent Garden, London, we are watching a new play called *Aphrodite against Artemis*, based on the story of Phaedra's desire for her step-son Hippolytus. The performance is the first production of a new group called the Literary Theatre Society.

At the centre of the play Phaedra has a long speech, of about three and a half pages, in which she reacts to Hippolytus' rejection of her advances and vengefully envisages his death, not by poison and knife 'But inorganic, with a weight of stone,/Crush him with accident casually; let doom/Be aimless as a landslip coming down' (Moore 1901). Her thoughts then turn to her own death and she says farewell to her absent children, remembering them as babies. Moving slowly, 'as numbed by pain', she goes into the yard and returns with a bridle: 'I am not mad, and can quite clearly see/Myself thus entering my home, and know/To which side life lies, tempted not at all/To suffer shameful years of emptiness'. Slipping the bridle over her head, she detaches from her previous self, 'My dear dead friend who loved Hippolytus' (Moore 1901: 18, 20), and leaves. As we stare at an empty stage come sounds, faint and far off, of her husband Theseus approaching; dogs begin to bark. As Theseus' shouts draw nearer, from an adjacent room Phaedra is heard hanging herself, then struggling to get free, then finally dying. Only once she is dead does Theseus arrive.

With such an episode at its heart this play was an appropriate vehicle for inaugurating the Literary Theatre Society (LTS). It is 'literary' in that it re-tells an ancient story, rather than representing contemporary life, and is in verse, specifically a verse that insists on its own presence as marked by density of imagery and syntax. In a speech as long as the one above that verse presence is felt as a primary entity on stage, not subsumed in business or spectacle. During its changes in mood Phaedra is directed to position herself in various ways within a door-frame. The movement is simple, as if under the control of the speech, in its rhythm. And for the climax there is no on-stage movement at all. The effects are done by juxtaposed sounds – dogs barking, Theseus' shouts coming nearer, Phaedra's cries for help, the clinking of the bridle. These 'literary' devices, verse and classical story, produce a prolonged, painful, as it were real-time suicide that is rather more uncomfortable than most effects provided by dramas of 'real' life.

Chapter 1 looked at some experiments with such dramas. In their different ways Barker and Barrie and Hankin, among others, were calling into question the accustomed modes of operation of 'real-life' plays. But they had contemporaries who thought that change could only come by starting somewhere different, not from inside fictions of real life but from outside. They wanted new sorts of stories on the stage and, above all, new sorts of expression of those stories. Only this would bring about what the author of *Aphrodite* called the 'renovation of the theatre'. In this chapter we shall explore these attempts to change the stage, the people involved, why they were doing it, what they were making and why it mattered.

The art of a clique

That call for renovation was made by Thomas Sturge Moore, a poet and illustrator, and the driving force behind the formation of the LTS. In his essay entitled 'The Renovation of the Theatre' Moore suggested various types of non-realist performance which would point the way towards a new theatre (see Chapter 2). But, in order to describe the engine which is going to drive that renovation, he begins by developing a point he made in an essay earlier that year, that 'a clique is the only force extant for the furtherance of art'. Cliques work on the basis of personal relationships. As their influence widens 'members of a clique become leaders of a party'. Thus 'The crowning test of a clique's wisdom is to recognise the right moment for constituting itself a public body' (Moore 1902b: 102).

When he published that essay in 1902 Moore had been working with just such a clique. Together they had given *Aphrodite* its copyright reading at the end of July 1901. We shall trace them from their beginning, as a group calling itself the Literary Theatre Club. The project had originated in Moore's relationship with the articulate and well-connected artist Charles Ricketts and his partner Charles Shannon (1863–1937). He met them in 1887, as an adolescent at art school, and their friendship gave him his principal aesthetic education. It was in their new journal, *The Dial*, that he first appeared in print, with poems and a story, in 1892. When Ricketts set up the Vale Press, Moore contributed wood-cuts and editorial work, and indeed he had a studio in Ricketts and Shannon's house on Beaufort Street.

Through Ricketts, in 1898, Moore – or Stoggy as Ricketts called him – met Laurence Binyon (1869–1943). A curator at the British Museum and well networked through literary circles, Binyon was a poet with an interest not only in writing plays but also in the reform of the stage. He took the opportunity in a review of Robert Bridges' poetry, and in particular his 'Mask' *Prometheus the*

Fire-Giver, to describe a new sort of theatre writing. By using a Greek model, he said, Bridges avoided the problem of prolix lyricism. Because it used the chorus alone for lyrical expression the Greek play was tightly focussed on action, which was central to all drama. In labelling *Prometheus* a 'Mask' Bridges drew on a native form which, fused with the Greek, offered a new model for drama that was simple, had proper action and relied on poetry for effect. That model was necessary because a regeneration of the theatre based solely on prose drama would not achieve the revival of the play 'as a beautiful form of art'. Such a revival would require the proper speaking of verse and scenery consistent with it, so 'a new theatre would probably have to be started' (1899: 203, 204).

To which end Binyon introduced Moore to his friend William Arthur Pye (1852–??), an art collector whose money came from an inherited wine business. Both Pye and his two youngest daughters Ethel and Sibyl were interested in new sorts of drama, indeed they built a collapsible stage at their house Priest Hill. Together these five turned themselves into the Literary Theatre Club. For it Moore wrote *Aphrodite* and Binyon *Paris and Oenone*. Into this mix arrived one further person. The Irish poet W.B. Yeats (1865–1939) moved to London in 1901 because his attempts to construct an Irish literary theatre in Dublin were being frustrated. The ideas he brought with him had their origin in the work of the Symbolists. In 1894 he had travelled to Paris to see de l'Isle-Adam's *Axël*. His subsequent review was, says Morash, his 'first major statement on theatre'. In it he assumed Ibsen was passé, and the enemy was the 'would-be realisms' of Pinero and Jones. As Morash notes, Yeats 'finds untenable […] theatre that functions as if unproblematic representation were a viable option' (2021: 45, 48). Representation always had to be problematic because, to do its work within the project of Symbolism, it necessarily depended on material means to show that which was immaterial, mythic, transcendental. It's a visual form which inevitably shows the inadequacy of the visible.

When, therefore, Yeats attended the Literary Theatre Club's copyright reading of Moore's *Aphrodite* he was much impressed by 'the beautiful constrained passion' (in Schuchard 2010: 48) of a play which, as we've seen, arrests the visible at a highpoint of the drama. This, together with Gordon Craig's Purcell scenography which he had seen a few months earlier, encouraged Yeats to believe that London could serve his purposes for creating an equivalent of his Irish Literary Theatre. Modelling itself on Antoine's Théâtre Libre a group was convened on 3 July 1903. They decided to call themselves The Masquers. Moore was of course there, along with Edith Craig, suffragist actress, and her brother Gordon; Walter Crane, whom we met at the formation of the Stage Society; Gilbert Murray, a political Liberal who had been on the committee of Grein's Independent Theatre; Pamela Colman Smith, suffragist illustrator and scenographer; and Arthur Symons, champion in England of French Symbolism and editor of *The Savoy*, a literary journal. The group's prospectus declared their aim 'to bring the stage back again to that beauty of appropriate simplicity in the presentation of a play which will liberate the attention of the audience for the words of a writer and the movements of an actor' (in Saddlemyer 1965: 101, with no source). While distinctly 'literary' in name, as a group the Masquers suggests the range of artistic and political interests committed to new theatre, together with its links into previous movements. But it lasted only a few months. Yeats and the rest went on to other work, as did Moore's friend Binyon.

The first play of Laurence Binyon, or Binny to his friends, had been in the Moore idiom, and he remained close enough to have his name on the announcement of the LTS inaugural event in 1906. But by then he had embarked on a journey that took him somewhere different. Having been introduced to the aspiring actor-manager Oscar Asche and his wife Lily Brayton in 1902, Binyon had drafted a play which would foreground both Asche's physique and his heroic acting style, *Attila*. Its opening performance on 4 September 1907 announced the beginning of Asche's career at His Majesty's Theatre, a venue famous for Beerbohm Tree's spectacular shows. And it continued that tradition, with substantial funding from Lord Howard de Walden and a score by Sir Charles Stanford, who did the music for Irving's production of Tennyson's *Becket*. The design was by Binyon's friend Ricketts, another famous name, now working for the first time in commercial theatre. Apart from Ricketts, the rest of the elements lined up Binyon with the very sort of theatre – quite apart from Tennysonian poetic drama – to which LTS, in its hired room, was offering an alternative. It also parted company with LTS in that the show was a success, with the *Daily Telegraph* praising it for having 'some of the swing and fire of our Elizabethan stage' (quoted in Hatcher 1995: 151). And there, for the time being, Binyon's output of poetic drama halted.

Moore himself, with The Masquers dissolved, remained set on creating a new group. Into the breach stepped Ricketts, eager, as ever, to see a new theatre practice developed. He gave Moore the proceeds from the sale of a Vale Press Marlowe edition. Moore then wrote on 5 December 1905 to Pye senior: 'I am joining with Mrs Emery and Mrs Bishop to start a theatre company more or less on the lines of Yeats Irish company [*The Irish Literary Theatre*]. It will be practically the New Stage Club transformed they were cooperative and consisted of 3 members as we shall, but we want to be a financial company as well' (978/1/5/38). That stress on the financial company, together with models of a possible structure and share arrangements, and an invitation to Pye to be financial director, show Moore planning how to turn a clique into a 'public body'.

His selection of his two other founding members was careful. Gwendolen Bishop (1874–1926), who later married the dramatist, Theosophist and son of a socialist philosopher, Clifford Bax, had been directed by Craig in Housman's *Bethlehem* and was a founder of the New Stage Club. Their significant production, in May 1905, was Wilde's banned play *Salome*, given its first staging in England. The director was 'Mrs Emery', better known as Florence Farr (1860–1917). Farr was in touch with, and positioned at, a range of points of innovation, as Litz (1996) and Schuchard (2010) so fully demonstrate. As actress she had played in works by Ibsen, Shaw and Yeats. She had an enthusiasm for Nietzsche, making her own translations from *Also Sprach Zarathustra* for chanted performance and becoming friendly with the Nietzsche-enthusiast A.P. Orage, one of the founders, with Holbrook Jackson, of the *New Age*, for which, in 1907–1908, she wrote 18 pieces. Through Orage she met the poet T.E. Hulme whose response to her lecture on chanting and Nietzsche at the Poets' Club in June 1908 constituted, says Schuchard (2010: 257), 'the first stage of the Imagist movement'. Together with this artistic activity she was a feminist whose book *Modern Woman* recommended pay for the separate jobs of wife, mother and housekeeper; a trade union for prostitutes; sex education for all; removal of stigma from those 'not capable of lifelong fidelity'. Above all she was blunt about the idealised marital state where 'it is possible to be the mother of a man's children merely by putting up with his caresses while one thinks about some other subject' (Farr 1910: 47, 34). Back in 1903, when she was first creatively encountering Nietzsche, she formed the Dancers, as an appropriately joyfully Nietzschean response to the collapse of the Masquers. With her in this work was Gwendolen Bishop, who went on to act in Farr's masque *The Mystery of Time*, done on 17 January 1905. These then were the two that Moore wanted for his new project.

In the inaugural production of *Aphrodite* Bishop played Aphrodite and Farr Phaedra. The third major female role was taken by another significant figure, Penelope Wheeler. In later years she would promote the staging of Greek plays, with her own touring company, but she also had a recurrent involvement with new work, including, for example, the staging of Schnitzler's *Green Cockatoo* (see Chapter 2). The significance of her participation on this occasion was that she was one of a group of actors, as indeed was Gwendolen Bishop, who more usually worked for Barker and Vedrenne's Court. Their loan to LTS for the inaugural show indicates how one experimental venture supported another. It also, though they didn't know it, pointed towards the near future when the Stage Society would absorb the LTS and provide Moore with a platform for his work. Before it got there, however, the LTS staged two more sets of productions, all designed by the supportive Ricketts. On 10 and 18 June 1906 they did Wilde's *Florentine Tragedy*, now completed with a first act that Moore was asked to write by Wilde's executor Robert Ross (1927: xviii), together with, rather significantly, a second outing for that banned play *Salome*. Then on 23 March 1907 it was Granville Barker's 'experiment in dramatic metre', *A Miracle* – an 'amateurish' piece according to Moore (978/1/5/38), but with the benefit of directly involving the powerful figure of Barker – followed by a prose translation of Aeschylus' *Persians*. And there LTS stopped.

But it had done enough to announce a new movement in the staging of poetic drama. The people involved were all in various ways plugged into new artistic and political thinking and the selection of plays declared this. As Levitas (2016: 353) says, production of *Salome* was a 'modernist signature'. To do a club performance of the banned *Salome* for the second time in a year was not only to be dismissive about state views of stage propriety but also, perhaps more daringly, to disregard, conspicuously, the scandal attached to Wilde's name. For they didn't do just one Wilde play but two. Selection of plays was something more than the statement of radical position. It was also a way of defining what they meant by verse drama or poetic theatre (the terms were interchangeable). For this there were several existing models. What they all had in common, initially, was a sense of remoteness from everyday life. The most remote was, in dramaturgic terms, the most radical. The selection of *The Persians* (albeit in prose) aligned LTS with the Court's exploration of Murray's Euripides. These plays were challenging in terms of theatre practice because they dealt with narrative and space in ways which were well outside the familiar domestic settings and social interactions of what Yeats called 'Journalistic drama' (in Morash 2021: 49).

As verse models the Greek plays carried both classical authority and innovatory promise. In this second respect they differed from the other major verse model, Shakespeare. His work may have been grandly authoritative but it was an institution, with years of accumulated conventions of performance. His works had been pummelled into submission by actor-managers who specialised in decorative spectacle and they set the model for verse dramatists who wanted to be both popular and appropriately arty. Their sort of product can be illustrated in general terms from Comyns Carr's *Tristram and Iseult* (1906). In Act 2 Iseult sings Tristram asleep, the hall darkens, a chorus of unseen spirits sings and the Vision of Iseult of the White Hands appears through drawn curtains. As the vision fades, the chorus help it off with a repeat of their number. The singing and scenic effects provide a vehicle for a theatre ready to invest heavily in spectacle, with a narrative organised to give priority to always evolving events and revelations, as opposed to reflection and exploration of character. The combination of elements produces a standard adventure story, but with a crucial difference: the verse. Carr writes a sub-Shakespearean verse, such as this from *King Arthur* (1895): 'of late our King/Hath oftimes asked for thee, and thou shalt learn/The noise of thy great deeds hath far outstripped/Thy good steed's swiftest course' (1895: 8). This does the job of larding on a glistening layer of Shakespeareness, thereby transforming the adventure story into Art. It confects a Shakespacular which taps into the unchallengeable artistic authority, the antiquity and the tastefulness while at the same time serving up lavish pictures and effects, like a grand piano dipped in honey.

It was not, however, ye olde Carr who was the leading figure but his occasional collaborator, Stephen Phillips. Although it was acknowledged that Phillips could write serious verse and tell a good story, as at least one contemporary observed the manner of Beerbohm Tree's spectacular productions had the effect of drawing attention from the verse to the picture, 'the emotion to its setting'. *Nero* was 'not a play but a series of tableaux' (Gwynn 1909: 350, 351). It was also hugely, briefly, popular. As such, Morra says (2016: 25), Phillips 'positioned his plays as the solitary vanguard' of a restored poetic drama. But Tree's spectacular staging gave them the look of what in 1909 Gwynn rather interestingly called 'thinking imperially' (1909: 347). Unsurprisingly such work produced from Moore a 'Stephen Phillipic' of scorn.

With the exception of the more institutionalised Binyon, Moore's response was shared by his friends. This is important to pause over as an historiographic detail. Recent work on this period has endeavoured to make more subtle, more properly complex, the image of commercial managers, to recognise that they were not hide-bound conservatives opposed to innovation. A good example is Lucie Sutherland's wonderfully detailed account of George Alexander. She argues (2020: 8) that: 'Although risk-averse, Alexander made new writing the defining characteristic of his management'. This is seen particularly in his extended relationship with Pinero. Pause now, and recall that Yeats thought Pinero was one of the clear enemies. The other 'new' writer favoured by Alexander was Phillips, which brings us back to Moore's scorn. Clearly there's new and there's new, and for Yeats and Moore and their friends a very sharp dividing line between them. Historiographically to blur that line is to produce a false – albeit comfortably cuddly – impression of the extent to which commercial management was artistically innovative, and, perhaps worse, to conceal the anger, and indeed riskiness, of those opposed to commerce.

The vivid difference of Moore's own writing is suggested by the vitriol which the champion of realism, William Archer, spat at *Aphrodite*. In a city where *Hippolytus* was being 'nobly performed night by night', Moore had created from the same story a play of 'feebleness, tactlessness, and ever-recurring vulgarity'. Its problem is that it does neither classical nobility nor journalistic realism: 'He seems to have designed to transpose the tragedy of Euripides into the key of domestic and even realistic drama. Yet he retains all the supernatural element of the story, and even exaggerates while he vulgarizes it'. This vulgarity and unintentional comedy are illustrated by Archer: Hippolytus' sexual advances towards the woman he takes to be Artemis are 'ill-becoming both his character and hers'; Phaedra's line – 'Thou dost not know what 'tis to be a girl' – is assumed to be comical (978/6/2/6). Thus blithely unaware Archer enunciated a set of ideas about the appropriate conduct of gender relations which was precisely the target of Moore's 'literary' and wilfully ignoble reworking of Euripides.

In its reworking the dramaturgy makes deliberate attempts to know what it is to be a 'girl'. We have seen already how Moore locks the audience into witnessing Phaedra's off-stage but real-time suicide. The crisis begins when she is taken over by her desire for Hippolytus: she says, in a phrase that the reviewer would have been compelled to find vulgar, 'we will throb together in the dark' (Moore 1901: 12). But it becomes clear that she is an unhappy young married woman, feeling neglected by her husband Theseus, whom she fears. Her story of past events, which Archer calls her 'masterpiece of absurdity' (978/6/2/6), begins with child abuse. It's followed by witnessing Theseus' readiness to dump his first partner Ariadne because he's fallen for Phaedra. Her consequent sense of herself is that while she was once beautiful she is now 'impure and prostituted'. After her death Aphrodite builds and lights a pyre under Phaedra's corpse, bidding the flames 'Roar over her, as in/Her veins that mighty tidal passion roared – /As that Atlantic on the world's end roars/Twice every day' (Moore 1901: 19, 36–37). With its central image of a burning woman – Brunhild-like – the play ends with an evocation of a female passion that far exceeds what Phaedra's duplicitous husband was capable of satisfying, that is as vast as the Atlantic, and just as natural.

If this is 'tactless' and 'vulgar', it was deliberately so. Moore was nothing if not forthright. He was also intellectually inquisitive, and among his extensive range of reading were up-to-the-moment books on psychology, such as Théodule Ribot's work on physiological drives, and on sexuality, such as Otto Weininger's *Sex and Character*. Of the latter he noted that the book's 'main thesis that genius or intellect is a form of masculine sexuality is I think probably false, and induced by his madness' (88957/1/66 f1). Moore's version of *Hippolytus* is, then, mediated through contemporary theories of the person, a belief that men are not superior and a poetic text that specialises in bluntness and difficulty. And it was performed in a company with a management core of two women and one man, and a cast in which Phaedra was played by one of the most well-educated and independent feminist actresses of her day. These various aspects of it begin to suggest why the LTS version of poetic drama was very different from other plays in verse and the theatres that housed them. By being 'literary' it could think and act differently. This is why it saw itself as being a potential instrument for renovating the theatre.

As instrument the company didn't last long, but its approach to performance and dramaturgy was sustained by Moore and his friends. This group and their work we shall now explore.

The people involved were Moore himself, his long-time friend Robert Trevelyan and newer acquaintance Gordon Bottomley. The latter two knew Lascelles Abercrombie, who was close to John Drinkwater. Their variously different contributions, from differing positions, when taken together show not just the art but also the theory and politics of the new drama. We begin with Moore.

Moore, light and scene

Although *Aphrodite* was based on Greek myth, Moore, though hostile to Christianity, tended to prefer the Bible as source. Its stories, he said, 'are superior even to those out of which sprang the Greek theatre, and, what is still more important for the purposes of a national drama, they are rooted in the best of this nation's past and are still familiar to the people at large' (1905: 622). The man who called for the renovation of the theatre had his eye on creating a 'national drama'. He was also picking a battle with a censorship that banned Biblical subjects, his treatment of which was designed not to be decorous.

Except for his experiment in a chronicle play of Absalom, Moore's preference was simple incidents, moments of confrontation, of limited number. This simplification of the action works in tandem with his approach to language. Both are contained in one of his favourite critical words, seen for example in this advice to a friend: 'you are unable to condense even when condensation is most called for and brevity the soul of success' (978/1/4/11). Phaedra's long speech in the middle of *Aphrodite*, with its switches in mood, is condensed, for all its length, because there is both focus on a single character, with no extended interactions, and language that is intensified in its syntactic structure and highly wrought images. Similarly Moore's plans for his play about Judas Iscariot (started 1910) had him on stage alone with everything passing in imagination. Such condensation concentrates focus and thickens up language, a machine for making present as it were. Advising another friend on his work, Moore said: 'I want more and hotter and cruder and more tremendously barbaric speeches and self-revelations all delivered from the heighth [sic] of towering passion, as the daughter, for the first time knowing, hates the father, and the father, for the first time considering, is dismayed at the daughter. You sketch and hint but do not realize' (88957/1/66 f208). Sketching and hinting were to be avoided. Impressionism was a dirty word. Moore's interest in staging passion had more in common with what elsewhere might be called expressionism.

That interest was not confined to language. Moore was a book illustrator who also wrote on the history of art. This specialism in the visual informed his engagement with staging. In an early draft for *Mariamne* he included diagrams of the scene, and for his late play *Medea* he did costume designs. His interest in the visual possibilities of staging was informed by his close friendship with Ricketts, but it also led him towards the most innovative scenographer in Europe, Adolphe Appia. While many English artists and intellectuals saw Appia's experiments with Dalcroze at Hellerau in 1912 and 1913, Moore seems to have been reading him since early in the century. A distant relative, Moore had met him in 1901 and 1902, the second time with Fortuny, and this may have given access to his ideas: among Moore's papers is a type-script in French of an Appia essay on eurhythmics, 'La gymnastique rythmique'. But it was Appia's thinking about light which seems to have influenced Moore's scenography. In *Tyrfing* (1921) the corpse of Agantyr is in a burial mound, but as it gets darker his form 'begins to appear through the mound as though the darkness rendered its turfs transparent' (Moore 1920: 49). I haven't found an exact precedent for this effect but it seems to draw on Appia's idea of how light can make the 'presence' of objects felt and 'thereby render them expressive' (2011: 56). One of Moore's friends was disturbed that 'the waning and waxing draws attention to it too constantly; almost makes the gasman one of the characters in the play' (978/1/7/21), a response that indicates the novelty of this foregrounding of scenic effect.

Moore's pioneering engagement with Appia was part of a larger exploration of scenography. Phaedra's suicide was heard but not seen. In *Mariamne* the corrupt trial of the heroine has her at the centre of a court-room stuffed with people. So that her husband Herod, sitting as judge, will not feel pity she has been shrouded from sight. She is also silent for the entire scene. The effect is of an assembled state apparatus sitting in judgement on a person that is constructed as an absence, neither visible nor audible. More extended use of masking and silence gives the power to Moore's most famous play *Judith*, written 1902 and dedicated to Wyndham Lewis on publication in 1911 but only performed, by the Stage

Society, in 1916. It is scripted for a simple curtained stage with the action playing in front of and inside Holofernes' tent. The sense of hidden depth is intensified both by lighting effect, with moonlight shining from the side, and by stage activity. When Judith enters the tent with Holofernes' weapon, to sever his head, there is silence, then the clink of the blade, then one sleepy line from Holofernes, a little cry from Judith, and silence. Into which breaks the noise of a soldier dragging his drunken and randy companion. After they have clumsily gone, there's silence. Judith appears and then returns inside. Her maid enters and calls to her. She hears Judith speaking 'with a strangely altered accent' from within: 'All that there was to do, is done, is done' (Moore 1911c: 65). The interaction between seen and unseen spaces combined with qualities of sound and silence cathects the unseen depth. The moment of killing is more or less silent. The perhaps more important subjective transformation of Judith into saviour of her nation is heard as completely new sound. The big effects are done by withholding spectacle.

The manipulation of what is seen, and how it is seen, reappears in a slightly different form in Moore's only published prose story, 'A Platonic Marriage' (1911b), for which he faced the threat of action from the National Vigilance Association. Its fictional ruse is that the woman loved by the narrator suddenly, overnight, shrinks in size. Her fiancé, horrified, departs, so the narrator marries her and takes much delight in making provision for her tiny, but thoroughly adult, body. At the end it turns out to be a dream, but the ruse allows for articulation of the mechanisms of desire and fetish. Moore's friend Gordon Bottomley (1874–1948) found it 'a valuable way of setting customary human relationships in unsuspected lights – so that the sources of passion and emotion can be better discerned' (978/1/7/18). The importance of those 'sources' is what excited Moore when he read Ribot's account of 'the subconsience [sic] in its relation to personality' (978/1/5/38). That the placing of the customary in an unsuspected light was intended in part to be provocative is suggested by Moore's plan for the Judas play. Depicting Judas as the leading disciple watching the dead rise in front of him would, Moore hoped, irritate both the orthodox and the sceptic.

The display of what should not be seen – inside a burial mound, a miniaturised woman – is the reverse of occluding sight of a horror that can be plainly inferred. Viewing is made problematic. The effect is then intensified by tortuously condensed poetic language intended to make present, in its rhythms and register, now and in front of us, the height of passion. Taken together both elements suggest that Moore's project for a national drama involved not only articulating but also making uncomfortable the expression of the subconscious. In this sense it was a sort of English expressionism.

The new literary theatre was thus very far from bookish. Moore used scene as much as word, and in doing so made a drama of ideologically provocative if not political effect. To see the political potency of verse drama enunciated more stridently, we have now to turn to the most radical of this group, Robert Calverley Trevelyan (1872–1951).

Trevelyan, music and politics

Bob Trevy, as his friends called him, had known Moore since 1894. He was a classical scholar, poet and political activist. He was also more financially secure than Moore. His father, a baronet, had held high offices of state. His Liberal politics were inherited by his sons, who radicalised them. Bob Trevy's elder brother Charles was a founder of the Union of Democratic Control, an organisation set up to press for transparency in British war aims and later became a Labour politician. As one of a circle of pacifist friends in Cambridge, including Bertrand Russell and Goldsworthy Lowes Dickinson, Bob joined the UDC. In 1918, to Moore's disquiet, he formally adopted the position of a conscientious objector.

Back in 1905 Moore wanted Trevelyan to join the steering group of the LTS because he shared many of Moore's views on the need for renovation of the theatre and was himself a writer of plays. Rarely if ever performed, these plays, so different from most others, were experiments that stretched both the form and the impact of verse drama.

The independence of Trevelyan's direction is felt in his sceptical attitude to contemporary writers. He thought Yeats a crank, albeit a sociable one. Binyon's *Attila* he judged to be too full of dramatic incident and inclined to bombast. And he refused to appear in an anthology alongside the Imagists and Kipling. In his specific field of classical translation he described Gilbert Murray's versions of Euripides as 'a little too fluid and sometimes metrically weak, and sometimes too Swinburnian, whereas Eur. is concise and clear-cut, and intensely intellectual' (978/1/4/3). In that picture of Euripides, the handling of metre is an image for, and part of, a rigorous intellectualism, which, in Trevelyan's case, is the foundation for a principled politics. Accurately disciplined classical metres are a way of thinking radically.

They are also a source of a sensual pleasure, exploration of which took Trevelyan's verse into a new association with music. The process can be seen in *The Bride of Dionysus* (1912). This tale of Theseus and Ariadne is handled less as character than as metrical interaction. For instance Minos' question 'Why riseth he not forth/From his waves in storm and wrath?' is followed directly with a chorus: 'Behold us, O ye just Gods, in whose hands are the fates of men!/Take pity on our desolation, on our misery look down'. Classical tricks such as the mid-line break are deployed in lines longer than the usual blank-verse pentameter. This variation in the lines spoken works to manage the voices which speak. So too does the distribution between solo voice and chorus. Some choruses speak in unison, some 'dispersedly'. It becomes more complex when Ariadne talks 'distractedly' over Dionysus' words, and still more complex when Ariadne and Phaedra both speak simultaneously aside during the course of Theseus' speech (1912: 11, 52–53, 22–23). While Trevelyan's preferred visual effects are generalised lighting states – mist, gloom, twilight, phosphorescence – his orchestration of voices is highly specific. For the dominant interest is in sound, both verse as music and verse in relation to music.

That interest was signalled when he subtitled *Bride* a 'music drama'. Behind that term reverberates the cultural influence of Wagner, whose work Trevelyan knew well. But this was not to do with imitating Wagner. It was driven by two local and specific imperatives. First was the need simply to get verse drama onto the stage. For managers, opera written in verse was acceptable. Thus Moore thought an association with music would solve the problem of actors who couldn't speak verse. His friend Bottomley, reacting to the excitement about the Russian ballet in summer 1911, wondered if it had the potential to establish 'a valid and accepted form of musically stylisated drama – which may lead us once more to poetic drama via an operatic means. I do think that when poetic drama comes into vogue again it will be in connexion with music' (978/1/7/18). That interest in the 'musically stylisated', in how verse could be stylised to work sonically, was the second imperative. For Bottomley what made Trevelyan's project exciting was precisely its exploration of music as an organising principle of verse. It began with Trevelyan publishing his *Sisyphus* as an 'operatic fable' in 1908. The next work, *Bride*, was conceived as a collaboration with his friend, the composer and musicologist Donald Tovey (1875–1940). In his analysis of the result, Tovey reviewed the historical tensions between musical form and dramaturgy. These informed his decision that, on the model of Wagner's later operas, 'the words are set in a manner best described as realistic' (1929: 3). This allowed for duets but not for repetition of words to complete a musical phrase. For in the collaboration of poet and composer, each has to ensure that neither lyric poetry nor classical form hampers dramatic action. At least that was the theory. Listening to it, Trevelyan's metrical experiments tend to be swallowed up by Tovey's musical architecture.

If that architecture drew on Wagner, another pair of poet and composer were, at the same time, aiming to improve him. Reginald Buckley and Rutland Boughton had a plan to reach back to the model of classic Greek theatre, and in doing so create a drama that established a new relationship with its audience and thus a new role in national life. The idea was set out in their 1911 book *Music-Drama of the Future: Uther and Igraine: Choral Drama*. Essays by both authors bookend Buckley's poetic drama.

Buckley (1882–1919) says that he was inspired by Wagner, in a world of philosophic quackery, to create 'a dramatic and poetic art, wherein the sane, healthy England might bathe, as in the pure, rhythmic sea of Cornwall' (1911: 45). The full work of which *Uther* is part was published as a Wagnerian tetralogy called *Arthur of Britain*. It comprises two sorts of text, verse drama and verse evocations of settings and atmospheres, with the latter intended for instrumental rather than vocal delivery. As with Wagner, at least in Buckley's reading of him, the Arthurian stories articulate – or perhaps Arthiculate – some universal themes, such as 'the coming of the Hero through Love, in itself lawless but controlled for the good of the race by Merlin; the founding of a democracy that must be national' (in Savage 2014: 81). In finding the composer for his poem Buckley met someone with a much more developed model for the function of music drama in the national life. Boughton (1878–1960) begins by defining the difference between opera and music drama, arguing that the former depends too much on physical activity and superficial sensuousness. Here we might recognise a similarity to Trevelyan's antipathy to bombast and busyness. For Boughton, the 'high tones of passion' are 'the essence of religious feeling and therefore of music-drama'. From this follows a dramaturgic requirement: 'a drama to be of real religious value, must present its characters on the typical or heroic scale with the heroic background of the mass'. Specifically, the relationship is dialectical. Strong characters, whatever their strength, 'act upon and are acted upon by the mass'. This model is derived from the ancient Greek chorus, now transmuted into the language of early twentieth-century socialism. Thus in their work on *Uther* Boughton and Buckley used the chorus 'to show the interaction of the individual characters and the mass-peoples'. Here they correct the mistake of Wagner who jettisoned the chorus, and in doing so give the new drama its purpose, for in 'a national festival drama' what is important is 'the mass-feeling of the chorus – the sense that the nation is gaining expression as well in the whole as in its more outstanding details of typical individuality'. Thus the 'orchestrated chorus' becomes the crucial player in, and defining feature of, the new music-drama, indeed the 'choral drama', and its national mission (1911: 20, 29, 30, 52).

In some respects Trevelyan was heading in Boughton's direction, with his interest in the interplay of chorus and individual. But his use of verse drama for political ends was less utopian, more polemical, if not agitational. It is also formally more innovative. Although Savage (2014: 82) praises *Arthur* as 'a ground-breaking attempt at an English *vers libre* libretto, written in what the poet calls "free melody"', it is nonetheless a throwback to Wagner coloured with Whitman. The other major music-drama cycle on national-mythic lines, *The Cauldron of Annwn* (1922) by T.E. Ellis (a.k.a. Lord Howard de Walden), based on the Mabinogion, was similarly Wagnerian. Neither, therefore, can strictly be said to be developing a new model. Trevelyan, by contrast, would not settle for verse story-telling, *libre* or otherwise, but was interested in the work done by poetic rhythms and textures as actively dramatic devices. Their wild effects animate *The New Parsifal* (1914), a reworking of Wagner's tale, begun in 1911. In the first act Klingsor arrives on Circe's island wondering if it might be the resting place for the Grail. When it's unveiled a mystical voice from within says that only when 'The self-propagating, fire-insured, five-centuried, fabular Phoenix' flies above will he know. The overblown grandeur of metre and register is punctured by alliteration and jokes. And the chorus don't know what it's talking about. Klingsor tells them they're fools, and that the Phoenix is real: 'Nay if perchance this were not so indeed,/Are not the best philosophers agreed/Truth is man-made, manufacturable at need?' There follows a lengthy imprecation to the Phoenix asking it to descend. A whirring is heard and 'a monoplane descends violently onto the lawn'. A young man in 'grotesque airman's costume' scrambles out: 'Christ, what a bump! Well, that was a close shave!' He looks around him, at Grail, Klingsor, Circe and Chorus: 'Great Scott! It seems we're in for something queer./Is it the Pope upon his honeymoon?/Or a pageant rehearsal? Well, we'll find out soon'. This radical change of register announces Percy (as in Parsifal) Smith, a bluff young Englishman. He thinks he has come across a group of players rehearsing their latest production and offers to sit quietly and smoke his cigar. The Chorus assume he is scoffing at 'our symbolic ritualism,/As though the Grail's high mysteries were a play,/Mere frivolous histrionism,/And all its knights and damsels merely players'. Percy still can't understand whether it's a prayer-meeting or a play. He wonders if he can buy the Grail. And when the Phoenix actually appears, fluttering magically overhead, he shoots it dead and then offers to pay compensation. While the Phoenix burns in the Grail, and reincarnates, Circe begs him to take her away from the 'Brainsick Grail-adoring asses' and he promises to return in his yacht (Trevelyan 2012: 116, 117, 120, 122, 128). Cynicism and stage spectacle are held in fine balance.

The fun with metre and register work within juxtaposed dramatic forms. This Grail story is Wagner plus Shakespeare plus W.S Gilbert. We have been primed for theatrical ironies by an Induction in which the Lord Chamberlain and the Examiner of Plays discuss whether this play should receive a licence and conclude it should, because it is in verse. They can find no adverse remarks about touchy subjects such as 'abuse of war, loose talk against the army or the Czar': 'It's all the merest literary twaddle'. At this point, the ghost of Wagner appears and demands that the play be refused a licence. Finding him tedious the state officials fob him off by referring the decision to 'a useful little advisory committee of Stage-managers and Professors, and prominent Silks'. But the joke is not only against Wagner. Percy returns with three companions: Professor Bruce, an academic specialising in comparative mythology, Gigadibs a critic and Futurist, and Hartley Quelch: 'A super-shavian post-dramatist/Formerly, now a conversationalist/Since conversations are an art-form higher/Than plays' (Trevelyan 2012: 108, 110, 145). The jokes are against a whole intellectual and artistic apparatus which is underpinned by wealth and weapons.

In Trevelyan's sharply radical step away from music drama into verse comedy he was exploring a new possibility for staged poetry. This form doesn't bury the specific characteristics of verse under music but foregrounds them as the mechanism for estrangement. That estrangement is necessary because the Wagnerian model, as interpreted for example by Buckley, opens the door to a romantic socialism that can live happily with eugenics and nationalism. Buckley's *Arthur* was conceived in the wake of the second Boer War with its introspective reflections on national unpreparedness. For him the hope promised by the Grail looked forward to a time when England's ancient traditional characteristics would resurface, a time that might appreciate Siegfried as Nietzschean superman. Trevelyan, by contrast, found Nietzsche somewhat comical (978/1/4/3). And by the time he began on *The New Parsifal* he faced a world very different from post-Boer War melancholy, a world now in a European arms-race replete with its beliefs in national superiority. This is the context for Trevelyan's Percy, an Englishman always ready with gun and cheque book. For an intellectual pacifist the political task was to weaken the hold of traditional myths and beliefs, undercutting ideologies not only of nation but also of the sacredness of art and aesthetics. In Percy's plan to take the Grail away, Trevelyan said he was figuring the liberation of art from ownership by an élite. It's an attack on art as institution which might have been recognised by any self-respecting avant-gardist. As might be the form of the whole: it's a seriously playful combination of diverse cultural elements bound up in a work that produces a high degree of reflection on itself as a form. Not until Isherwood and Auden two decades later would English verse drama manage again such a degree of satiric formal complexity, and perhaps not even then.

When he wrote the sequel the mood, and the achievement, were different. As the war progressed Trevelyan's sense of alienation from England grew more intense. Reacting to E.D. Morel's *Morocco in Diplomacy* (1912), a commentary on the Agadir Crisis which showed Britain and France to be more warlike than Germany, Trevelyan said: 'I find it very hard not to be something very like a pro-German, at least pro-English I can never now be' (88957/1/87 f160). By this time the majority of other intellectuals and artists were lined up behind a straightforwardly anti-German position. For example in 1914–1915, Laurence Binyon had produced a propaganda drama, *Bombastes in the Shades,* featuring Sophocles, Heine, a cartoon Prussian and the suggestion that all professors are secretly militarists, which comes a tad strangely from someone who was a British Museum curator, though it obediently followed the government's propaganda line as did attacks on German scholars by Gilbert Murray and Ford Madox Hueffer (Hynes 1990: 71–72). This unpleasant little piece was published in the Oxford Pamphlets, a series of very short texts about aspects of the war which were the University's gallant contribution to the war effort, written by professors whose secret militarism was presumably of an allowable kind.

This is the context in which, in 1916, political verse comedy finds its necessity, for both political and personal reasons. Trevelyan was an active member of the No-Conscription Fellowship, and indeed beaten up for it. 'I give vent to my feelings by writing an Everyman, partly serio-comic, partly serious. I have already had my fling at some things, including warlike parsons' (88957/1/87 f136). But Everyman gave way to the return of Percy Smith, *The Pterodamozels.* As he was writing Trevelyan was expecting some of his friends to be imprisoned for refusing conscription: 'I have now lost the last vestige of patriotism I possessed' (88957/1/88 f45). In the play Prometheus 'has created a new race of bird-men and women to destroy and succeed mankind', though in the final version Prometheus' creations, significantly enough, are only female. What happens is that 'Percy flying away from civilization in his aeroplane in disgust at the war, comes to island [sic] where Prometheus is creating the new race, and after nearly being lynched, pleads for humanity as not being really so bad as it seems, and gets it reprieved, and Prometheus and the bird men somehow manage to stop the war. It is more in the comic vein than Everyman, though I can treat present things almost more freely, for that very reason' (88957/1/87 ff210–11).

Among those 'present things' are the entire English hegemonic order and its ideological efficacy. In the debate as to whether mankind is naturally vicious Percy argues that it is made so by 'fears,/His credulous nature and sheer thoughtlessness'. 'He's bullied, brayed at, patted on the back/By patriot phrase-mongers, pamphleteers,/Journalists, poets, parsons, dons and peers'. He suggests that the 'butchering business' will be ended if a group of important people were removed: 'First all belligerent cabinets [...] Then a good haul of journalists,/Fleet-Street conspirators and diplomatists,/Professors, royalties, war-profiteers,/Armament-firm-promoting financiers' (Trevelyan 1916: 25–26). The invective is given force by the metre. The more accurate and elaborate, the more fierce. It is as if by enacting the intense 'intellectualism' displayed in the rigorous metre Trevelyan can create the necessary political distance from a state he despised. But by now the conditions of war were such that it was difficult to make that distance as playful as it is in *New Parsifal*, with the consequence that *Pterodamozels* is theatrically less rich though politically more explicit. Taken together these plays represent an achievement for both verse comedy and the politics of verse drama that none of the other verse dramatists got anywhere near, for decades. And, naturally, neither was performed.

Bottomley and the only fundamental theatre

Getting performed was the problem for all of them. Indeed, as Moore said, it was difficult even to get published. Trevelyan, who could afford it, paid to have *Pterodamozels* printed privately, fortunately. Moore, thanks to Ricketts, had been able to do a few productions with the short-lived LTS. The only place where the new verse drama seemed to be regularly staged was outside London, in Birmingham.

There a small amateur group had started playing in the family home of Barry Jackson (1879–1961), going public in autumn 1907. The following year the Pilgrim Players, as they called themselves, began performing at the Edgbaston Assembly Rooms with an aesthetic influenced by Poel. On the strength of their increasing popularity Jackson made plans for a permanent theatre. This opened as Birmingham Repertory Theatre in February 1913. One of their number, the poet John Drinkwater (1882–1937), was given the formal title, and pay, as Company Secretary from 1909 and he retained a key management role in the Rep. This position gave him influence on the selection of plays and as such he was regarded by most of the verse dramatists as their only route to a production of their work. That idea was substantiated when Drinkwater mounted *The Adder* by his friend, the journalist and poet Lascelles Abercrombie (1881–1938).

In staging it Drinkwater was championing the work of one of those whom in 1921 he regarded as 'our group' (88957/1/39 f42). Other members of this 'group' were the poets Wilfrid Gibson (1878–1962) and Gordon Bottomley. What this group had in common was that they had emerged from, or worked in, areas well outside London. Drinkwater was the most southerly, Abercrombie had worked in Liverpool before moving to Gloucestershire. Like Gibson, originally from Hexham, Northumberland, he became associated with the 'Dymock' poets. Bottomley was a Yorkshireman who had moved, at an early age, to Cumbria. In the case of these last three, in plays such as *The Adder* and Bottomley's *Midsummer Eve*, local register and regional vocabulary rhetorically signal social and cultural distance from the metropolis. For Bottomley that distance was enforced. His chronic lung illness – 55 haemorrhages in 19 years – for long periods confined him to his home, sometimes immobilised on his bed. But this also seemed to give him ideological distance. London for him was an enclosed culture capable of self-delusion, imagining that theatre had been regenerated (88957/1/24 ff58, 23). But the job was incomplete. His own project was to make a more fundamental change.

In this Bottomley was more persistent, and radical, than other members of Drinkwater's 'group'. Of those others Wilfrid Gibson seemed least interested in being staged. Like many poets he wrote dramatic poems such as *Borderlands* (1914), moving on to a full-length work, *Krindlesyke* (1922), though that was not conceived 'with a view to stage production' (1926: 524) and is structured as a set of Books. In works designated plays, in *Kestrel Edge and Other Plays* (1924), there is little sense of the possibilities of stage space. *Lovers' Leap* opens with a nine-page dialogue between mother-in-law and wife, broken only at the end with noise of two new farm girls arriving, followed by the men. Abercrombie by contrast really did want productions and would indeed have liked to run a theatre himself. As well as exploring possibilities with Drinkwater he also tried Iden Payne and Basil Dean at Liverpool, though he found the latter somewhat cautious. That caution was perhaps well advised. Abercrombie was good at strongly expressive language, but the dramaturgy consisted of large swathes of dialogue chopped up in speech paragraphs. Drinkwater himself, after a short series of not uninteresting verse plays, turned to somewhat sentimental prose history plays such as *Abraham Lincoln*.

By contrast with the others, despite Drinkwater's fancy about his 'group', Bottomley was on a slightly different journey. His closest artistic friends after 1909 were Moore and Trevelyan. Like Moore he specialised in the history of visual art, and like Trevelyan he had an interest in contemporary music. And like both he was highly critical of what passed for 'modern' theatre. Reporting to Moore in 1910 on his reading of Barker's plays and Galsworthy's *Justice*, he said: 'I am profoundly annoyed that works such as these and Shaw's should be taken as fulfilling a renascence in English drama. People can always be eventually persuaded to agree to a rehabilitation of the drama of every-day life by the injection of a little modish philosophy and new observation, but the enlargement of its scope by the substitution of middle-class, bourgeois, existence for the once everlasting "drawing-room in Mayfair" is not enough. No modern conveniences and improvements in realistic drama can, apparently, lead to the renascence of the poetic, the only fundamental theatre' (978/1/7/2).

Bottomley's commitment to this fundamental theatre began with the work of Wilde, from whom he learnt the power of words. His sense of effective poetic theatre was shaped by Craig's early productions and by Maeterlinck, after whom he encountered the work of Yeats and Moore. Although his verse plays would be very different what he shared with them was the aim of side-stepping realism. Noting that in the modern theatre, 'No one wants anything but current everyday interests' (978/1/7/2), Bottomley, like Moore, Trevelyan and the others, drew on stories which were conspicuously distant from the everyday. His first two plays (1900–1901), for example, depict encounters with supernatural forces. This was not an aesthetic choice made by dramatists who were 'old-fashioned' or conservative. As Danby argues (1999: 9), 'the "revived" romance was in part a distinctively *modern* phenomenon'. Moore mixed with Imagist poets, he took part in a recital by Marinetti. Bottomley played music by Bartok, Schoenberg and Satie and hugely admired Joyce's *Portrait of the Artist*. They all lent each other books, keeping up with the latest writings. From Trevelyan Bottomley borrowed, among many others, Virginia Woolf's first novel, which he liked, Clutton Brock on William Morris and the 'Sade-Masoch volume of Havelock Ellis' (88957/1/87 f219). He also enjoyed receiving UDC pamphlets. In using old stories they were writing drama for a new sort of stage which could not be mistaken for 'modern theatre'.

To stage the non-everyday story the key formal vehicle for Bottomley's theatre was the one-act play. Learning its potency from Yeats he found it, in 1909, 'the most symphonic and homogenous in structure of all dramatic forms' although he wanted it to be closer in length 'to the proportions of Greek tragedy' (88957/1/24 f4). The form compelled a concentration of the action into sequences of evolving episodes, seen, for example, in *The Riding to Lithend* (1909), which opens with three house-women in a tenth-century Icelandic household speaking as chorus first about the 'forsaken quiet house,/This late late harvest, and night creeping in' (Bottomley 1920: 87), then about the doings of their master Gunnar. This gives way to their mistress Hallgerd arguing with Gunnar and defiantly letting down her hair. As he exits, she sits in the 'high-seat' and her women express anger with the way he treats her. At its simplest this sequence positions women as abused within a patriarchal structure and simultaneously both self-analytical and forceful, as it were produced by abuse.

The rhythms and repetitions of the opening chorus and the extended image of the hair are both devices for characterising their separate episodes, and each is then further developed as a way of organising the subsequent stage images. In the battle which kills Gunnar his verse rhythm gets faster: 'O, smite and pulse/On their anvil heads'. It is taken up by his opponents as they surround him so that only his weapon can be seen rising and falling. The rhythm is scripting movement. For Bottomley this 'blend of rhythmic speech and movement was something new in the British theatre' (1948: 12). Its effect is most formalised for the insecurely human Beggar-women who appear just after the midway point. Hallgerd drives them out and as they leave they chant together: 'We shall cry no more in the high rock-places'. When Hallgerd falters in her attack, 'they turn as they chant, and point at her'. It is a sort of dance (Bottomley 1920: 124, 111).

As forceful as the rhythmic effects, and perhaps most characteristic of Bottomley's work, is the bluntness of the language. In explaining to her women why she will not leave the house Hallgerd says: 'Without a man a woman cannot rule,/Nor kill without a knife'. She then explains how she tested his strength: 'I have planned thefts and breakings of his word/When my pent heart grew sore with fermentation/Of malice too long undone'. Imaged here are both a set of irrevocable social circumstances, the gender structure, and personal feeling which is driven by the force of inevitable biological process, the fermenting malice. And the one produces the other. The attitude of the woman to her given circumstances is a sort of gleeful passivity in the face of the irrevocable. As Gunnar's enemies approach Hallgerd tells his mother: 'Watch and be secret,/To feel things pass that cannot be undone' (Bottomley 1920: 96, 118).

Hallgerd here exemplifies Bottomley's attempt to get away from 'novelistic' character. He suggested to Abercrombie that 'drama in England is too much burdened by the depiction of character [...] a bad habit learnt from the novel [...] poetic drama cannot flourish again until stage-characters have leave to become types as well as individual accidents' (88957/1/24 f5). Thus Hallgerd combines the specific and the typical, her private fermenting feelings and her place as any woman in a patriarchal structure. This dramaturgic method, applied more widely than character, constitutes Bottomley's particular innovation in verse drama. Advising Abercrombie that the one-act play should have one central action, he specified that this should be at the spiritual level. Thus in Hallgerd is imaged a general outcome of patriarchal abuse. More metaphorically, in sonic terms, the choric rhythms suggest larger processes beyond the localised, the 'night creeping in', and visually the images do several things at once. Hallgerd's release of her hair is an act of defiance, sensual in its detail and prolongation, expressing her youth, her widowhood, her sexuality; her structural position and her potency. Rhyming with it is a moment in the battle scene when Gunnar asks for two locks of her hair to replace his broken bowstring. Tossing back her hair, she refuses. This at last is her moment of vengeance for a blow he gave her. His mother sarcastically speaks of 'priceless' widow's hair; Gunnar describes 'gold upon her head' treated as gold. Her hair is a specific attribute of her person, a sign of self-preservation and an instrument within the dynamic of historic abuse. The dialectically organised image inhibits simple localised response.

For his subsequent play *King Lear's Wife* (1915), Bottomley removed choric speaking, dance and complex sound effects in order to arrive at what Moore would have called condensation. But it differs from Moore's staging of the ferocity of passion in that Bottomley's dramaturgy works dialectically, making the specific and typical, personal and structural pull against each other.

The play is prequel to Shakespeare's tragedy. During the course of the single act Lear's wife Hygd is dying. Her husband paws the maid servant, to the outrage of his daughter Goneril, a huntress who respects her mother. Cordelia, an off-stage presence, is heard as a spoilt child. When Drinkwater did it at Birmingham Rep the critics were ferocious, as Bottomley reported: 'Shakespeare dragged into the divorce court; a loathsome drama of blood & lust; beastly in the strict sense of the word' (88957/1/87 f207). Although the majority of the audience liked it, the critics' response articulates horror at damage done to the vigilantly guarded status of the national Bard, rabbits and all. The setting is without glamour, its mode of life mean and brutal. Lear's attitude to women and sex, previously mitigated by his distant tragic pentameter grandeur, is now unavoidably egotistical, lecherous and cruel.

But the provocation may well operate at a deeper level. Once Hygd dies two elderly female corpse washers arrive, wearing black costumes with sleeves flapping like birds' wings. They curtsey to the corpse; one checks the pockets of the robe for money. While the elder of the two folds the bed linen, the other roughly tidies the body. The elder sings: 'A louse crept out of my lady's shift', the younger finds a jewel, they fight over it. This handling of the corpse comes after a sequence of brutalities. Before the corpse washers arrive, Goneril pushes to the ground her father's lover Gormflaith, a servant who wears Hygd's crown. She is forced to stumble on her knees towards the bed and lay the crown upon it. Even more abrasively than *Riding* the play shows woman-on-woman violence within a structure where all authority is wielded by the male monarch. As Hygd said earlier to her daughter, 'woman is a thing of a season of years,/She is an early fruit that will not keep,/She can be drained and as a husk survive/To hope for reverence for what has been;/While man renews himself into old age,/And gives himself according to his need'. Of that biological inevitability the woman is entirely conscious within a structure she cannot change. It's not just the corporeal bluntness of the image, but also the self-awareness, the insistence on speaking it, which gives its force. And that force, pressing against the irrevocable circumstances, is a source of violence not against the untouchable man but against other women. Early in the play Lear asks the Physician what is wrong with Hygd and is told 'it may be/Some wound in her affection will not heal'. As she dies Hygd tells Goneril: 'Daughter, pay Gormflaith well'. Which Goneril does, by stabbing her (Bottomley 1920: 43, 16, 9, 33). The localised violence follows its logic within a clearly familiar structure of relations, with the re-worked Shakespeare intensifying the effects. These are both the events of a grand antique story and the grubby everyday interactions produced by recognisable circumstances. The verse dramaturgy condenses, focusses, the action while simultaneously forcing recognition of the larger shapes. That antique brutality always brooding in the work of the national Bard is yet among us. The always dialectical poetic form refuses to settle into either the grubbily everyday or the nobly distant.

Apart from the dramaturgy the other reason it feels like (deliberately) soiled Shakespeare was that although the character names recall the rich Bardic tradition of verse drama these interactions were not acted out within the beautified pictorial settings that had been so efficiently used to turn Shakespeare into spectacle. The Birmingham setting showed stripped-down pictures in a semi-realist mode. The problem, as Bottomley saw it, was the basic proscenium arrangement. It held the performers away from an audience and, above all, obscured the sound of the text.

This is why the new poetic drama couldn't work well theatrically. His analysis was vindicated when his plays were taken up by experimental new directors. Theodore Komisarjevsky did *Crier by Night* and *Lear's Wife* in February 1921 and Terence Gray did three of them at his new Cambridge Festival Theatre in the mid-twenties, using rostra and screens much in the visual mode of European expressionism, for which the plays, written perhaps ahead of their time, had been waiting.

Meanwhile by that time Bottomley had become involved with the Oxford Recitations, an annual competition of spoken poetry. There was no apparatus of theatre, simply a platform. For this Bottomley developed appropriate written texts which required nothing other than an open space. These laid the basis for the scheme which, in 1943, he called a 'Theatre of Poetry'. It was an auditorium based on both the Greek and Wagnerian models but smaller, and with the fixed stage replaced by an empty floor stretching back around 10 meters to the rear wall. In its roof would be a well-equipped lighting rig. In Wagner's theatre, Bottomley noted, there was a gulf in front of the stage, accommodating the orchestra. In his own the empty space was behind it, operating as a 'gulf of mystery' (1948: 69), receding into the darkness out of which creativity emerged. It's a model that facilitates both the sound of poetry and that dialectical tension between distance and nearness which gave the power to so much of Bottomley's work, and was, he might argue, only available in a newly born theatre of poetry.

Expanding the whole being

Which brings us to a question. We have looked at the work of a group of innovative verse dramatists but we have not so far asked why it had to be verse.

The fullest and best answer to this question could work as commentary on Bottomley's method. If prose drama, it says, imitates only the external, poetic drama imitates the 'core'. 'Or rather, it seeks to imitate in you the *effect* which would be produced if you perceived with certainty and clarity the grand emotional impulse driving all existence'. Verse drama 'uses for its texture a verbal process which […] is inescapably recognizable as *symbolic* of the emotional reality of life. The primary emotional urge of our being is conveyed directly, immediately into our apprehension'. This argument was put by Lascelles Abercrombie (1912: 112) in a special issue of *Poetry Review* published in March 1912. Not the best of the dramatists Abercrombie was the best analyst of how verse drama did its work on spectators.

The crucial instrument is metre, 'for metre gives to the poet's words a *form* which is itself a direct expression of the emotion which the words enclose. Not only does the underlying consistent beat keep our answering emotions in the necessary state of excitation, but the sudden varieties and modulations of metre, the momentary deviations from consistency are most powerful suggesters of shifting changes and unexpected upward rushes of emotion'. From here his analysis explores that 'excitation'. Initially the spectator develops enhanced self-consciousness: 'to witness the triumph of dramatic order over life causes, by a kind of induction, a more shapely orderliness in ourselves'. But self-consciousness is more than orderly. It is 'a state of being in which we find it something of an exultation to know that we are ourselves'. Indeed 'the fundamental importance of drama is its power of forcing us into a state of astonishment – astonishment that glows to perceive with unexpected force that terrific splendid fact, the fact *that we do exist*'. Self-consciousness is thus a state approaching ecstasy, which is *not* unconsciousness but 'Being supremely and superbly knowing itself for Being'. In summary drama functions as '*intoxication*' (Abercrombie 1912: 112–15). And the best intoxicant is poetic drama because it produces aesthetic desire for rhythm and order and moral desire for courage and exultation.

A similar argument about dramatic poetry's efficacy was formulated by Sturge Moore in a lecture probably delivered sometime in 1920. He claimed that 'poetry's most essential function is to speak to the whole man [...] his whole harmonized capacities, or as is commonly said to "his soul" though what is vulgarly meant by "soul" is only part of this whole harmonized nature'. What he means by 'harmonized capacities' seems to be that poetry 'expands the whole being and demands for the moment our whole energies of apprehension, of nervous sympathy and of aesthetic admiration'. Great poetic dramas 'distend both the physical and the psychical faculties to their full before they can be entertained and appreciated' (978/2/6/33).

For Moore, as for Abercrombie, the interest was in real-world impact of verse drama, not by reflecting aspects of given living conditions but opening up possibilities of a new way of being, or, as Abercrombie neatly put it, 'the drama of life in place of the drama of facts' (88957/1/24 f75). The importance of Abercrombie's work is that he sought to locate this potency in the materiality of poetic language. Two years after the work on metre, he focused on poetic diction. This 'somehow manages to hold more meaning, more of its originating intention, than other kinds of language. [...] it contrives to imply a deal of more or less related and, as it were, surrounding meaning, quite independent of grammar and logic'. To explain the mechanism of this implied 'surrounding meaning' he used terminology developed by Arthur Ransome (1884–1967) in 'Kinetic and Potential Speech' (1913), first published in *The Oxford and Cambridge Review*. 'He proposes that we should take over from mechanics the names for the two kinds of energy – kinetic, the energy of motion, and potential, the energy of position. The driving force of a sentence is what the grammar and logic of it have to say; that is the kinetic of words. Quite distinguishable from this, the potential of words is due to the way they happen to come up against one another'. While Ransome's essay, with its Symbolist origins, used this binary to distinguish tasteful readers from others, Abercrombie envisages effects which are indiscriminate: 'What we are after now is the concealed and stored-up power of, so to say, suggesting beyond themselves which words reveal instantaneously on contact with other words' (1914: 4, 5).

These arguments were echoed and developed over the decade. Bottomley shared the idea that poetry had 'powers of nameless and intangible suggestion', but introduced a new element when he argued the powers came from rhythm which is 'primarily a function of music', and thus poetry takes on the 'functions of music' (978/1/7/18). For Drinkwater too rhythm was a key quality but conceived now as a force: 'The difference between fine prose and fine verse is fundamentally rather one of urgency, of intensity, than of beauty'. While suggestion and urgency are different effects, both depend for their production on the specific material qualities of drama: 'A play focusses into two hours the selected and concentrated experience of many lives, and it finds an expression that is correspondingly artificial and purged. [...] It is for this reason that the greatest drama is the poetic drama, where the expression reaches the highest artificiality' (Drinkwater 1917: 229–30, 234). Arriving here the discussion about verse drama begins to echo the discussions in such journals as *Rhythm* about the qualities of post-impressionist art. That too was conceived as an anti-realist form that made its visual effects by abstract and rhythmic means. The poetic play can affect profoundly precisely because it is highly artificial.

Rhythm in paintings did not, however, face the same obstacle as it did in drama. Plays have to be performed. And in performance if poetic words are to release their stored-up power they must be given their own space. In general on the commercial, and the new realist, stage there was too much movement, unnecessary gesture, redundant handling of props. The stage imagined by verse drama, by contrast, emphasised simplicity, measure and poise. When Moore rehearsed Sybil Pye for Binyon's *Paris and Oenone* he instructed: 'the fewer gestures the better. Large, slow, rhythmic movements are [...] the secret of dignity on the stage' (in Legge 1980: 196). This was part of what we can call a dramaturgy of stillness.

In performance of this dramaturgy the key issue, for Moore, was proper vocal delivery: 'elocution is that means of representation in which the poet should be proficient' (978/2/6/33). Most contemporary performers did not understand the art of 'elocution'. They either subjugated the verse text to characterisation, speaking it in a way which would not compromise the illusion of a credible character, or used it as a vehicle for a display of expressivity in clear excess of what was required. In neither case did they trust the rhythms and language of the verse and speak them precisely. This constituted a blockage so damaging that Abercrombie thought the theatre could only be regenerated if professional actors were all removed.

The renovated theatre's difference from dominant practices would be displayed in the development of a new actor who could do proper 'elocution'. For this reason Yeats, Moore and their associates enthusiastically embraced Florence Farr's experiments in chanting verse. Working within the restricted range of tones of an instrument specially made for her by Arnold Dolmetsch (1858–1940), a central figure within musical experiment, she intoned the words. As distinct from singing, which focusses on the melody of a phrase, her method recognised that 'each word has a melody of its own, which starts from a certain keynote on which it is uttered'. The effects of this are seen when the repetitive chanting of

Eastern priests begins to work on a chattering crowd: 'their bodies sway to the rhythm and melody of the words, their souls melt under the breath of the inspiring spirit'. But it's not only the listening body which is affected. In speech the sound is functional and thus naturalised while song demonstrates submission to the discipline of music. Chanting foregrounds the work of the individual voice as a physical entity. So too its focus on individual words 'as *sounds*, not merely as symbols' (Farr 1909: 17, 18, 21) physicalises those words. This embodiment made chanting consistent with the central activity in Farr's Dancers group. Like dance, chanting to an audience has the capacity to relate directly from body to body, sharing sound and rhythm. Thus verse, actively spoken as verse, is more than a medium for invoking the immaterial world. For those promoting 'literary drama' the word was not merely symbol but was also, here and now, materially present.

While Yeats and Moore were excited by the possibilities of chanting, it was a fairly minority taste and perhaps of only dubious relevance to performing verse drama. When Moore's close friend Trevelyan saw Farr in *Aphrodite*, for instance, he noted that she 'constantly seemed to me to spoil the beauty of the lines by exagerated [sic] emphasis on some word or phrase [...] and in general by too little respect for the line as a rhythmical unity' (978/1/4/6). So after the chanting fad faded, the exploration of a technique for dramatic elocution continued for several decades. In 1923, after watching a performance of Bottomley's *Gruach*, done by the Scottish National Theatre Society, with voices trained by Marjorie Gullan (1879–1959), a pioneer of choral speaking and speech training, John Masefield established his Oxford Recitations, to promote the speaking of poetry. Coming from another direction, in the relatively new domain of academies for actors, Elsie Fogerty (1865–1945), founder in 1906 of the significantly named Central School of Speech Training and Dramatic Art, emphasised skill in recitation as a major part of the actor's tool-box. But the problem of speaking was about something very much more than appropriate performance technique.

When Bottomley began to develop scripts inspired by the set-up of the Oxford Recitations they involved performers doing choric delivery. The creation of a group that speaks in unison requires a loss of individuality into the discipline and interaction of a multi-individual entity. This curtails the possibility of an individualist approach to performance, an approach produced and sustained by the commercial system, its competitive careers and its production of celebrity. Moore argued that an actor who cannot give 'poetical effect to the poet's words' makes them appear unnecessary and replaces them with 'star-acting' (978/2/6/5). Bottomley agreed: 'I have long felt that performers' insistence on "personality", and the serious value they put on it, has been one of the causes of the decay of public art'. He was discussing Moore's idea for placing speakers behind a curtain. Bottomley speculated: 'Would not the "personal" show-reciter, when deprived of the appeal of face and gesture and dress, be likely to develope [sic] a higher organisation of tricks of voice, in order to make his "effects" carry (and be recognised) through and beyond the curtain?' (978/1/7/18). It's a prescient hunch about the obsessiveness with which celebrity, even unseen, insists on itself, like a nasty smell in a handbag.

Stars and their glistening productions were not just agents of commercialism and spectacle. They also curtailed the positive function of poetic theatre. Where poetic language embodies force and suggests meaning beyond the everyday, the star's failure properly to speak that language eviscerates it, changes its effects, confines the spectator to the superficial and everyday. The spectator is in the most negative sense alienated. Poetic theatre was opposed to such performance because its role, as Drinkwater put it, was, in the face of 'a strongly organised and capitalised industry', to return to 'Passionate life' (1917: 221). The mechanism of that re-awakening was described by Bottomley, and it can serve as a summary of the ideas described in this section.

Writing towards the end of his life he said that he chose verse drama not because of the great tradition but 'because I desire more speech and sound on my stage than the present all-pervading form of colloquial drama can give me'. Sound is important in its own right, as a phenomenon, because 'poetry's unearned increment upon sense causes the sound of the words which compose it to be part of their meaning'. Thus 'when poetry is performed between persons, the fact that their intercourse is raised to the poetic tension often causes the action to be on the spiritual level; and, when that is the case, the words become the action [...] a sound can stir the blood, a sound can paralyse or release' (1948: xiii–xiv). Bottomley uses a basically phenomenological argument to demonstrate how being in the presence of verse drama can work on the body, as sensation combined with spirit, to retrieve the spectator, consumer of spectacle, from the status of object among objects. This, then, is the political function of activating a person's whole harmonised capacities, and the reason why a renovated theatre needed verse.

But almost the whole of the rationale for verse has so far depended on the effects of sound and diction and rhythm. Verse could, however, do more than this. To discover what we must turn to a poet dramatist who mainly moved outside the groups around Moore and Drinkwater.

Experiments in tragedy

In his autobiography John Masefield (1878–1967) tells how he set himself to learn the craft of writing drama by playing with a model box and trying out the shapes of scenes (1952: 169–70). For him drama was not a development from the dramatic poem, as for Abercrombie or Gibson, but an art which begins with three-dimensional spaces. An interest in how those three dimensions can work informed the series of dramatic experiments in which he aimed to model a version of tragedy appropriate to contemporary times. In following that project we discover the various potencies of verse dramaturgy.

It began with prose. Although it was not the first of his plays, the title of *The Tragedy of Nan* (1908) marks it as the formal start to his project. Set in rural Gloucestershire, the use of local dialect and invocation of tradition-bound local community suggest the influence of the key figure up to that point in Masefield's life, the poet he sought out and visited in Woburn Buildings, and to whose views on poetic delivery he eagerly listened, Yeats. *Nan* is a Gloucestershire version of Yeats' plays of Celtic rural life. But if it emerged from the link to a poet *Nan* also delivered Masefield into the hands of a theatre-maker. It was first done by the Pioneers theatre group under the direction of Granville Barker, with Barker's wife Lillah McCarthy playing the lead. And it was Barker's touch which effaced Yeats from the play to which Masefield turned next.

In her biography of Masefield Smith (1985: 95) tells how he stayed with the Barkers while he was writing *The Tragedy of Pompey* (1910), suggesting they assisted with thinking through its dramaturgy. This dramaturgy was a very much more complicated matter than *Nan*. The play depicts Caesar's eventually victorious military campaign to wrest control of Rome from Pompey and in this imperial context stages discussions about democracy, ethics and war. Pompey's daughter Julia, for example, urges him to confront Caesar: 'it is better to have war than to see law set aside. Law is such a wonderful thing. The will of Rome' (1913: 26). In the months during which the play was gestating the British press was concerned about increased production of German battleships. In May 1909, for example, Garvin recommended (1909: 806) that what was needed was 'inflexible moral steadfastness and a decisive development of our Imperial strength on sea and land'. In shaping a tragedy for those tense years Masefield seems to connect his dramatic language to the discourses around him. And here again Barker was useful, for Masefield much admired his 'fine supple style that has a play and a glitter on it like a sword of the best temper' (in Smith 1985: 113).

That remark, and the *Pompey* project, display Masefield's distance from the other verse dramatists. The movement from *Nan* to *Pompey* is away from the condensation and passion recommended by Moore. The stripped-back language of debate and tactics, noticed by reviewers, displays precisely what Bottomley despised – Masefield's almost journalistic plainness, his 'anxious diligence to call a Spade a Bloody Shovel every time' (978/1/7/18). And to admire Barker was to admire someone apparently wedded to realism. Verse plays built on this foundation would be very different from the Literary Theatre and its like.

The first of them was in similar territory to *Pompey*. The one-act *Philip the King* (published in September 1914) shows Philip of Spain awaiting news of the success of the great armada he has sent in 'God's cause' (Masefield 1918: 14) to defeat the English. It was an appropriate moment for such a tale. The arms-race rhetoric since at least 1909 nearly came to actual conflict with the Agadir crisis of 1911. Although it was averted, warnings proliferated about the developing feud with Germany and the need for naval power and a better army. Then war was declared in August 1914. This sets the frame for the sixteenth-century monarch's pride in the strength of his fleet. But his relationship with contemporary affairs is made complex by Masefield's decision to use verse and conspicuously theatrical devices such as ghosts. We hear the talk of weapons and strategy and simultaneously hear something beyond it.

Various figures from the past appear to Philip including the brother he killed to advance his career and the man who built his fleet for him. But it's typical of Masefield that the first of these is a group of Indians killed in the brutal conditions of the Spanish gold mines. 'The evil men do' they say 'gathers behind the veils/While the unjust thing prevails' (Masefield 1918: 20). From behind such veils, these are voices of those destroyed by militarism and empire. This sense of a world always beyond, and not necessarily the one imagined by rulers, is strengthened by the use of offstage crowds, first celebrating apparent victory, with monks chanting, and then the sad singing of defeated sailors. It all comes onstage in the single person of the messenger who describes the sinking of the armada and final collapse of dreams of military triumph. The episode draws its power not from stage activity or spectacle but from narrative verse, done at great length and increasingly formalised, with rhymes. It is a set piece of bravura delivery, a display of extremely skilful human expressivity, and at the same time a tale of the destruction to life wrought by militarism, two interlocked possibilities of human potency. As a dramatic device, it's come from one of the earliest modes of verse drama, that of ancient Greece.

This Masefield explored more fully in the play after *Philip*. Begun in 1914, it was interrupted by war work, visits to the battlefields and a book about the disastrous landings at Gallipoli. Completed in 1916, deep into a war that didn't seem to end, its subject matter seems somewhat distant. Called *Good Friday* it tells the Biblical story of the death of Jesus. It is not, however, a religious play. Indeed Masefield himself at this point was not religious. The Bible story is used much as other sorts of historical story, as a vehicle for a play about militarism, colonialism and power.

It opens with an argument between the Roman governor Pilate and the Chief Citizen as to what should be done with Jesus. The decision has to do with the balance of power between Romans, Jewish priests and the crowd. It's a conversation between coloniser and colonised, where the coloniser has to depend on an existing infrastructure in a restless country.

In the relationship between the violent crowd and the Romans the play spells out the effects of ideology. Pilate tells the Chief Citizen 'These ancient prophecies/Are drugs to keep crude souls from being wise'. This apparently civilised Roman rationality has its own ideological constraints, however, as demonstrated in Pilate's conversation with his wife Procula. She says Jesus should be spared. Pilate explains: 'Roman laws forbid/That I should weigh, like God, the worth of souls./I act for Rome, and Rome is better rid/Of these rare spirits whom no law controls' (Masefield 1925: 10, 36). From this legal destruction of Jesus Procula dissociates herself. To expunge the ethical stain, she stabs her own arm. It is the only physical violence in the play, shockingly sudden and, with the blood, visually striking. And, in the narrative, entirely redundant. Placing the liberal opposition to both popular prejudice and colonial law in the mouth of a woman, Masefield shows her to be rhetorically powerful and politically ineffectual.

This is a play about the management of ideology within conditions of colonial rule and racial antagonism. When reviewers observed that it failed to transmit Christian faith they firmly had the wrong end of the stick. Jesus is kept offstage, never offered for empathy. Nonetheless the cruel outcome of the political machinations is emphasised. Longinus describes the crucifixion: 'the heavy blood-gouts dropped and ticked/On to the stone; the hill is all bald stone./And now and then the hangers gave a groan' (Masefield 1925: 43). There is in this something of Masefield's picture (1916: 74–75) of the destruction on the slopes of Gallipoli, where a casualty might lie 'bleeding in the scrub, with perhaps his face gone and a leg and an arm broken, unable to move but still alive, unable to drive away the flies or screen the ever-dropping rain', until 'nothing is left of him but a few rags and a few remnants and a little identification disc flapping on his bones in the wind'.

Longinus' images have force partly through their vividness and partly, also, through their theatrical framing. This is made clear in a letter Masefield wrote to his wife on 26 February 1917. He says that with six months more he could have improved the play, 'scrapping all the first half of it, & making it a complete Greek structure, as of course it is, the death of Dionysus, after a contest, the messenger, & then the transcendence or reawakening' (Masefield 1985: 201). Longinus delivers a Greek Messenger speech within a context not of a Christian play, but of *The Bacchae* with Christ as Dionysus.

As such it becomes more potent than a play of faith and goes far beyond 'social' drama. By using the Biblical story Masefield attempts to engage with populist ideology and imperial rule without participating in the language of either, and to invoke the pain of destroyed bodies without being pictorial or sensationalist. The rationale is set out in the Introduction to the 1925 *Verse Plays*:

> If playwrights were concerned solely with the characters and events of everyday life, they might find prose a sufficient instrument: but the playwright's art is not so limited: often a playwright is not concerned with the events of everyday life, but with the dealings of the Gods, elements in the soul of man and the fables of a nation. He is then not writing of the accidents and incidents of personality, but of the heart of life as it is displayed at great moments. His theme then demands a language and movement other than those of daily life: it becomes of the nature of religion and demands a ritual.
>
> (1925: v)

An effect of seeing the heart of life is produced just over halfway through *Good Friday*. A character called simply the Madman has a conversation with a Sentry about Jesus. He 'told the crowd/That only a bloody God would care for blood'. After the Sentry leaves the Madman speaks a poem: 'The wild-duck, stringing through the sky,/Are south away./Their green necks glitter as they fly,/The lake is gray'. It's not simply the new verbal formality that makes the contrast with the preceding dialogue sharp. The poem invokes a wholly new landscape.

After three stanzas the form changes for eight short rhymed lines, then returns closer, but not precisely, to the play's dominant form: 'Darkness come down, cover a brave man's pain'. The stage darkens. 'I have been scourged, blinded and crucified,/My blood burns on the stone of every street'. It darkens more. 'Beyond the pain, beyond the broken clay,/A glimmering country lies/Where life is being wise' (Masefield 1925: 32–34). This is the point in the play where Jesus, offstage, is crucified. Masefield halts the dramaturgic progress. Unseen worlds are invoked. The Madman in front of us speaks as one who has died on the cross. It's a set-piece display of the operation of human empathy, moving into new spaces, inhabiting a different body. There is no other expression of feeling like this in the play.

Masefield is here putting to use Moore's aesthetic of simplicity and condensation, the verse play's characteristic dramaturgy of stillness. But he takes it further. As a response to the horrors of the time at which it was written, to get at the heart of life – and death – the verse play becomes even more formalised. Within the Greek tragic model, and a dominant mode of rhyming couplets, it's a Madman's formalised speech that is a poem of empathy. Here is the verse play arriving at a new model of tragedy appropriate to its bloody times.

In following Masefield's journey here, albeit sketchily, we have traced the relationship between verse drama and the existing genre of tragedy. But Masefield's work can also take us into another key interaction for verse drama, that with Oriental culture.

Experiments with Eastern forms

The journey begins with Masefield's close friend Laurence Binyon. As Assistant Keeper of prints at the British Museum Binyon promoted knowledge of and enthusiasm for Japanese aesthetics through the extended range of his acquaintances, particularly the artistic group which gathered regularly at the Vienna Café in London. Among them was Ezra Pound, and it is the consequent effect on Pound's writing that informs Arrowsmith's claim (2011) that Binyon, and indeed the British Museum, played a role in developing the artistic language and ideas of 'Modernism'.

Significant as that claim may – or may not – be for literary history, the story of engagement with Asian culture at this time is bigger and richer. The interest was not confined to Japan and there were more agents than Binyon. Knowledge of the 'Orient' came not just from artworks and books but also from personal or artistic networks, imperial service overseas and travels. To take examples from the writers we're looking at here: Bottomley knew the poet Yone Noguchi and arranged for English publication of his book *Pilgrimage*; just about everyone knew, and raved about, the Bengali writer Rabindranath Tagore, and Moore wrote unpublished commentary on his work; Moore had been interested in Japanese prints since the 1880s and had two Hokusai prints on his walls; his close friends Shannon and Ricketts had a substantial collection, indeed Ricketts knew sufficient to be asked to assess the quality of the British Museum's Oriental holdings; Pye acquired Chinese and Japanese art through his son who worked for an East Asian shipping company; Bottomley had become interested in Javanese dancers having seen photographs sent by Bessie Trevelyan's brother who was stationed there; Bob Trevelyan, together with Lowes Dickinson and E.M. Forster, took an extended tour in 1911–1912 from India through China and Java to Japan, sending regular postcards of artworks as they went.

None of this, of course, need have made any difference to the drama. Commercial English theatre, from *The Mikado* to *Chu Chin Chow*, was well capable of using a generalised 'Orient' to titivate its tedium without changing its practice. Even for someone as scholarly and serious as Binyon himself the cultural engagement didn't lead to a new drama. His play *Ayuli* (1911) simply has an Oriental theme without much Oriental practice. By contrast there was his work on *Sakuntala*, a Sanskrit text that a friend of Tagore, Kedar Nath Das Gupta, wanted to show in London. Binyon met Das Gupta in late 1918 and agreed to do a dramatised version of his basic translation. But the work remained a Sanskrit drama, not a new form of English practice. For that we have to turn to more skilled dramatists.

Which brings us back to Masefield, and his play *The Faithful*, started in 1913. It was based on a story from an 1871 classic, Algernon Mitford's *Tales of Old Japan*, which, along with Lafcadio Hearn's books between 1894 and 1904, was a standard of the Japan fad. But use of a 'Japanese' story need have no impact on dramatic techniques, as *The Mikado* showed. The significance of Masefield's work is its apparent attempt to use Japanese aesthetic principles. I suspect these derived from Binyon's recently published 1911 book about Oriental painting, *The Flight of the Dragon* (they were friends, and the dates are close). Binyon opens by identifying a problem. The assumption that art is 'imitative and representative' of nature no longer has force, but there is no agreed alternative. Among possibilities, the only viable one is Oriental aesthetics, of which the foundational 'Six Canons' have, as their most important, 'Rhythmic Vitality, or spiritual rhythm expressed in the movement of life' (1959: 9, 11).

'Rhythm' is not mere poetic metre but the organisation and balance of elements in any sort of artwork. That proposition is elaborated more fully by an author who influenced Binyon's ideas, Kakuzo Okakura, whose *The Ideals of the East* was published in 1904. His version of that first Canon, 'The Life-movement of the Spirit through the Rhythm of Things', relates back to Shakaku, who first formulated it: 'art is to him the great Mood of the Universe, moving hither and thither amidst those harmonic laws of matter which are Rhythm'. By 700–800 (CE) 'art becomes largely a reaching forth towards the visualisation of the vastness of the universe' (2007: 37, 73). As Binyon put it, 'the artist must pierce beneath the mere aspect of the world to seize and himself to be possessed by that great cosmic rhythm of the spirit which sets the currents of life in motion' (1959: 11–12). The artist, having focussed her or his perception, yields to absorption into a cosmos.

In the present day, as Okakura saw it, two forces competed for the Japanese mind: 'One is the Asiatic ideal, replete with grand visions of the universal sweeping through the concrete and particular, and the other European science, with her organised culture, armed in all its array of differentiated knowledge, and keen with the edge of competitive energy' (2007: 126). That contrast has been politically sharpened already by Okakura's characterisation of some historic Asiatic societies as socialist or communist. Thus the alternative to the unsatisfactory realism of European art is, at least for Okakura, not simply to do with aesthetic regimes of abstraction against representation but also with the universal against the differentiated and competitive.

Masefield engages all elements here. He instructs that *The Faithful* be played without a break on a stage divided into two scenes, the front bare except for a screen painted with a Japanese landscape and, behind, 'a room in a Japanese palace', beautiful but 'bare' (1915: vii). These are quoted images. It is a tragedy, not an authentic Japanese play, with the transition between scenes derived from Barker's Savoy Shakespeares (1923: vi). Nonetheless it is interested in the dramatic effects created by a foregrounded bareness. The speech is mainly stripped-down prose and the movement sometimes formalised into ceremonial discipline. One such ends the first act. Asano has been tricked into striking his devious greedy enemy during a ceremony. For this he is sentenced to death. Alone on a ceremonial white mat he speaks: 'Sometimes, in wintry springs,/Frost, on a midnight breath,/Comes to the cherry flowers/And blasts their prime' (1915: 53). The stillness is both physical and verbal, held by the rhythm of the sudden verse. It emits a sense of larger natural process, beyond the deceptions and aggression of greedy men. The moment of conspicuous formalisation of the words is simultaneously the moment of apprehension of that which is universal.

Later Asano's scattered followers regroup after wandering for a year. As they narrate their experiences they move into verse. One tells how his wife stabbed herself, another how his children starved to death: 'We lay on the reeds/In the marshy places,/They cried for food,/For the sweet cakes of old'. Gathering up their weapons to burn them, they speak in unison: 'Burn, with our hopes, to ashes, all is past,/The waiting in the snow,/The year-long pain,/The faith that equal justice falls at last' (Masefield 1915: 102–7). In the verse modes Masefield has something in common with other Japanese-influenced contemporaries, the Imagists. As Earl Miner says, the play's last poem 'is composed in the syllabic fives and sevens of Japanese poetry with which Amy Lowell had experimented' (1966: 218). These sorts of Imagist intensification depart from speech norms to communicate a sense of larger forces at work, what Asano calls the 'machine of this world' (Masefield 1915: 44). That communication, more than superficial imitation of Japanese forms, most closely approximates to Binyon's image of the artist piercing the surface to be seized by cosmic rhythm. Together the European characterisation and the foregrounded bareness and formality create a dramatic language very different from journalistic social drama.

It was also very different from the most well-known encounter at this period between poetic drama and Japan. The oft-repeated story is that Ezra Pound, having been introduced to Oriental art by Binyon, in turn introduced Yeats to Ernest Fenollosa's unpublished translations of Nō plays, which he had been sent by Fenollosa's widow, and they spent the winter of 1915 in Sussex reading together, from which emerged the first of Yeats' plays for dancers, *At the Hawk's Well*, begun in February 1916, and Pound's edition of Fenollosa, *Noh, or Accomplishment* (1916), with Yeats' Introduction 'Certain Noble Plays of Japan'. As Pound saw it (1916: 152), the discovery of Nō provided the formula which verse dramatists had been seeking since the beginning of the century: 'The beauty and power of Noh lie in the concentration. All elements – costume, motion, verse, and music – unite to produce a single clarified impression'.

But, despite Pound's self-positioning at the forefront of things, the process of theatrical engagement with Nō had begun somewhat earlier. In his retrospective *A Stage for Poetry*, Bottomley said that by the early twenties he had been interested in Japanese drama for years. One of his sources was Osman Edwards' 1901 book *Japanese Plays and Playfellows*, which included a Nō drama. Edwards (1864–1936) was interested in a range of forms of new writing – he wrote on Verhaeren for the *Savoy* magazine, for example – and was particularly alert to theatre practice. The features of Nō he lists are the use of a significant suggestive object, the communication of feelings by 'dirge-like song' and 'lugubrious' postures and dance, all with the capability of suggesting the largest ideas in a very small physical space: 'The gods become marionettes for an hour, without wholly losing their godhead' (1901: 35, 37). Alongside this Bottomley may also have learnt from his friend Yone Noguchi who had written a piece in 1907, published in Japan, comparing Yeats' theatrical ideas with Nō. His 1909 *Riding to Lithend*, as we have seen, opens with a choric narrative, uses simple props and gestures to carry complex meaning, has a dance at the centre of its action and a story that is offered as culturally ancient.

A later significant case of interaction with Japanese drama was that of Stanley Jast (1868–1944). Based in Manchester, he was a chief librarian whose most famous output is the Manchester Central Library, together with its theatre (Fry and Mumford 1966). The vision for that theatre grew out of Jast's experience with the Unnamed Society which he co-founded in 1916 with Frank Sladen-Smith (1887–1955), son of a music-hall musical director and a textile designer who trained at Manchester School of Art. There Sladen-Smith met Karl Hagedorn (1889–1969), forming a tiny art club, Der Künstler Zwei, in 1908, which laid the basis for the Unnamed Society's distinctive links with visual artists. Both men went to Paris, the centre of progressive art. Here Hagedorn embraced the modes of Cubism and Fauvism and brought them back to exhibit at the second exhibition of Manchester's Society of Modern Painters in October 1913, to the horror of reviewers (Whitworth Art Gallery 1994). A few years later they were working on Unnamed productions.

A couple of years after its formation the Society began performing at Madge Atkinson's Studio at 259 Deansgate. Atkinson (1885–1970) pioneered a form of dance which she called Natural Movement, which used natural forms as stimuli (Fensham 2015), a technique which Jast would draw on for one of his shows. Comprising an alliance of experimental practices the Society was a conscious refusal of northern realism: 'Its aim is not to reveal Manchester, but to forget it [...] It envisages the play as a compound of drama, stage setting and acting' (Jast 1924: 3). This compound motivated Jast's 'lyrical ballet-masque' *The Loves of the Elements*, where the simple story of the four elements is a ruse to explore the interaction of the stage's expressive elements: body interacting with light, voice speaking to music, voice marking dance rhythms, contrasts of verse and prose, contrasts of vocal and physical texture – the Undines' speech is 'rippling', the Gnomes' 'harsh' and their dancing 'angular' (Jast 1923: 75, 56). This 'dancing play' was choreographed by Atkinson with music by Georgia Pearce and design by another student of the Manchester School, Lilian Reburn (1887–1973), whose costumes and masks were inspired by Kathak dancers.

It was one of four Jast plays using dance among the six staged between October 1918 and October 1921. Another was 'a play of poses', and one 'an application of what I conceive to be the fundamental principles of the Japanese Nō' (Jast 1923: vi). This play, *Harbour* (premiered October 1921), was done against a simple blue curtain, with costumes by Karl Hagedorn. It depicts a Pilgrim preparing himself for admission to Nirvana by first denying the body and then the mind. He spends most of the play kneeling, with minimal and 'ritualistic' movements. A chorus sits cross-legged. The chorus comments, represents various temptations and can speak for the Pilgrim, but is never really in dialogue with him. Delivery was also denaturalised. *The Times* (27 February 1922) noted the actors 'broke up their words as a spelling-book breaks them'. Towards the end, the curtain is drawn to reveal the figure of Buddha in a blaze of light. Like the *Elements* this story of progressive withdrawal from bodily and mental engagement explores the interaction of thoroughly material and indeed sensual devices of theatre. It shows how highly disciplined, restricted movement and speech, together with conspicuously simplified lighting, can themselves be a source of pleasure, a sensually exciting disciplining of sensuality. In these respects Jast seems to tackle Symbolist theatre's problem of showing immateriality by material means. He gets there by assimilating and then re-functioning Japanese convention.

This explicit refunctioning was very different in purpose and effect from Yeats' appropriation of Nō. While he seemed to embrace the most obvious features of Nō's restrained dramaturgy and apparatus, with its masks and curtain-bearer, Yeats invented, as Morash (2021: 106) says, a role for the musicians as a sort of chorus. This was actually a proliferation rather than stripping back of the elements, and his friends were somewhat sceptical about its superficiality. For them Nō was a form that had its own resistance to being colonised by simplistic imitation. Moore, Trevelyan and Bottomley were all friends of Arthur Waley, another British Museum curator, who knew Japanese. Waley told Bottomley that the plays were 'impossible to translate', and only an idea of their staging could be suggested (88957/1/114 f147). His view of Pound's Fenollosa volume, as

Moore reported, was that none of the plays in there was 'really complete'. This uncertainty about translation was by now built into Nō scholarship. In Marie Stopes' 1913 book, based on a previous article from 1909, she discusses at length the problems of translation, noting what is sacrificed by every decision. This all relates to the larger issue of how Nō could be understood formally. In the preface to *Arthur* (1914: xii), Buckley likened it to 'Greek, Shakespearean, and Wagnerian music-drama'. Percy Scholes in 1917 added in the English miracle play (Savage 2014: 114).

In the face of this diversity Yeats pinned the slippery thing down to what he needed it to be. For him it was a model, on which 'I have invented a form of drama, distinguished, indirect, and symbolic' (1989: 221). For these reasons in *Hawk's Well* the Old Man moving to music is directed to be like a 'marionette'; in *Dreaming of the Bones* the images in the musicians' songs are offered as Significant, though it's not clear of what, and the characters' journeying is marked by a circuit of the stage where the exact repetition each time works like a ritualising device, though it's unclear what for. The effects seem to amount to little more than a performance of being symbolical. Or rather a performance of being distinguished, obscure, and élite. Moore, Yeats' friend, and inveterate critic (Bridge 1953: xvii), was not taken in: Yeats' notions about Nō drama 'are all second hand and misty at that. He never shakes his mind free from theories which are founded on his personal peculiarities'. As Bottomley saw it the problems had started earlier. In July 1909 he commented to Moore that 'When Yeats published Deirdre I began to feel that his impeccable form […] was achieved at too great a cost, the sacrifice of energy was too invariable, style and concinnity were attained by a narcotizing of all those great primitive heroes and high-hearted women' (88957/1/24 f4). Thus when Yeats began imitating Nō, he seemed not to comprehend the importance of the sheer physicality essential to the dance on which the form is based.

When therefore Moore tried his own hand at a Nō play he was aware of Yeats' limitations. Yeats would return the favour by being highly critical of it. Moore's *Medea* (1920) begins on the Yeats/Nō model with the entrance of a male curtain-bearer who addresses the audience before two female curtain-holders enter to unwrap the curtain for the performance. Note already Moore's use of female performers in what was traditionally a male form. These two will supply the voices of Medea's dead children. Medea then enters accompanied by a female companion, Proto, whose initial role it is to be sceptical about the sounds Medea thinks she can hear. Then we too hear children as the two folders speak 'without moving, in a childish voice' (Moore 1920: 15). They visually remain in role as folders, even while they perform the children. Medea rehearses her original murder of the boys, but Proto still cannot hear them and Medea, wanting rid of her, charms her to sleep. Proto sleeps standing up.

Once she's asleep Medea thinks she's alone, but then the curtain-bearer begins to speak: 'I speak for silenced visions in thy mind'. Telling her it's the 'second failure' in her life he has her re-visit her life-history. This episode ends with her praying to Artemis and resolving to ask forgiveness from the children. She seeks for them in the trees, which they treat as a game, wanting her to shoot arrows as they run about. This leads to two episodes of dance in which Medea tries to track the children's movements and then aim her arrows while the curtain-bearer narrates the scene. Only Medea moves, among four still bodies. She then collapses and Proto awakes feeling 'moved, but blank' (Moore 1920: 16, 25). Seeing the collapsed Medea she feels pity, despite having disliked her. And the curtain-bearer and folders then extend the curtain, behind which the stage empties.

This version of the Nō apparatus allows Moore both to stage psychic intensity and to keep it at distance. Medea, in the grip of memories, regrets and desires, is compelled to repeat her actions and never be satisfied. But it's watched as game and dance, with articulation of her feelings split between her and the curtain-bearer. Hers is the single body expressing distress among bodies that frame and watch it as performance. In some ways it's like watching someone undergo a form of therapy, which can never eradicate the passion. Moore, with his interest in psychic processes, has adapted the ritualised Nō into a more contemporary form of ritualised therapeutic encounter.

Overall, then, the engagement with Nō, like that with tragedy, was an exploration of the possibilities for verse dramaturgy. Just as importantly it was a way of showing that modern verse drama could be significant and serious in its form and effects. But there was one further development. Partly arising from the work with Nō, partly deriving from the medium of verse itself, poetic drama pushed towards a new concept and function of stage space.

Sonic spatiality

In *Good Friday* Masefield instructed that there be only one setting, with exits either through bronze doors at the back, for the Romans, or stone steps at sides and front, for all the rest. His use of a Greek model drove an exploration of the functioning of stage dynamics. While in *Philip the King* ghosts share the same space as historical characters that space is anchored down by our primary identification with Philip as dramatic centre: we're seeing the visions he sees. Where the dramatic centre is dislocated or even removed the space becomes freer from narrative ordering. This happens with the ambivalent status of the Madman in *Good Friday*. Moore, who had joined the Stage Society council in 1912 (Gwynn 1952: 41) and worked on this production, astutely observing that the play lacked 'a central interest' commented: 'that absence of a central interest or shall I say a dramatised interest is fairly common in Noh plays. That the thing should have happened is considered itself important, so that your sympathies are quite free inside that interest and do not need to be absorbed by any one player or identified with any one point of view actually presented. This is a great quality. Truly poetical' (88957/1/67 f72).

Moore's alertness to what Masefield was doing had its roots in his own dramaturgic experiments with occluding the central visual interest. In 1912, in a lecture on 'The Reading of Poetry', he recommended 'a curtain to hide the speaker [...] to reduce him as nearly as possible to a voice' (in Morrisson 2001: 66). In 1920 he used this arrangement not for a reading but for a play. In *Niobe* (1920) there are three characters: Niobe and her children. The children speak in terror, facing death. They die. Niobe laments and rages. None of the characters appears on stage. The whole thing is heard while we look at a bare platform. Stanley Jast tried something similar with *The Room*, where we look at a hotel landing, seeing a shadow but no bodies. Moore goes further by cancelling all visual representation. We become acutely aware of the stage's capacity to conceal as well as reveal, a capacity more brutally enacted in the darkness around the spot-lit mouth of Beckett's *Not I*. Half a century or so earlier even Moore's closest friends found this development too extreme. Yet it was but a continuation of the logic of 'literary' theatre.

Produced by a small group of poet dramatists that theatre led, as we've seen, to some fairly profound developments. It proposed that the verse play, much more than social drama, could communicate something spiritual, universal, beyond the everyday. This inspired experiments in tragedy and Nō, with the latter in particular intensifying a drive towards simplification and abstraction. With the emergence of new dramaturgy came a new sonically ordered space.

By way of drawing these observations together, we again take our seats in the theatre, to observe one of the high points at which verse drama arrived. We are in the Oxford Playhouse in early June 1923. A single woman walks forward on a bare stage and speaks directly to the audience in verse, telling us how she plans to deal with unrest against her weak husband the king. Her name is Jezebel. The actress is Penelope Wheeler, who, way back, played Moore's Artemis. She is part of Masefield's company the Hill Players, named after his Oxford village of Boar's Hill. This is the opening of his play *A King's Daughter*.

Jehu, a military commander, aims to overthrow the royal couple who are despised for making peace with their Syrian enemy. He has an ally in the Prophet who uses his status, and violent rhetoric, to support military aggression. Within the community Naboth is stirring up trouble because the monarch wants to take control of his vineyard to strengthen the defensive capability of the town. In refusing this demand Naboth rejects both community values and state interests. This dramaturgy reverses the customary Biblical values, where Naboth is seen as the righteous man deprived by a corrupt power and Jezebel as the archetype of a wicked woman, and a foreigner to boot. The casting in this role of Wheeler, an actress associated both with art theatre and with entertaining the troops, helped unsettle assumed ideas about the evil female ruler.

The audience at this unsettling had been through the war. This context layers new associations onto the Biblical story. For her attempts to avert war by negotiated settlement Jezebel is accused of trying to buy peace for Syrians because she is herself Syrian. This feels specifically reminiscent of the accusation by the militarist British press that Lord Haldane's attempts to seek a diplomatic solution to the war were motivated by his being pro-German. That war-mongering press is generally suggested by the language of the Prophet. Characteristic of that language is the assumption of a religious mission, with God being incontrovertibly recruited to Team GB. Thus the reversal here of assumed Biblical values becomes politically important. In his book about the Boer War, *Jingoism*, J.A. Hobson had argued (1901: 29) that the privately-owned press was 'the chief instrument of brutality' in whipping up nationalist feeling. In 1916–1918, Masefield and those like him thought similarly about the war-mongering press. When Naboth invokes his divine rights to private ownership as against the interests of the community we hear the Biblical narrative estranged by a New Liberal if not socialist standpoint.

The interest in rhetoric and ideology is emphasised by the formal device of the figures who end each act with a narrative which tells of revisiting the battlefield of ancient Troy. For most of the play these two speakers are detached from the world of the main story but in the final act become maids to Jezebel, albeit still retaining their choric formality. While the Biblical story is an embodied action, the Troy story is told as narrative. And while the Biblical action tells of the build-up to war the Troy narrative tells of its aftermath. These two dramatic elements are brought together as the play works towards the death of Jezebel, who is thrown from a window. We hear her trampled to death by horses outside, and then the usurper Jehu enters. He promises more slaughter, drinks wine, sings a song, and goes off to make sacrifice. The short epilogue is given by a seer who concludes that 'the ways of the gods […] are dark, they make me afraid' (Masefield 1937: 228).

Where earlier verse drama had mainly depended on the poetic text to suggest the universal, something beyond, Masefield has taken the form into a more dramaturgically open state. The embodied action and the recited narrative each have equal weight, each deal with something different. But in dealing with the before and after of war, they are not in balance. The knowledge of the aftermath makes the arguments of the lead-up look superficial and selfish. With what we have to call a dialectical relationship between these two elements – always yoked together, always pulling in different ways – Masefield has begun to discover for verse drama its transition into something which would shortly, and elsewhere, become known as 'epic theatre'.

It got there because in its vehement rejection of realism verse drama had striven for a dramaturgy that showed intersections of particular and general, individual and universal, the 'heart of life'. In doing so it invited a new thinking about stage space and created new modes of complex viewing. Most of this was a direct product of or largely facilitated by the specific medium of verse. And thus it is that verse drama played its particular part in renovation of the theatre.

But was this something that we might usefully call avant-garde or even – heaven help us – modernism? Well, that depends on how you define it…

References

Unpublished

88957: The British Library; Gordon Bottomley papers
978: Senate House Library, University of London; Thomas Sturge Moore papers

Published

Abercrombie, Lascelles 1912 'The Function of Poetry in Drama' *The Poetry Review: Dramatic Poetry* volume 1: 107–18
Abercrombie, Lascelles 1914 *Poetry and Contemporary Speech* London: The English Association
Abercrombie, Lascelles 1922 *The Adder* in *Four Short Plays* London: Martin Secker
Appia, Adolphe 2011 *Texts on Theatre*, ed. Richard C. Beacham London: Routledge
Arrowsmith, Rupert Richard 2011 'The Transcultural Roots of Modernism: Imagist Poetry, Japanese Visual Culture, and the Western Museum System' *Modernism/Modernity* volume 18, number 1: 27–42
Binyon, Laurence 1899 'Mr. Bridges' "Prometheus" and Poetic Drama' *The Dome* volume 2: 199–205
Binyon, Laurence 1906 *Paris and Œnone* London: A. Constable & Co
Binyon, Laurence 1907 *Attila* London: John Murray
Binyon, Laurence 1915 *Bombastes in the Shades* Oxford Pamphlets 1914–1915 London: Oxford University Press
Binyon, Laurence 1923 *Ayuli* Oxford: Basil Blackwell
Binyon, Laurence 1959 *The Flight of the Dragon* London: John Murray
Bottomley, Gordon 1920 *King Lear's Wife and Other Plays* London: Constable & Company
Bottomley, Gordon 1948 *A Stage for Poetry: My Purposes with My Plays* Kendall: Titus Wilson & Son
Boughton, Rutland and Buckley, Reginald R. 1911 *Music-Drama of the Future: Uther and Igraine: Choral Drama, with Essays by the Collaborators* London: William Reeve
Bridge, Ursula (ed.) 1953 *W.B. Yeats and T. Sturge Moore: Their Correspondence 1901–1937* London: Routledge & Kegan Paul
Buckley, Reginald R. 1914 *Arthur of Britain* London: Williams & Norgate
Carr, J. Comyns 1895 *King Arthur* London: Macmillan and Co.
Carr, J. Comyns 1906 *Tristram and Iseult* London: Duckworth and Co.
Danby, Nicholas 1999 *Modernism, Romance and the Fin de Siècle: Popular Fiction and British Culture, 1880–1914* Cambridge: Cambridge University Press
Drinkwater, John 1917 *Prose Papers* London: Elkin Matthews
Drinkwater, John 1925 *The Collected Plays: Volume I* London: Sidgwick & Jackson
Edwards, Osman 1901 *Japanese Plays and Playfellows* New York: John Lane
Ellis, Thomas E. 1922 *The Cauldron of Annwn* London: T. Werner Laurie
Farr, Florence 1909 *The Music of Speech, Containing the Words of Some Poets, Thinkers and Music-Makers Regarding the Practice of the Bardic Art Together with Fragments of Verse Set to Its Own Melody* London: Elkin Matthews
Farr, Florence 1910 *Modern Woman: Her Intentions* London: Frank Palmer
Fenollosa, Ernest and Pound, Ezra 1916 *'Noh' or Accomplishment: A Study of the Classical Stage of Japan* London: Macmillan & Co.
Fensham, Rachel 2015 'Designing for Movement: Dance Costumes, Art Schools and Natural Movement in the Early Twentieth Century' *Journal of Design History* volume 28, number 4: 348–67

Fry, W.G. and Mumford, W.A. 1966 *Louis Stanley Jast: A Biographical Sketch* London: The Library Association
Garvin, J.L. 1909 'Imperial and Foreign Affairs: A Review of Events' *The Fortnightly Review* volume 85: 805–22
Gibson, Wilfrid 1926 *Collected Poems 1905–1925* London: Macmillan and Co.
Gwynn, Frederick L. 1952 *Sturge Moore and the Life of Art* London: The Richards Press
Gwynn, Stephen 1909 'Poetry and the Stage' *The Fortnightly Review* volume 85: 337–51
Hatcher, John 1995 *Laurence Binyon: Poet, Scholar of East and West* Oxford: Clarendon Press
Hobson, J.A. 1901 *The Psychology of Jingoism* London: Grant Richards
Hynes, Samuel 1990 *A War Imagined: The First World War and English Culture* London: The Bodley Head
Jast, L. Stanley 1923 *The Lover and the Dead Woman and Five Other Plays in Verse* London: George Routledge and Sons
Jast, L. Stanley 1924 'The Aim' in *The Unnamed Book* Manchester: Sherratt & Hughes
Legge, Sylvia 1980 *Affectionate Cousins: T. Sturge Moore and Marie Appia* Oxford: Oxford University Press
Levitas, Ben 2016 'The Theatre of Modernity' in Vincent Sherry (ed.) *The Cambridge History of Modernism* Cambridge: Cambridge University Press
Litz, A. Walton 1996 'Florence Farr: A "Transitional Woman"' in Maria DiBattista and Lucy McDiarmid (eds) *High and Low Moderns: Literature and Culture, 1889–1939* New York: Oxford University Press
Masefield, John 1913 *The Tragedy of Pompey the Great* London: Sidgwick & Jackson
Masefield, John 1915 *The Faithful: A Tragedy in Three Acts* London: William Heinemann
Masefield, John 1916 *Gallipoli* London: William Heinemann
Masefield, John 1918 *Philip the King and Other Poems* London: William Heinemann
Masefield, John 1921 *The Tragedy of Nan and Other Plays* London: Grant Richards
Masefield, John 1923 *The Poems and Plays of John Masefield: Volume Two: Plays* New York: The Macmillan Company
Masefield, John 1925 *Verse Plays* New York: The Macmillan Company
Masefield, John 1937 *The Collected Works: Plays: Volume II* London: William Heinemann
Masefield, John 1952 *So Long to Learn: Chapters of an Autobiography* London: William Heinemann
Masefield, John 1985 *John Masefield's Letters from the Front 1915–1917*, ed. Peter Vansittart New York: Franklin Watts
Miner, Earl 1966 *The Japanese Tradition in British and American Literature* Princeton: Princeton University Press
Moore, T. Sturge 1901 *Aphrodite against Artemis: A Tragedy* London: At the Sign of the Unicorn
Moore, T. Sturge 1902a 'A Plea for an Endowed Stage' *The Monthly Review* volume 6: 119–31
Moore, T. Sturge 1902b 'The Renovation of the Theatre' *The Monthly Review* volume 7: 102–16
Moore, T. Sturge 1905 'Causerie of the Week. The Bible and the Stage' *The Speaker* 30 September: 621–22
Moore, T. Sturge 1911a *Mariamne* London: Duckworth & Co.
Moore, T. Sturge 1911b 'A Platonic Marriage' *The English Review* volume 7: 299–320
Moore, T. Sturge 1911c *A Sicilian Idyll and Judith: A Conflict* London: Duckworth & Co.
Moore, T. Sturge 1920 *Tragic Mothers* London: Grant Richards
Morash, Christopher 2021 *Yeats on Theatre* Cambridge: Cambridge University Press

Morra, Irene 2016 *Verse Drama in England, 1900–2015: Art, Modernity and the National Stage* London: Bloomsbury

Morrisson, Mark S. 2001 *The Public Face of Modernism: Little Magazines, Audiences, and Reception, 1905–1920* Madison: University of Wisconsin Press

Okakura, Kakuzo 2007 *The Ideals of the East with Special Reference to the Art of Japan* Berkeley, CA: Stone Bridge Press

Phillips, Stephen 1906 *Nero* London: Macmillan and Co.

Ransome, Arthur 1913 *Portraits and Speculations* London: Macmillan and Co.

Ross, Robert 1927 'Preface' in Oscar Wilde *Salomé, La Sainte Courtisane, A Forentine Tragedy* London: Methuen & Co.

Saddlemyer, Ann 1965 'The Heroic Discipline of the Looking "Glass": W.B. Yeats's Search for Dramatic Design' in Robin Skelton and Ann Saddlemyer (eds) *The World of W.B. Yeats: Essays in Perspective* Victoria, BC: University of Victoria Press

Savage, Roger 2014 *Masques, Mayings and Music-Dramas: Vaughan Williams and the Early Twentieth-Century Stage* Woodbridge: The Boydell Press

Schuchard, Ronald 2010 *The Last Minstrels: Yeats and the Revival of the Bardic Arts* Oxford: Oxford University Press

Smith, Constance Babington 1985 *John Masefield: A Life* London: Hamish Hamilton

Stopes, Marie C. and Sakurai, Joji 1913 *Plays of Old Japan: The 'Nō'* London: William Heinemann

Sutherland, Lucie 2020 *George Alexander and the Work of the Actor-Manager* Cham, Switzerland: Palgrave Macmillan

Tovey, Donald Francis 1929 'Analysis' in Robert C. Trevelyan and Donald Francis Tovey *The Bride of Dionysus: An Opera in Three Acts* Edinburgh: Townsend & Thompson

Trevelyan, R.C. 1908 *Sisyphus: An Operatic Fable* London: Longmans, Green & Company

Trevelyan, R.C. 1912 *The Bride of Dionysus, a Music-Drama, and Other Poems* London: Longmans, Green & Company

Trevelyan, R.C. 1916 *The Pterodamozels: An Operatic Fable* London: Printed for the author at the Pelican Press

Trevelyan, R.C. 2012 *The New Parsifal: An Operatic Fable* in Brian Keith-Smith *Essays on Richard Wagner and Parsifal, Including Robert Calverley Trevelyan's Drama The New Parsifal* Lewiston: The Edwin Mellen Press

Whitworth Art Gallery 1994 *Manchester's First Modernist: Karl Hagedorn 1889–1969* Manchester: Whitworth Art Gallery

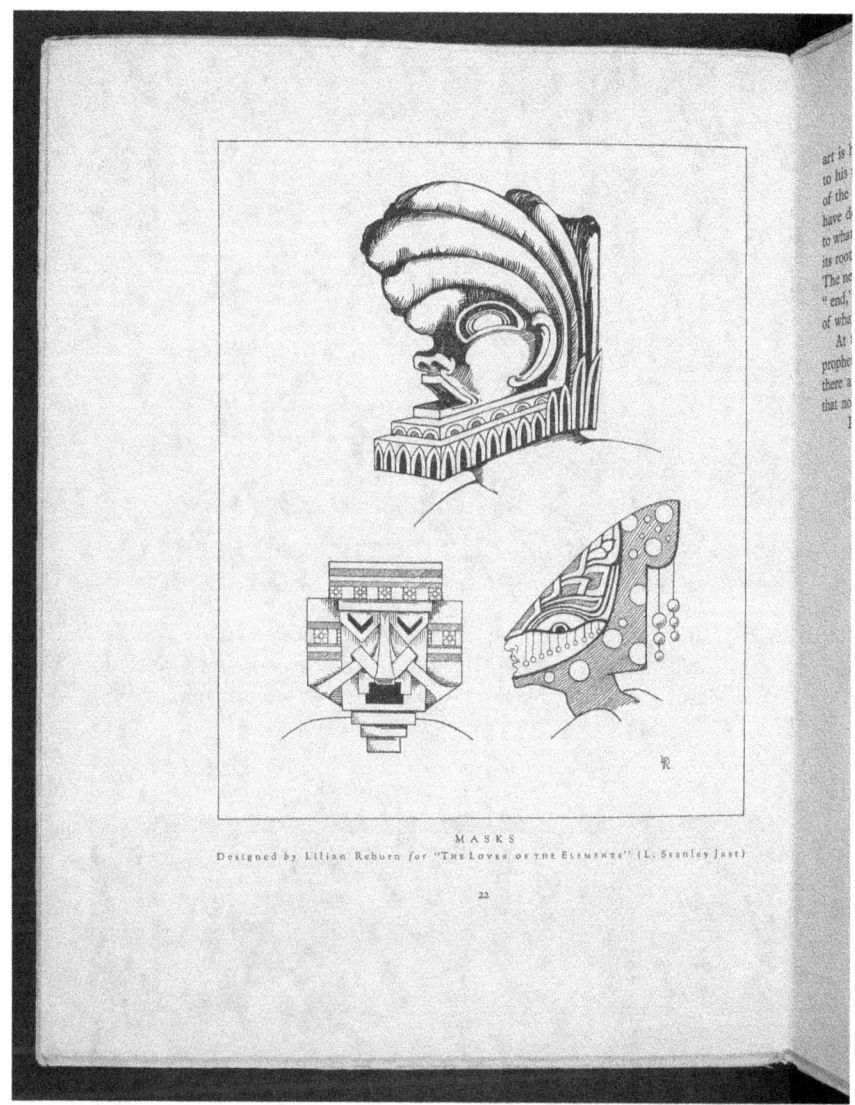

FIGURE 3.1 Lilian Reburn, mask designs for *The Loves of the Elements*, 1919. *The Unnamed Book*, 1924.

FIGURE 3.2 Claud Lovat Fraser, The Forest of Arden, design for *As You Like It*, 1919. Claud Lovat Fraser and Grace Crawford Lovat Fraser Collections, Bryn Mawr College Libraries. Reproduced by permission of Bryn Mawr College Libraries.

FIGURE 3.3 Claud Lovat Fraser, Rosalind's Cottage, design for *As You Like It*, 1919. Claud Lovat Fraser and Grace Crawford Lovat Fraser Collections, Bryn Mawr College Libraries. Reproduced by permission of Bryn Mawr College Libraries.

FIGURE 3.4 Paul Nash, design for *The Truth about the Russian Dancers*, 1920. Gordon Bottomley papers, Add MS 88957/4/10. The British Library.

FIGURE 3.5 Karl Hagedorn, design for *Harbour*, 1921. *The Unnamed Book*, 1924. Reproduced by permission of Sue Cowan and Nicholas Harris.

4
ADVANCED GUARDS

Stepping outside the auditorium of the newly established Oxford Playhouse we run into the back-end of a controversy. The Vice-Chancellor of Oxford University, who had a reputation for banning any events which might be radical or entertaining, censured the founder of the Playhouse for embarking on such a project without consulting him. The city, he said, exists for the university, and 'the university exists for the purposes of study'. In the exchanges which followed the prestigious theatre critic of *The Times* A.B. Walkley hoped that if the Playhouse were established it would not be on the grounds that it was a substitute for Latin translation. Walkley apparently 'loathed the very idea of drama as an academic discipline' (Chapman 2008: 34–35).

The tension between the long-established academic institution and the theatre producing new art on its doorstep was an example of a relationship which had been described over a decade earlier by the social scientist, and champion of New Liberalism, J.A. Hobson (1858–1940). In his essay on 'The New Realism' from 1909 he argued that for half a century 'the "educated" public of England' had been prevented from 'facing the deep searching questions lying at the foundations of our institutions'. This was ensured 'by a persistent avoidance of certain lines of thought', seen in the way universities controlled the curriculum, shutting out 'newer branches of natural science' and indeed English literature. The control was facilitated by increased specialisation, the narrowing down of enquiry so that larger connections are no longer seen. 'For this systematic "doping" of all studies to which the new disturbing thought might obtain access, there is no other explanation that that this is the distinctive self-defence of vested interests and established causes' (Hobson 1909: 548–49).

Now, however, there is challenge to the 'old fixed faiths', the 'clear-cut convictions of the permanency of a single type of monogamous family, of the sanctity of individual property, of the limits of government, of the private

DOI: 10.4324/9781003033295-4

control of industry, of the conception of a God and of personal immortality'. All are being eroded by 'modern intellectual forces'. These can be collectively summarised as a drive to replace faiths by facts, a drive fuelled by the spirit of 'realism'. This is not, says Hobson, an adequate word, but in effect it meant, in our terms, a challenge to and deconstruction of dominant ideologies. When he lists, in the domain of art, those who have made such challenges, it's clear he is not talking about literary realism. Wagner, Whistler, Nietzsche, Whitman, Ibsen, among others, once treated as 'freaks', have 'a new and common spirit in their work'. So too there is 'the new spirit in science'. With the emergence of the various instances of new spirit what is needed among those who are so inspired is 'a recognition of their unity of purpose and a fruitful co-operation'. This won't function to 'secure adhesion to any common formulae or any creed, but only to a common temper and common outlook' (Hobson 1909: 549, 552–53).

Hobson, as usual, was slightly ahead of the game. Three years or so later a set of books proclaimed that sense of the new, particularly, as concerns us, in relation to the theatre. We have already encountered Horace Samuel's *Modernities* from 1913. The same year saw Craig's *Towards a New Theatre* and Holbrook Jackson's *The Eighteen Nineties*. While that last work doesn't have 'new' or 'modern' in the title, Jackson's argument was that the 1890s, the supposed great age of the 'New' – with its New Woman and New Drama – was by 1913 no longer so, if it ever was. The real new drama came in the decade Jackson was writing. This was the period in which Hobson, writing in 1909 about Liberal politics, saw an 'historical crisis' confronting 'what we term the advanced guard' (1988: 79).

Someone who consciously positioned himself in the role of an advanced guard was Huntly Carter, author of *The New Spirit in Drama and Art* from 1912. We've seen earlier that his book calls for English theatre to renew itself by opening up to European influences. Its main thrust is a sustained polemic arguing for a new English drama and the theatre to house it. The new drama in its finest form will be 'a rhythmic form of theatre', combining music, colour, line, space and movement. The 'purely literary theatre', which lacks the lyrical element and has no rhythmic design, will be replaced by 'aesthetic theatre'. Once achieved the finest drama, through its rhythmic design, will connect us to 'the great rhythm of life', it will offer 'mental visualisation of mystical states'. The theatre will be a temple (Carter 1912: 30, vi, 43). Carter would go on to elaborate the spirituality and sublime possibilities of a new drama in a series of essays published in 1914 in a journal called *The Egoist*, often associated with Ezra Pound and Richard Aldington.

Before the new drama emerges, however, the agencies which protect and promote a deadly dominant art have to be destroyed. Primary among these agencies is the 'Repertory Theatre movement', which began with Grein's Independent Theatre and then the Stage Society. The latter is defined as a 'propagandist organisation' the activities of which 'completed the dullness of the English Sunday'. But the sins are more than aesthetic. The Court Theatre as a Repertory Theatre was 'instituted to exploit budding dramatists in the bourgeois drama business'. Note here how the aesthetic assault becomes an attack on the class which favours those aesthetics. When by contrast Carter celebrates the openness to innovative work of Annie Horniman's 'Manchester enterprise', 'the admirable Glasgow Repertory Theatre' and the Liverpool Repertory Theatre, it becomes clear that in addition to his attack on class he is attacking the metropolis (Carter 1912: 38, 39). If the London Repertory Theatre could but follow the lead of Manchester and the rest, there won't be any need for the National Theatre for which Barker and his friends were campaigning.

In reaching this point, where an aesthetic attack combines with an attack on cultural institutions, even apparently progressive ones, and the social order which they supposedly serve, Carter's book begins to sound like one of those polemics classically associated with an avant-garde. And this is why it's interesting. It forces us to ask some fundamental questions.

Carter's clear assumption was that there was no contemporary avant-garde theatre in England. This assumption has been shared by almost, though not quite, all historians of theatre and English culture. But while for him the 'new spirit' was only to be found in Europe there were others, as we've seen, who saw it also in England. And thus the first questions arise: in our accounts of this period, what might be the exact features of the thing for which we're looking? And if something's actually there how have we persistently missed it?

To answer these questions we have to attend to the assumptions we make and the stories we tell about the material we're studying. It's the job of this chapter to review these assumptions by looking at definitions of an avant-garde, the circumstances in which it arises and the likelihood or not of English theatre fitting the definition. We should then be able to suggest an answer to the overarching question: is it reliable and useful to speak of an Edwardian theatrical avant-garde?

Being avant-garde

For that we'd need to know what sort of thing we're talking about. Crudely speaking, avant-gardes might be seen as groupings that pressurise for cultural innovation. Since about the mid-nineteenth century there seems to be a whole set of them in various shapes and sizes. It depends where you look, because different arts practices, different academic disciplines, have their own distinct versions as to what constitutes an avant-garde and when it occurs. Let's begin with a couple of examples.

Writing from within art history Orton and Pollock insist that an avant-garde 'is the product of self-consciousness on the part of those who identify themselves as, and with, a special social and artistic grouping within the intelligentsia at a specific historical conjuncture. [...] An *avant-garde* is a concrete cultural phenomenon that is realised in terms of identifiable (though never predetermined) practices and representations through which it constitutes for itself a relationship to, and a distance from, the overall cultural patterns of the time'. They emphasise the specificity of the phenomenon because within the practice of art history avant-garde 'is now a catch-all label to celebrate most twentieth-century art and artists'. This gives the appearance of constant change, which is actually an illusion. Apart from the original cultural avant-garde formed in Paris in the 1850s–1870s, 'there has been only one other, successful *avant-garde* moment [...] This occurred in New York in the late 1930s and early 1940s', with the emergence of a style of painting known as Abstract Expressionism (Orton and Pollock 1985: 167–68).

In the second example we change discipline and immediately encounter a small problem. While Orton and Pollock say there was only one successful twentieth-century avant-garde, Armstrong, writing within literary studies, tells us that, also in the twentieth century, 'it is with Ezra Pound and Imagism that the sense of a programmatic avant-garde begins'. The same point is made by Nicholls (1995) and Peppis (2000). Crucial to this formulation is that word 'programmatic'. In late 1912 Pound and T.E. Hulme proposed Imagism as a programme with 'its aesthetics centred on notions of instantaneity, immediacy, the elimination of waste, and a plasticity of style based on the "prose tradition"'. But Pound insisted that it was more 'a movement of criticism' than of 'creation'. That's to say, in Armstrong's words, 'it begins as an attack on existing style'. From here Pound moved to draw in others, including most significantly Wyndham Lewis. They initiated the broader movement of Vorticism, with, in 1914, its own journal *Blast*, which, true to its name, was both violent and short-lived. In the pages of *Blast* there is a checklist of appropriately modern issues: 'an obsession with periodization [of literature], with what is dead and what newborn, and with influences from abroad'; 'aggressive attacks on prudery and censorship, a championing of sexual candour, women's emancipation, and the values of self over those of the machine-like crowd' (Armstrong 2008: 28, 29–30). Working much as Orton and Pollock describe, Pound continued to build his self-consciously 'special social and artistic grouping', anchoring it in another journal, *The Egoist*, to which he appointed T.S. Eliot. The names may now be famous, largely thanks to their own efforts perhaps, but this special grouping was also very tiny. Subscriptions to *The Egoist* diminished to about 750. By 1920 the group had nearly disintegrated.

Armstrong is clearly not using 'avant-garde' as a 'catch-all' term. His account of Vorticism very tidily fits Orton and Pollock's description of the characteristic features of an avant-garde. They make much of the fact that the context in which Abstract Expressionists painted was informed by the theorisations and polemics being simultaneously published in the journal *Partisan Review*. In a similar way Armstrong (2008: 30) points to the role of *The Egoist* journal in constructing a 'definable group' around Ezra Pound. Someone else might make reference to Marinetti's polemics and the art of Futurism.

Indeed several twentieth-century avant-gardes can be taken to be 'successful' although they may not be 'programmatic' in Armstrong's sense. We are dealing with a slippery term. To arrive at a workable cross-disciplinary definition is difficult. One of the most carefully argued attempts to do so is that of Peter Bürger from 1984. Bürger insists on both historical specificity and function.

The avant-garde emerged after, and as a consequence of, Aestheticism which had dislocated art from life. This opened the way for an art that reflected on itself. Previous modern art, however 'new', was, without this reflective capacity, still necessarily bound into its own institutionalisation. It's only the avant-garde which makes a radical break with tradition by launching a wholesale critique of, and challenge to, the institution of art in bourgeois society. Of this Dada is an exemplary instance.

This is a clear model, but it has a couple of problems. Both of them recur in much writing about avant-gardes. The first concerns assumptions about what avant-gardists make. Rather than talk of 'work' Bürger suggests, on the model of Dada, that we speak of 'manifestation' which, working as provocation, may be designed to produce public disturbance. Avant-gardist art negates both the category of individual creation and that of individual reception. The problem here is that his analysis of avant-garde art is focussed mainly on Dada, Duchamp and Surrealism. It is not explained why these are selected for more attention than others, such as, say, Abstract Expressionism, nor why it is either legitimate or useful to extrapolate general principles of avant-garde art from these particular cases.

The second problem is more implicit. Within the narrative 'avant-gardists' figure as coherent and separated groupings. But in England for example Laurence Binyon was a friend of Ezra Pound, Sturge Moore a friend of Wyndham Lewis but neither Binyon nor Moore was a Vorticist. When Moore participated in one of Marinetti's readings, he was not necessarily becoming a Futurist. When Lovat Fraser worked alongside both Craig and Gaudier-Brzeska to illustrate Haldane MacFall's *The Splendid Wayfaring* (1913) he didn't become a Vorticist. These were groupings that were permeable. According to Clark (1982) artists such as Rimbaud, Stendhal, van Gogh, Cézanne hovered around the edges of the Parisian avant-garde, identifying with it at junctures where it was useful or necessary to do so, and then sliding out again. Apparently Whistler, travelling between London and Paris, adopted a strategy that 'necessitated at the very least two distinctive career trajectories and masculine identities which were responsive to the alternative currencies of avant-gardism as they operated within each metropolis' (Stephenson 2000: 138). In these circumstances, affiliation to a grouping could be put on or taken off like a performance. But then the question arises as to why this performing feels important or necessary.

To answer that we need an historical account rather more fluid than Bürger's. We have noted already that in England by the 1890s people were consciously labelling their activities 'new', even, later, conceiving of entities that might be described as 'advanced guards'. In his account of that decade Holbrook Jackson says that the initiatives that were 'new' were the ones that aligned themselves with temporal progress: they were intending to be 'modern' and to drive the progress towards modernity. For him, as for his contemporaries, the emerging new work could best be described as 'modernist'. This sense of themselves needing to be modern was produced by large-scale economic and social changes. The various explosions of new work mainly happened in Paris, London and Berlin, coming later in New York. The first three of those cities had all been made similarly wealthy by the empires they controlled. In this sense, as some have remarked, avant-garde art is a by-product of imperialism. The metropolitan wealth facilitated, and created, an appetite for publishing, exhibiting and discussing artworks. But other factors gave a specific form to the artworks and discourses about art, to that sense of modernity, which did not obtain in other periods. These are described by Perry Anderson, writing from a Marxist position associated with New Left Review, 'as a cultural field of force triangulated by three decisive coordinates'. The first of the coordinates is 'the codification of a highly formalized *academicism* in the visual and other arts, which itself was institutionalized within official regimes of states and society still massively pervaded, often dominated, by aristocratic or landowning classes'. The second coordinate is complementary to the first: 'the still incipient, hence essentially novel, emergence within these societies of the key technologies or inventions of the second industrial revolution: telephone, radio, automobile, aircraft and so on'. The third coordinate of this 'modernist conjuncture' was 'the imaginative proximity of social revolution. The extent of hope or apprehension that the prospect of such revolution aroused varied widely: but over most of Europe, it was "in the air"'. This was the case even in Britain, which 'was threatened with regional disintegration and civil war in the years before the First World War' (Anderson 1984: 104).

These three coordinates had their own specific effects. Anderson argues in the case of the first that the institutionalised academicism, and the old order associated with it, 'provided a critical range of cultural values against which insurgent forms of art could measure themselves, but also in terms of which they could partly articulate themselves'. Their opposition to this institution provided something in common between the various avant-gardes and new practices: 'their tension with the established or consecrated canons in front of them is constitutive of their definition as such'. They also had in common a hatred of the structure and operation of the capitalist market-place. In their resistance to it, new art practices drew on the resources and traditions of the old order with which they were also in tension. Anderson cites Imagism reaching back to Roman lyric poetry, but we might also think of Wilkinson's Greek vases or Trevelyan's Euripides. The influence of the second coordinate is seen in artists' imaginative engagement with 'a new machine age'. Anderson cites Parisian Cubism and Italian Futurism. That engagement, he notes, is with techniques and artefacts, not with the structures of production that make them. Finally, there was 'the proximity of social revolution', the visions of which gave an 'apocalyptic light' to those groupings most ferociously opposed to the entire social order. Here Anderson instances German Expressionism. In summary, says Anderson, the new art practices of Europe in the early years of the twentieth century 'flowered in the space between a still usable classical past, a still indeterminate technical present, and a still unpredictable political future. Or, put another way, it arose at the intersection between a semi-aristocratic ruling order, a semi-industrialized capitalist economy, and a semi-emergent, or -insurgent, labour movement' (Anderson 1984: 105).

Anderson's account begins to tell us more about how avant-gardes happen, though at the same time it reinforces a narrative that there was all too little of this activity in England. His single example, as for Armstrong, is Imagism. As a general account, however, this narrative offers an informative context for the work we're studying and thus, before anything else, it needs rehearsing.

The richest of the imperial cities, London, saw the gradual emergence of a professional class which enlarged the constituency of those who participated in the consumption, discussion and patronage of art. But such stimulus didn't, apparently, produce striking new practices. The cause of this is attributed to a specifically English situation. Here the increased ability to participate in art-related activity was part of a process whereby the professional class, indeed the bourgeoisie in general, were absorbed into alliance with a governing landed gentry. The consequence of this, as Nairn (1981) argues, also from an NLR Marxist position, was that Britain, uniquely among the great powers, could avoid the threats of various sorts of revolution. This avoidance was in part facilitated by a key group, the intelligentsia. Now Nicholls (1995: 163) observes that Britain lacked a powerful *academic* culture, though Hobson still felt in 1909 that academic institutions had conservative effects. But the intelligentsia as such may be thought of differently. These were not the 'state-fostered technocracy' of the French nor the 'alienated' intelligentsia of Russia. In Britain, says Nairn, the intellectual class 'was formed by civil society itself, not the state', in the 'public schools' and old universities. This was only possible in England because of what Nairn calls the 'powerful, pervasive informality of England's civil élite', with their patrician liberalism. Similarly Robert Colls (1987: 50) notes: 'For those at the top, the new role of the public schools and ancient universities as tutors in leadership provided a common code and grounding [...] Here, the interpretation of the national interest lay not in the democratic State, but was encoded in a network of personal contacts and informal understandings beyond and behind that State'. The formation of a liberal intelligentsia was thus an expression of the alliance of landlordism and the bourgeoisie. As such it operated to preserve the British form of rule and its articulation in a conservative liberal ideology. Nairn summarises: 'such adjustment as proved necessary to maintain the system in being was conceived, publicized, and largely enacted by this exceptionally active, confident and integrated intellectual class. If the external secret of old England's longevity was empire, the internal secret lay here: in the cooptive and cohesive authority of an intelligentsia much more part of the state, much closer to political life and more present in all important civil institutions than in any other bourgeois society' (1981: 33–36).

The cultural operation of that intelligentsia can be seen in the guest-list for Barrie's Cinema Supper at the Savoy in 1914. Among the guests was the Prime Minister, Asquith, whose Liberal government had won a landslide election in 1906. Alongside him, apart from his wife, were theatre managers, occasional aristocrats, composers, playwrights and stage celebrities, together embodying the established order and, here, ready to participate in an unusual event organised by a favourite dramatist, though, as we know, Asquith thought Barrie had gone too far. At a more local level, the cultural operation may be illustrated by the Prime Minister's daughter-in-law, Cynthia Asquith. Herself from a family of aristocrats, she was both a friend of Barrie, becoming his private secretary, and a close friend and supporter of D.H. Lawrence. Overall, then, this doesn't seem to be an upper order that could be as clearly and negatively characterised as a persisting *ancient régime* on the European model with its associated institutionalised academicism. Consequently it didn't provide so clear a force or structure to oppose and thus, if we return to Anderson's model, the first coordinate that shapes an avant-garde seems, in England, weaker in effect. Similarly the Cinema Supper indicates why his third coordinate, the proximity of revolutionary action, was apparently absent in England. A main player in the event was Shaw, known for his Fabian views about which he was both principled and loud. But as a Fabian he was opposed to revolution if not the labouring classes as a whole, revolutionary or otherwise. The people had to be led to their improved lives by enlightened members of the intelligentsia, all those people who enjoyed conversations about the contradictions in capitalism when they were securely framed on a stage, which might also, of course, include the king.

In general terms, then, this history of English society seems to validate Anderson's analysis that the conditions for an avant-garde barely existed. But that's not how it was seen by some of those who were there. Writing about Marx's *Capital* in 1907 Holbrook Jackson said that its main effect was not on the working class but on the bourgeois: 'It was the revolting sons of the bourgeoisie itself [...] all, like myself, bourgeois crossed with squirearchy – that painted the flag red' (1909: 101). His analysis suggests Nairn and others are right about the composition of the intelligentsia but wrong in their slightly mechanical assumptions about how it consequently behaved. Another example suggests the same. Robert Trevelyan, second son of a titled Liberal father, was a member of the National Liberal Club, mixed with Cambridge philosophers, was a verse dramatist closely connected to Moore and Bottomley, and active within the Union of Democratic Control to which he recruited Bottomley. As an activist with the No-Conscription Fellowship he was beaten up on at least one occasion by a mob hired, he said, by the Daily Express (always on the side of the angels). In January 1916 he thought 'a big strike or revolt' was needed to change England (88957/1/88 f6) and he looked to the trades unions, rather than the Labour Party, to lead this.

Despite the Labour Party, despite Fabianism, Trevelyan's example shows that revolution could be regarded as both thinkable and necessary. So Anderson's third coordinate was not so very distant. Nor, if we listen to Holbrook, was his first. 'Half of Shaw's so-called attack on Shakespeare', he said (1909: 171), 'is the old antagonism of the free mind with the academic mind'. If we are looking for a constraining 'academy' at this period in England that role seems to be filled by the institution of Shakespeare. To this might be added state censorship. We have seen that there was a clear rejection of what had constituted itself as 'art' theatre, with its sub-Shakespearean verse and picture-frame Shakespaculars and so too there were polemics against and direct challenges to the institution of Censor. Here surely was 'tension with established or consecrated canons'. And alongside it the attack on commercial theatre displayed a hatred of the market-place. In their break from it theatre-makers drew on ancient if not classical techniques such as Greek theatre and the 'simplicity' of the early-modern platform. All of this seems to fit with Anderson's model of how avant-gardes are meant to behave in relation to his first coordinate. This leaves only his second one – the engagement with a new machine age. Here, instead of thinking about telephones and radio, we might equally think about explorations in new technologies of the stage, the interest of Barker, Moore, Rutherston and Wilkinson in stage light, for example. And all of this was accompanied by plans, polemics and indeed manifestoes for a renovated stage.

So, without devaluing the overall narrative about the specific characteristics of English society, we can use Anderson's model to show that there existed the conditions for, and characteristic behaviour of, the very thing he barely admits, avant-garde activity that spreads beyond Imagism. An obvious question then arises. How did this omission happen? I suspect it's because these sorts of synthetic, and highly informative, narratives are woven together, quite legitimately, from secondary sources. They know about Imagism because English literary history strongly features Imagism. By contrast a search of theatre history will find hardly any information about the work we're looking at here. The single exception of which I'm aware (and I apologise if I'm being ignorant) is Dennis Kennedy's 2009 account of the Stage Society and Barker's Court Theatre. With customary perceptiveness Kennedy uses Bürger's modelling to argue that what the various European avant-gardes had in common was a concern with shaping audiences and managing reception of their work. Along these lines both the Stage Society, with its restricted membership, and Barker's Court Theatre, with its mainly female matinée audiences, appear as avant-garde. The Stage Society, says Kennedy, 'established the model for the New Drama' while at that 'theatre of intellectuals', the Court, the 'unconventional spectators […] constituted a self-defined and distinct culture' (Kennedy 2009: 62, 68). Indeed an artistically well-informed contemporary, Desmond MacCarthy, likened the Court to the Théâtre Libre. Despite the fact that the audience for experimental work could not financially sustain the Court, Barker, notes Kennedy, refused to compromise his position, unlike, say, Antoine or Brahm.

This account is useful in part because it recognises the slipperiness of 'avant-garde' as a concept. In trying to pin it down more rigorously, through a focus on reception and audience management, it pays a price however. The essay gives little sense of the range of work that was being made beyond the 'New Drama', itself in need of definition given Jackson's scepticism about it. Nothing is said, for example, about the Literary Theatre Society or the Unnamed Society. Nor about Barker's interest in 'fantasy' plays which persisted into the early 1920s, with the active and knowledgeable support of his too frequently maligned second wife.

But the major problem is outside Kennedy's control. Seven years after his book appeared Ben Levitas published an overview essay on 'The Theatre of Modernity' (2016). We've seen already that English drama of the first decades barely features here, apart from an enthusiastic slaver over Shaw. The round-up of European stagings of that emblematically modern play *Salome* omits both English productions, thus effectively effacing any mention of the Literary Theatre Society. And certainly there's no mention of Stage Society or Court Theatre as being potentially avant-garde. It may be that Levitas wasn't convinced by Kennedy's case, although he doesn't say so. But as it stands Kennedy's argument hasn't managed to dent, let alone revise, the stock account of English theatre at this period. So we have to begin to wonder. Does the problem of identifying an English theatrical avant-garde reside with the practices of the theatre or with the discipline that manages the ideas we have about them?

Stories of theatre

There are two powerful stories that are told about the theatre of this date. These stories work to define and control our ideas as to what we're looking for and what we're looking at. Let's take an example of each.

Christopher Innes' book *Avant Garde Theatre* begins with the origin of the term, borrowed from military terminology to give the title in 1878 to Bakunin's anarchist journal *L'Avant-Garde*. It has subsequently been applied to artistic groups so diverse that they seem united only by their shared rejection of that which is socially or aesthetically dominant. Nonetheless, says Innes, in the case of theatre there is an 'identifiable unity of purpose and interest' which he summarises as 'primitivism': 'Along with anti-materialism and revolutionary politics, the hallmark of avant garde drama is an aspiration to transcendence'. At the same time primitivism is linked to 'aesthetic experimentation designed to advance the technical progress of the art itself' by asking basic questions as to what a theatre or an actor is. On this basis Innes unfolds a neatly tidy linear narrative which begins with Bakhtin's interest in carnival and the exploration of ritualistic practices. Of these some 'highly traditional/primitive cultures' offer models which come close to theatre, such as Balinese dance (1993: 1–3, 12). From here we head to 1890s French Symbolism, Maeterlinck and Jarry, and then to its Scandinavian version exemplified by Strindberg. With him in place the way is clear to German Expressionism, Artaud, Grotowski, Uncle Tom Cobley and all.

With so many famous names in such tidy order this feels a satisfying account of what we should be encountering when we look for avant-garde theatre. Except that its basic premise has done a minor melt-down in the opening pages: 'aspects of primitivism', says Innes, 'have been so widespread in twentieth-century theatre that the boundaries of the avant garde are amorphous'. That's to say that the very thing which two pages earlier gave clear definition to the theatrical avant-garde is now the very thing which makes it blurry. Sensing his dilemma Innes has another shot: the 'mainstream of the avant garde' is not just defined by stylistic qualities; it 'is essentially a philosophical grouping' (1993: 4). Philosophies are so varied that this enables no greater precision than defining something as an 'imaginative' or 'reflective' grouping. And then the key word 'primitive' crumbles in our grasp at the point where it is applied to a society which spawns something as complex as Balinese dance.

Innes' problem has several causes. One, as he more or less concedes, is that he is seeking to base his definition of avant-garde on theme as well as style and avant-garde groupings tend to share the discourses of their contemporary culture. Secondly, the description of theme is too generalised. In the notion of 'aspiration to transcendence', what is being transcended? Presumably this could include plays about fairyland. Thirdly, there is very little reflection on the organisational and economic features which avant-garde groupings may or may not have in common. Such reflection may enable us to distinguish between a group organised to a purpose and a string of theatre-makers linked simply by being 'philosophical', a string that could be extended at will to include Seneca, Dryden and Tennyson and anyone else we fancy. With its problems of definition this story is of little use in approaching the English theatre of 1900–1925, yet it's had damaging effect through its claim to tell us what we should be looking for.

The second, more thoughtful, story has the slightly different effect of defining what we're both looking for and looking at. It has been told in various forms by Raymond Williams. The version I shall use here is his essay 'Theatre as a Political Forum' in his posthumous *Politics of Modernism*. The argument is that there are two points of major transformation of the theatre, one in the 'Renaissance' and the other in the mid-eighteenth century. That second transformation was based on recognition that the contemporary and the indigenous were legitimate materials for dramatisation, a dramatic language which used contemporary speech forms and incorporated an extended range of social classes, and lastly a drive towards secularisation. Most subsequent drama is shaped by these developments so the job is to explore the 'variations and tensions within these norms', which then enables consideration of the 'real nature of the avant-garde revolt'. In this narrative 'the Naturalist variation is decisive'. Naturalism, intensively restating the features of the eighteenth-century transformation, was 'the first phase of Modernist theatre' and in the work of Ibsen, early Strindberg and Chekhov it challenged dominant bourgeois order. That challenge was compromised in two respects. Naturalism's preferred vehicle for showing how human lives are shaped was a representation of the bourgeois household. Its dramatic language was thus incapable of showing either the social forces that worked on that household or the crises of the inner lives within it. So the three 'major Naturalist dramatists' began to explore new languages, with Strindberg, for example, inaugurating the methods 'later known as Expressionism, which were to be main elements of the drama and theatre of the avant-garde'. From here Williams tracks the two options that presented – an exploration of the sites of social power or of inner consciousness – beginning with German theatre and then moving in one direction towards early Soviet theatre, Piscator and Brecht and in the other towards Surrealism and Artaud.

Having put this in place he turns to England and observes that, in contrast with Germany, the theatre 'of the twenties and thirties never acquired any real political momentum. The dominating figure was Bernard Shaw, but his drama of ideas lacks the leading edge of formal innovation' (1996: 83–91). The closest parallel to German Expressionism was the work of Sean O'Casey after 1927 and then Auden and Isherwood from the late 1930s.

Like Innes, Williams tells us what we're looking for. He specifies the 'real' nature of avant-garde revolt and associates its 'main elements' with the characteristics of Expressionism. Hence anything that doesn't look like Expressionism is unlikely to be avant-garde. But Williams is also effective in telling us what we're looking at. His central narrative has the three 'major' Naturalists leading the way in innovation and from them flow other developments, with recognisable names slotting into place. This organically coherent canon of names does an efficient job of shutting out anything outside it. In particular, it shows convincingly how avant-garde innovation as if by its very nature must bypass England. For the only available representative of English drama is at the opposite pole of anything that might be associated with Expressionism: Shaw. And there the story has remained. In 2004, kicking off his account of 'The London stage, 1895–1918', Postlewait has Shaw, with a photo for added emphasis.

Although Williams' declared topic was drama as 'political forum', and Shaw a conspicuously political figure, the sole focus on Shaw is nevertheless unwarranted and distorts our sense of the theatre we're looking at. As we have seen several of Shaw's contemporaries thought his work old-fashioned and undramatic. We may disagree with them but if we want to know about the period it would not be useful to dismiss without discussion their concept of a progressive theatre which did not include Shaw. The problem for us now is that Shaw's efficient and energetic self-production, his genuinely earnest attempt to be involved in multifarious progressive activities, together with an ego that remorselessly claimed its own place at the centre of all initiatives, had the effect of effacing, or indeed replacing, the contribution and importance of others. For contemporaries the most significant instance here was Ibsen. Carter argues that after Archer introduced his work to England Ibsen was assimilated by a 'race of realists' who misunderstood him: 'Ibsen was ruined in this country by his English interpreters'. Among those interpreters Shaw played a key role in creating what Barrie's Judy called 'bearded drama'. For Carter the task was to reinterpret Ibsen, properly instate him in an aesthetic theatre and kill 'the fatal heresy that art is imitation' (Carter 1912: 32, 36, 41). For the promotion of that heresy he blamed both the Stage Society and the 'Repertory movement'. Both were associated with Shaw and his Fabian politics. Indeed at the Court Theatre Shaw's plays were done so frequently it might have been called the 'Shaw-Spielhaus'. And because of the influence of Shaw the mode of imitative drama was dominant.

Driving these claims is Carter's desire for the wholesale destruction of imitative drama. He had no place for Holbrook Jackson's careful distinction between Shaw's old-fashioned mode and the newer work, which, as we know, in the hands of Barker and Barrie was causing realism to revise itself if not implode. And in his attack on 'literary' theatre Carter ignored the fact that its adherents were also strongly opposed to realism. But in these divisions of opinion what we're looking at is a theatre conscious of what was at stake in its explorations of dramatic form. To these explorations Shaw was seen as largely irrelevant. Thus when Williams positions him as the 'dominating' figure he not only misrepresents the actual situation as contemporaries saw it, but he also obscures from view the ideas and work of those contemporaries, thereby effectively controlling what we think we're looking at in theatre of the period.

The paradox here, as with Anderson, is that Williams' analysis inadvertently makes the case for the very thing he doesn't recognise. If, instead of focussing on Shaw, Williams' characterisation of the 'first phase of Modernist theatre' is applied more widely, a different picture begins to appear.

The 'new languages' of the three major Naturalists led, Williams says, to exploration of sites of social power and of inner consciousness. He selects his examples among canonical European writers. But he could also have cited uncanonical examples of English verse drama in which Moore or Bottomley dramatised internal states. So too he could have cited Barker's *Madras House* which begins in a bourgeois household, then moves to the workplace, then moves to the market-place of commodities both object and human, and then back to a bourgeois household but now experienced as the site of difficult private attempts to find a language to speak of internal states. No two acts are in the same place; the bourgeois household is part of a larger economy and producer of a private world. In citing Barker he would have included a dramatist whom one contemporary likened to Chekhov. In citing Bottomley he would have included a dramatist who discussed and critiqued Strindberg. Alongside the other activities described in preceding chapters these could be taken as signs that the English drama, as much as the European, was on the path of modernisation, and in similar directions.

We know that Kennedy characterises some of this activity as avant-garde. Now, having recognised the limitations of theatre histories, we should be placed to see if Kennedy's picture can be extended to include more of the material described in this book. In order to make that assessment I draw once again from Williams' *Politics of Modernism*. His essay on 'The Politics of the Avant-Garde' is useful because it avoids an analysis based solely on formal or thematic features, which led Innes to become unstuck, while being more historically specific than Bürger and more detailed about artistic practice than Anderson. Williams seeks to ground discussion of creative activity within historical processes, and specifically within the material formations, the resources as well as organisation, of cultural production. For him the avant-garde can be pinned down to a precise phase in the economic development of the west. It was part of the larger phenomenon often called Modernism which has to be defined, he says, not in terms of 'themes of response to the city', which may appear in artworks anywhere from classical civilisations onwards, but instead in 'the new and specific location of the artists and intellectuals of this movement within the changing cultural milieu of the metropolis'. This milieu meant that alongside the traditional and authoritative academies housed in the metropolis there was enough cultural space for dissident artists to develop communities around their own practice. Just as importantly there was now an increased ability to cross frontiers and in doing so to reject the world as it was shaped by the old order. Thus, says Williams, 'The true social bases of the early avant-garde were at once cosmopolitan and metropolitan' (1996: 44, 59).

Instead of Innes' account of what Williams calls 'singular men', however interesting or indeed female they may be in themselves, Williams maps a succession of cultural formations that rapidly developed from the late nineteenth century onwards. These moved through three possible phases: 'Initially, there were innovative groups which sought to protect their practices within the growing dominance of the art market and against the indifference of the formal academies. These developed into alternative, more radically innovative groupings, working to provide their own facilities of production, distribution and publicity; and finally into fully oppositional formations, determined not only to promote their own work but to attack its enemies in the cultural establishments and, beyond these, the whole social order'. Defence becomes self-management becomes attack. It is in that third phase that the avant-garde begins (1996: 50–51).

The attack on the whole social order had various targets. Most noticeably there was the rejection of tradition, 'the insistence on a clean break with the past'. Earlier formations had seen an interest in revival of forms from the past but the emphasis of the avant-garde was on entirely new making. One resource for that was provided by the social order itself. Imperialism brought knowledge of so-called primitive forms from other cultures and these were used in the work of making art that felt new in the west. It is this activity on which Innes founds his whole thesis. But alongside it, as Williams quickly reminds us, 'there is a virtually unprecedented emphasis on the most evident features of a modern industrialized world: the city, the machine, speed, space'. Another target was the bourgeois. The characteristics and effects of this class shifted in relation to whether it was viewed from above, with the aristocracy, or below, with organised labour, so attacks on it took different forms, but what avant-garde groups had in common was the claim that they were anti-bourgeois. Most of the artists were not themselves in fixed class positions and their activities and politics slide in and out of different aspects of the bourgeoisie. There was opposition to the market-place which turned art and labour into commodity but creative art was seen as inherently different from the products of simple labour. In seeking to control their own property and production many artists behaved like good bourgeoisie of a particular phase, especially in their celebration of what Williams calls 'that central bourgeois figure: the sovereign individual' (1996: 52–53, 55). As Sell (1998) puts it, the innovative bourgeois maker has the effect of opening up new markets. At a later phase, says Williams, the bourgeoisie consolidated their success in a discursive insistence on the morality of property and social order. It was within this context that there developed a specific and very obvious target, the bourgeois family. But, again, such an attack could go in different directions. There were those who campaigned to liberate women and children from a system of control and there were those who wanted to free men from women. There was also, as we shall see, an attempt to dislocate relations between the sexes from their supposed reproductive imperative.

This was all happening, Williams says, in a period 'from around 1910 to the late 1930s' (1996: 67). This statement reminds us that, once again, we're dealing with one model among many. Williams' claim that his periodisation is 'conventional' is not one that might be echoed by someone working within the conventions of visual art, the narrative of which reaches back to Paris in the 1850s. Indeed the Société anonyme coopérative des artistes peintres, sculpteurs, graveurs – in other words the Impressionists as they became known – fits very precisely with, indeed almost uniquely precisely with, the conditions Williams describes. Apart from the fact that it predates them.

A reminder of the variety in the models of the avant-garde is salutary. It underlines that our business is not to match the features of cultural activity with a fixed template but instead to look for tendencies, repetitions, accumulations of similarity within those features. If we can suffer its inelegance, we might say we're seeking gatherings of avant-gardishness.

For that search Williams' detailed model provides a useful tool. Using it we can briefly note some examples from the preceding chapters. Moore, who believed in the value of coteries, gathered his friends into a Literary Theatre Society with the intention of renovating the stage. Jast and Sladen-Smith, connected to Manchester School of Art, formed the Unnamed Society to show new art and repudiate realism. Masefield, with his immediate family and friends, founded the Hill Players to do work that mingled amateur and professional players. On a larger scale the Stage Society formed explicitly to be 'experimental', and Barker and Vedrenne's Court Theatre trialled the new repertory model. All in different ways sought to go beyond the market-place of commercial theatre.

The metropolis in particular facilitated creative networks. Ernest Oldmeadow's Unicorn Press brought writers such as Binyon, Craig, Fry, Housman, Moore and Symons into contact with one another, launched their work and provided a platform for opinion in the aesthetic journal *The Dome*. Ricketts and Shannon were linked to the Slade School of Art and reached backwards in time to Wilde – who called then the Heavenly Twins – Rossetti and Morris, funded Moore's theatre project, ran an occasional journal *The Dial*, and had a publishing press which brought artists together. Moore worked for them and was published by them. The Vienna Café on London's New Oxford Street was used regularly by staff and researchers of the British Museum. These 'Anglo-Austrians', as he called them, might have been taken, said Henry Newbolt, 'for a Bohemian society of students' (in Hatcher 1995: 44). Binyon was a regular in this group. Other regulars included Roger Fry and Bob Trevelyan, John Masefield, Ricketts, William

Rothenstein and Yeats. Wyndham Lewis joined in often and there, thanks to Binyon, began his friendship with Moore. In another part of the room a discussion group gathered regularly around the Nietzsche translator Oscar Levy (Thatcher 1970: 235).

This metropolitan culture was also cosmopolitan. There was not only conscious importing of the newest European work, translation and staging of it. Ricketts, Moore, Binyon and Bottomley also had interests, even specialisms, in Japanese, Javanese and Indian art and performance. And there was travel to see new art. Barker went to Berlin and Moscow to meet Reinhardt and Stanislavski and to look at theatre design. Moore read Appia's essays in the British Library and travelled to meet him at least twice. Trevelyan went sightseeing in India, China and Japan. Masefield used a 'Japanese' model for a play which attacks greedy and aggressive acquisition of land. Trevelyan experimented with metrics derived from classical Greek in plays that attacked the nexus of politicians, capitalists and owners of the press. Indeed the whole development of verse drama can be seen as an experiment in finding a public language that was not compromised by the available languages of state discourse, newspapers or the already-existing 'journalistic' social drama. And whether in verse or prose there were repeated and probing attacks on manifestations of moralistic bourgeois culture, on its control of women and on the presumed superiority of heterosexual masculinity. All these elements taken together might perhaps offer an example of what Williams describes as 'rejection of the existing social order and its culture [...] supported and even directly expressed by recourse to a simpler art' (1996: 58).

But much hangs on the force attached to 'rejection'. These activities might be said to amount to nothing more than Williams' second phase of development towards the avant-garde, the self-management of artistic production but not the full-on rejection of cultural enemies. Certainly the theatre-makers didn't produce anything like Wyndham Lewis' wholesale Blast of repudiation, at least not in public. Privately Moore railed against 'the snobby rich and callous commercial classes'. He told Bottomley: 'I feel sometimes as if I should be driven into Flauberts mood of hatred of all governments and parties whatsoever'. And later, in the same letter, he accuses 'professors and M.A.s and "well paid & able pens" who are really savages as far as literature is concerned there clothes are there [sic] only real connection with it, the fashions that have been forced upon their minds' (88957/1/66 ff200-2). Elsewhere, still privately, his language gets Lewis-like: 'This sacrificing of the live work of art to the dead idea that once was is anathema. it is pokey, spewky, muling, degenerate, billious, and should be spat on spewed on, shat on and left behind for ever' (88957/1/66 f144). Bottomley, meanwhile, thought in October 1914 that Lewis' journal *Blast* 'looks amusingly stale and old-fashioned already' (Bottomley and Nash 1990: 75).

But the public discourse of the theatre-makers, including Moore, was largely, and rationally, directed to a highly specific enemy, the system of theatre censorship, against which in 1909 the more established authors, including Barrie, founded a new organisation, the Dramatists' Club, and co-ordinated active protest. Their published denunciations were intended not simply to argue against a state office but also to repudiate the whole culture of puritan morality which was seen as endemic to the English dominant order, what Hobson (1909: 547) called 'the inward fortress of conservatism'. Such denunciation looks less strident than Lewis' because it takes the form of the printed essay rather than a graphically shouting manifesto, but it can also be said to be more closely argued and therefore more searching in the analysis of what it repudiates. For example Laurence Housman (1910: 852) suggested that the argument over censorship was not a simple division between radical and conservative but between 'commercial interests' – the theatre managers – and 'dramatic talent', which was constrained by limits placed on its expression. This was merely preface to the real substance of Housman's essay, which was to suggest a new form for handling the licensing of plays. Gilbert Murray had suggested something similar. Typically, theatre makers accompanied their assault by positive proposals for new sorts of material organisation.

This theatrical challenge to the dominant order was in a way more risky than that of the Vorticists. Lewis' blast, however ferocious the language, was a printed object as it were graphically performing on his behalf. But it dwindles into superficiality alongside the making of performances which defied censorship. The delivery of censored lines requires that actors physically commit themselves, not so much by using their voices but by simply being there, in front of a live audience, embodying the defiance of restraint. And for the others who come as voluntary witnesses to this act there are those prolonged moments of intensely felt difficulty as they – we – sit in an auditorium and witness, quite close to us here and now, not so much wilful ideological perplexity as the insistent confrontation with, for example, abortion, suicide, female desire, the memory of the prosecuted sodomite. It's not the topic so much that matters. It's the need to have it acted out and to witness that acting out. That's where the energy of full-on rejection is to be found. And to recognise it is perhaps to see that we are indeed looking at Williams' third phase, the avant-garde itself.

Nonetheless there remains a difference between blasting others and speaking blasted lines. They are different sorts of performance, and they imagine different sorts of social interaction. It is in exploring the difference between them that we encounter something that we might call a new sort of avant-garde.

Beyond the art-gang

In Vorticism's mode of organisation one individual, Ezra Pound, was at the centre of a network, lecturing, publishing and perhaps above all coordinating teams around journals such as *The Egoist* and, with Wyndham Lewis, *Blast*. If the model were altered, replacing the journal with a theatre, what differences result? Like the journal, the theatre is a vehicle for showing work authored by a range of people. Its operation and production depend on the work of a team of people, repeating activities over a period of time. It has a vision shaped and guided by those in the role of editors, the managers of the theatre. In this adapted model, the Court Theatre replaces *The Egoist* and Granville Barker replaces Wyndham Lewis. But one of the significant differences between the two versions of the model is that many more people were involved with the theatre, as both makers and audiences, than with the journal.

One of the effects of increasing the numbers of those involved is that the sense of purity of avant-garde purpose gets muddied. Lewis and Pound and their immediate associates were in a defined group which could, apparently, police its separation from wider society and culture, keeping itself pure. One of those very interested in the work of the Court was J.M. Barrie but Barrie was linked to commercial theatre through his long-standing relationship with the American theatre manager Charles Frohman at the Duke of York's. So this complicates our sense of the purity of the Court's position. But the complication continues. Barrie was close to Frohman because Frohman would take artistic risks, and Barrie persuaded him, after the Court's collapse, to sustain its artistic project by offering a repertory season at the Duke of York's, with Barrie and Barker among others in artistic control. The new artistic initiative was funded by the entrepreneur, though it still failed commercially, thereby acquiring perhaps some taint of purity.

These sorts of cultural transactions, rather than the preferred image, were the lived reality. And they almost all involved blurring of lines and muddied purities. Pound, as we know, was led to Oriental art by Binyon, a curator in that most proper institution the British Museum. Along with Lewis Pound would appropriate Binyon's *Flight of the Dragon* as a Vorticist text. For those who see Imagism/Vorticism as a tight coterie aggressively positioned against a dominant culture, it's important to recall the image of Lewis and Pound mingled among British Museum staff and the range of other artists who used the Vienna Café. More interesting still is the case of Edward – Eddie – Marsh (1872–1953). Marsh is famous for more or less inventing a school of poetry with his anthology of contemporary work published in 1915 and rather blandly called by the name of the current monarch, 'Georgian'. Marsh seems to have known, certainly known about, almost everyone who was making contemporary art of any sort. And he actively supported its production and dissemination. He commented in detail on the finished text of Bottomley's *King Lear's Wife*, which he regarded as a 'masterpiece', had it read at his house by Henry Ainley to members of Barker's company and then sent the script to Barker himself. His rooms at Gray's Inn became a meeting-place for young painters such as Gaudier-Brzeska, Mark Gertler and Stanley Spencer. He was a friend of T.E. Hulme, the 'Imagist' poet, who took him to hear Pound read. They became friends and Pound asked him for advice on quantitative verse, which he then ignored. Although Pound was later to be very critical of Georgian poets, he hoped in 1912 that he himself might be included in a future Georgian anthology. Of Lewis Marsh 'suspected him of pose, so we shan't make friends' (Hassall 1959: 278–79, 187, 193, 258). All this cultural activity took place alongside, indeed was financed by, Marsh's day job, working as Private Secretary to Winston Churchill from his first Ministerial position in 1905 through to his role as First Lord of the Admiralty.

These various interactions may complicate the picture of a cleanly segregated avant-garde. But they also seem to make it possible. As Kennedy says (2009: 49): 'An avant-garde can only exist when surrounded by a discourse about avantism'. And that discourse is anchored in material practice. Watson's *Strange Bedfellows* describes the network of the poets and artists of the first American avant-garde, specifically including 'those who organized its events, articulated its theories, and made its work known to the public'. In its early days it was 'just a loose skein of tangled social circles' (1991: 7–9). In a similar way England had its own loose and complicated network of those who made, knew, promoted and supported avant-garde practices. The moments of acutely felt artistic innovation happen as points of intensity within that larger network of connections, both of persons and artefacts. But the manifestation of those points of intensity varies. The scandalised response to Barker's 1912 *Winter's Tale* or Fraser's 1919 *As You Like It* is different from a Wyndham Lewis *Blast* manifesto. The latter rhetorically announces itself as an attack and thereby creates sharp separation between the author and the larger group. As manifesto the text is too vague to function as a programme of action. Instead it works as a performative text, and the job of work it does, using its particular selection of words and print graphics, is to authenticate the disaffection of the individualised writer. The *Blast* manifestoes – together with his mode of dress – are a performance whereby Wyndham Lewis publicly positioned himself as the opponent of the dominant. Marinetti's Futurist manifestoes work in a similar way, as does much of Dada.

Manifestoes apart, as Cooper (2004) observes, writers who consciously positioned themselves as leading exponents of 'modern' writing tended to produce texts which separated them as 'intellectuals' from the mass audience of market society. For example, the Vorticists may have emerged by carefully drawing the right – sometimes very right – people into the circle, but much of their impulse was towards exclusion, conspicuous rejection of those who didn't fit. The aim and mechanism of this process are explained by Thomas Strychacz (1993: 27) using an analogy with the simultaneous development of professional writing: 'If a body of formal knowledge underpins a professional's power within a mass society, then the idiom of modernist writing – arcane allusion, juxtaposition, opaque writing, indeterminacy, and so on – performs precisely the same function'. Similarly the 'particular strategies of modernist texts give their writers a cultural prerogative to be heard – to speak, as it were, for literature'. Such speaking functions, as much as does club membership, to delimit the audience: 'The modernist emphasis on the "materiality and density" of language and complex narrative strategies requires from its readers skill, patience, and competence' and in this way 'organizes a special kind of relationship between text and reader'. This activity could be interpreted by contemporaries as self-production. Having just read T.S. Eliot's *Sacred Wood*, Bottomley remarked: 'He seems to despise Pater a good deal, but the great difference between him and Pater is that Pater would only write on men and works which he liked, while Eliot seems to prefer to write of men and works which he wants to disparage. I felt there may be something ill-natured in him which loves to belittle men and their works' (978/1/7/22). The aggression implicit in writing that announced its own prerogative tended to foreground the individuality of the writers, and it is perhaps no coincidence that in so many cases these happened to be young male individuals. Behind their performances of shouting shimmers the picture of the playground bully, surrounded by his small group of aspirant bullies. In this respect this version of the avant-garde looks something like an art-gang.

And this, for many, has been, over and above formal characteristics and social interaction, its defining feature. The word 'avant-garde' is at heart a military term and that association persistently, silently, suggests that its cultural innovation is done in a military – or at least quite shouty – way. Thus the expectation is that properly avant-garde artists take sides, talk warfare and yell at their enemies. By contrast, although Edwardian theatrical innovators adopted models associated with various avant-gardes, they performed what they were doing in a different way. Sturge Moore, conforming to the classically accepted model, believed in the usefulness of coteries. His friend Gordon Bottomley disliked 'coteries in the London sense', preferring a small group of poets that had 'cohesion' (88957/1/87 f175). Granville Barker, further to the left perhaps, defined the medium in which he worked as a necessarily communal one. His innovative repertory system ensured that dramatic roles were shared out in such a way that actors played small parts as well as large. All elements of the production were treated as mutually dependent. To accompany this work Barker wrote texts which modelled a theatre of the future. Although these texts deeply questioned the structure and operation of the entire commercial theatre, they were written as rational argument rather than belligerent posturing. Barker thought that writing should aspire to values of simplicity and clarity. His close friend Masefield was sometimes dismissed for writing poetry with plain language, calling a spade a shovel as Bottomley snottily said. 'So far he seems to me a journalist', noted Maurice Hewlett to Eddie Marsh, 'but his ear is perfect' (in Hassall 1959: 205). Barker and Masefield consciously worked to strip back and simplify language, to thin out its density. Theirs were not approaches to art-making which were either exclusionary or wilfully difficult. They certainly didn't shout. So can this be called appropriate avant-garde behaviour? Or is it something else?

An alternative avant-garde

In 1909 J.A. Hobson welcomed the new spirit which would challenge both conservatism and narrow specialisation. 'We have had', he says, 'little schools of intellectuals who have soared into some loftiness of thought where they have claimed to find the one and absolute'. But they are 'in an atmosphere so high and dim that unity seems only got by blotting out diversity, not by harmonising it'. 'What is needed is [...] not so much a single faith, religious, ethical, intellectual, aesthetic, practical, as a single spirit in the conduct of life'. While philosophers may explain the universe or the pattern of human history, 'What men are seeking for is a wholeness without strained unity, a freedom of thought, of feeling, of conduct'. This search appeared to be simultaneously happening in all fields of human activity. Across these what was needed was 'a recognition of their unity of purpose and a fruitful co-operation'. This could be enabled, at what we might note was a time of increasing nationalism, by not seeking allegiance to any particular creed 'but only to a common temper and a common outlook' (Hobson 1909: 551–53).

It is precisely a common outlook which is the goal of a theatre defined as communal endeavour. Hobson's new spirit seems to inhabit verse drama's attempts to create through rhythm a new wholeness of the person. So too it was there in the visions of directors such as Barker. Seven years on from Hobson's essay in an article about American community theatre Barker argued that drama was a communal art that enabled communities to express themselves: 'look to the so-called Neighbourhood and Community Playhouses (again to the simplest of them, where art, if it is mentioned at all, has no capital A), unpretentious little places to which gather, their day's work done, the butcher and baker and candlestick-maker and amuse themselves by singing and dancing, by staging and acting little plays'. While such things cannot yet be called a 'national art form', nonetheless 'we have here quite genuinely the people trying to express themselves; and that, surely, is the foundation of all true art'. In particular, he celebrates an Icelandic play done in North Dakota, an example of immigrants bringing their culture to the place they now live. In language reminiscent of Hobson he says: 'It is in the blending of many and diverse races that the spiritual strength of America will lie, but if – and only if – they really can be blended. And certainly from such a blending the richest art may spring, but if – and only if – each people brings its genius generously, humble-mindedly, content to lose its soul with faith to find it'. It will only work if, as Hobson said, there is no adhesion to any particular creed. 'Certainly in that blending, in the clash of emotion and idea which must precede and go along with it is all the stuff of drama'. In conclusion: 'first and last, and in general and particular, it is by this co-operation that the drama lives. Pipe we never so wisely, the souls of our hearers will not dance unless the sense of drama is living in them too. And the need for self-expression – personal, communal, national – is a need that must be filled if democracy is not to be a byword for the fooling of the people' (in Shepherd 2021: 17–19). Three years later he agreed to become Chair of the new British Drama League, an organisation committed to the promotion of drama activities in communities, large and small, across the country. But even as Barker was formulating these ideas another disciple of what he saw as new spirit was arguing completely the opposite.

In a series of articles in *The Egoist* in 1914 Huntly Carter defined the nature of drama, as he saw it. In March he attacked the anthropologist Jane Harrison and her contention that art is 'social in origin'. She knows nothing, says Carter, of primitive man: 'Art, Drama and Religion to primitive man mean his individual feeling of relation to the world of emotional reality. When man became civilised or mass-man he lost this sublime feeling' (Carter 1914a: 115). In August he developed the point: 'Drama is something which proceeds from the union of the soul of the author with the spirit of the universe'. Hence, 'Drama is the great mystery of which the author alone has the key'. In a manner which the Symbolists might have desired, drama can thus 'flow uninterruptedly and emotionally from author to spectator'. This lays the basis for an attack on the 'middleman', effectively the whole apparatus of theatre (Carter 1914b: 298). That attack is worked through in his December essay. Drama, he says, is not so much artwork as subjective experience: 'drama is a medial organ in and by which our relations with reality and the interaction of its spirit on our own, is perceived by us. The glimpses of reality and its truths, which it flashes upon us, are peculiarly our own. [...] Drama promotes each of us to creative authorship in a spiritual sense'. If this 'individualistic basis' is the truth of drama, then what is false is any notion that drama is about either social communication or theatrical practice: 'the author supposes the spectator, another false value [...] a large transference of his Self to something contained in the auditorium of a theatre. Absurd!' The producer, actor, composer, designer, costumier all contain bits of the essential Self of the dramatic author. This scattering of that self has been caused by the middleman system of theatre. Theatre is thus demonstrably part of the 'slave ideal' which strips individuals of their will. Against this the ideal situation is where individuals become their own author and actor, where every man (sic) will experience 'in and by and through himself, a perfect form of drama, say, the Transfiguration'. The argument pushes beyond the self to its necessary transcendence. Carter recommends experiments with the impersonal actor. Marionettes are too personal. Instead there need to be 'mummers who can so subordinate themselves to the initial flow of Drama as to speak and act by no will of their own' (Carter 1914c: 461–62).

One of Carter's favoured writers, the East-End poet John Rodker (1894–1955), wrote similarly in his theatre manifesto published in *The Egoist* in November 1914. 'The theatre is the staging for emotion' and has no need for words. Hence in his sequence of scenarios gathered as 'Theatre Muet' the wordless actions of Pierrot and Columbine are described. Where conversation is written it 'need not be materialised'. But theatre is also spectacle, and spectacle can distract from concentration on the emotion. In order to avoid this problem theatre should be made by marionettes, 'conventionalised figures which do not draw attention to their idiosyncrasies'. To that end, says Rodker, he wants to rent a theatre in London and use for the plays 'either human marionettes of the Dutch-doll type or naked humans, or to clothe them in a sort of cylindrical garment' (Rodker 1996: 177, 29, 177–78). That cylindrical garment sounds a bit like the anecdotal barrel in which Yeats wanted to put actors, and, back beyond Yeats, the Symbolist anxiety about theatre's materiality. There's something quite old behind the modernity of *The Egoist* and it's producing a version of drama that not only wanted to de-socialise it but, more deeply, to strip out the bodily human agency.

That contrast at the level of theory between Egoism and Barker's model of co-operation can be put alongside a similar sort of contrast in practices. Around the time of Hobson's Realism essay Gordon Bottomley made a plan: 'as I may not go to London, and as no one in London will play the things I want', he told Moore, 'I begin to ask myself why there should not be a Festspielhaus in Cartmel, to play all the lovely things I want to see' (978/1/7/2). His choice of word invokes the memory of Wagner. Meanwhile, much further south, Wagner's influence was also working on Reginald Buckley. In association with the composer Rutland Boughton he was planning a so-called 'Temple' theatre, a Festspielhaus, in Glastonbury for the purposes of showing music drama. Buckley's view of the origins of drama was more that of Jane Harrison than Carter. It emerged, he says, from dance and 'folk-dancing was the first communal expression of religious feeling and human joy in life'. So for the future, 'the living principle of folk-art calls for modern expression, and provides us with the best hope of a contemporary drama' (Buckley 1911: 49, 54). This thinking underpins the 'Articles' for the Temple Theatre: 'The building of a theatre in connection with an agricultural commune. [...] The theatre to serve primarily for the enjoyment and expression of the community' (Boughton and Buckley 1911: 94). The idea was repeated in his proposals for a Shakespeare theatre at Stratford: 'those working for the theatre should be united by a common bond. In connection with the theatre would be a handicraft guild and a farm colony', with artists and 'stage-hands' working outdoors (Buckley 1911: 127).

Neither Bottomley nor Buckley got their Festspielhaus, but something on a less ambitious scale was achieved by John Masefield who started putting on plays in the music room at his house on Boar's Hill near Oxford. His immediate family were involved, on stage and off, and it grew into the Hill Players, consisting of local amateurs and visiting professionals. They may have done their plays in a 'music room' but their lead male performers were all farmers and performances had to be scheduled around more important activities such as harvest. With this we can contrast Yeats' plans for his Nō-influenced 'plays for dancers' begun in 1915. He found his ideal space for their performance in the drawing-room of Lady Cunard: 'I have invented a form of drama, distinguished, indirect, and symbolic, and having no need of mob or Press to pay its way – an aristocratic form'. Performances will then be given for 'the pleasure of personal friends and a few score people of good taste'. In the same way, previously, he had hoped that the Irish Literary Theatre would attract all the 'right people' (Yeats 1989: 221–22, 166) For Ezra Pound, sitting with other selected literati such as T.S. Eliot, this was presumably all absolutely, as one might say, right. His opinion of Nō was that 'These plays, or eclogues, were made only for the few; for the nobles' (Fenollosa and Pound 1916: 5).

As Yeats settles into the aristocrat's house, as Masefield schedules rehearsals around the farming year, we have in front of us two different understandings not just of how to do drama, but also of how drama works, what it's for. And each of those understandings is arguably part of an avant-garde practice. Carter's attack on middlemen is as much archetypically avant-garde as Yeats' desire radically to limit his audience to what he, and presumably Pound and Eliot, regarded as the culturally competent. And, on the other hand, as Kennedy argues, both the Stage Society and Barker were characteristically avant-garde in their commitment to experiment and their attempts to control their conditions of reception. Among their experiments were productions of Masefield. So too Bottomley's plays were taken up by later avant-garde directors. Twenty years after the founding of the Stage Society it was clear that a whole other sort of experiment had been going on in parallel, an experiment in the organisation of theatre practices, not just in theatre management and repertory playing but in developing an infrastructure to facilitate drama-making in new places with new communities. It was a project with a communal form which, if it were to happen at all, depended on achieving common temper and common outlook.

If we've got at least two sorts of avant-garde practice here, how best to characterise them? Barker thought a drama that expressed community would make democracy meaningful. Carter thought that drama which involved anyone else would strip individuals of their will. Yeats snuggled up to an aristocrat while Masefield concerned himself with the farming community and Buckley with new garden towns. Alongside this political distinction, we can observe another. According to Bürger (2007: 53) a characteristic avant-garde event would generate responses that 'range from shouting to fisticuffs'. Yeats claimed that his writing of plays 'has been the search for more of manful energy' (in Schuchard 2010: 206). And not only him. Armstrong (2008: 41) observes – if that's the right verb here – that Pound and others 'understood creative activity in terms of masculine aggression and spermatic fecundity'. This might readily link up with the Blasting and belligerence, the posing that so alienated the homosexual Marsh.

Which takes us to the opposite pole from unproblematised masculinity. In the alternative, as it were non-Egoistical, avant-garde the bodies are more variously gendered and sexed. A number of the proponents and sponsors of avant-garde practices were women. We've met Florence Farr and Gwendolen Bishop, even Lady Cunard. But the list is much longer. In their various discussions about getting their plays staged, the verse dramatists mention Mrs Patrick Campbell, famous for doing Maeterlinck's *Pelleas* and Hofmannsthal's *Electra* (Peters 1984); Lillah McCarthy, Barker's first wife, celebrated both for acting in 'experimental' plays and producing them – the plans for a Verhaeren play, for example; Gertrude Kingston who tried, unsuccessfully, to make a London art theatre at the Little Theatre in the Adelphi; and Madame Strindberg, who established a 'cabaret' for art theatre and founded The Cave of the Golden Calf, a club with a reputation, as Cook says (2008: 120), for 'tolerance of same-sex relations'. The cabaret and the club together suggest another feature of this avant-garde. It happened in a network in which seemingly uncensured homosexuality was part of the landscape. Ricketts and Shannon lived openly together as did their friends Katherine Bradley and Edith Cooper who wrote together under the single name

Michael Field. Ricketts knew them as Michael and Henry, they called him Fay. All of them were opposed to marriage. Indeed Ricketts was very cross when their protégé and lodger Sturge Moore decided to get married. Among their friends none of this seems to have been worth comment. Barker worked closely with Laurence Housman whose homosexuality was well known. Almost everyone knew Eddie Marsh and was happy to be associated with him. Harold Monro, rather more covert, was unproblematically at the centre of a group of poets. Perhaps more astonishing is when Bottomley, writing to Moore in January 1911, described his admiration for Wilde and, 15 or so years after that very public trial for sodomy, comments only that he had a sheltered upbringing and 'when Wilde's trouble came in 1895 [...] I did not understand, or even conceive, why Wilde was being prosecuted: but I saw quite clearly that the enmity of men's minds, if nothing else, would hinder him from creating any more of the beautiful things that had meant much to me' (978/1/7/2). Some were prepared to sustain Wilde's memory even with the more risky material. There were those two *Salome* productions for example, with the first of them involving some of the friends of homosexual campaigner George Ives (Cook 2008: 185). The ease of these mutual penetrations, as it were, between avant-garde theatre and homosexuality is nowhere embodied more concisely, and more literally, than the hairless chin of the male. As Cook notes (2008: 61) facial hair symbolised late-Victorian respectable masculinity. The hairless chin was associated with 'fashion, bohemianism and an avant-garde' – and with homosexuality. Respectable homosexuals such as Housman, Ricketts, Shannon all had beards. Shaw, aggressively heterosexual, was prolifically bearded, as the moustachioed Barrie mockingly noted. Barker throughout his life, apart from the obligatory military moustache, remained militantly clean-shaven. The pacifist radical Trevelyan had his Pterodamozels joke about hairy men.

On the one side, then, the women entrepreneurs, the female audiences for experimental matinées at the Court, the sexually various network. On the other, the costumed self-production of young male Egoists, puffed up with rhetorical aggression, insisting on their throbbing individualism but disliking the staged body. What name do we find for an avant-garde that doesn't perform their way? In the communally focussed, accessible work of co-operative theatre-making, in the variety of sexed bodies, we find something that can be said perhaps to be a non-phallic avant-garde.

As it sidles into view we're compelled to ask: why did we not see it before?

First, the generally accepted theatre history has made a mistaken assumption about what we're looking for when we're looking for an avant-garde. Second, the received version of the history of this drama sees Ibsen, modulated Naturalism and Shaw as the only significant features. And third, there's pressure from the canonical assumptions of the English literary tradition which designate Imagism and Vorticism as the only definable pre-war avant-garde, with Yeats' dramatic experiments as a solo side-line to his poetry and 'Modernism' – with a very large capital letter – beginning properly with Eliot post-war. The story has all the 'right' people lined up as tidily as they sat together in Lady Cunard's drawing-room. And it's all reinforced by another story, that of the Great War as an apocalyptic event that changed society for ever.

One narrator of that story, Samuel Hynes, suggests that the effect was such that by autumn 1915 'the war had virtually stopped the English Modern movement'. In 1916 in London one could not find 'anything new, experimental, avant-garde, challenging'. This must be true, because it was the opinion of one of the 'right' people. Ezra Pound noted that he was 'the only person of interest left in the world of art, London', an opinion that Hynes, a man of literature, quotes without demur (1990: 65, 102, 101). Pound was ignoring the fact that his friend Moore had a Stage Society performance of his play *Judith* in January 1916. And he presumably didn't know that in 1915–1916 Granville Barker had developed his ideas about drama as community expression. Nor that he had formulated an idea of everyday life as performance – which anticipated by about fifty years Erwin Goffman's restatement of the same idea. And after Pound said things had stopped the Stage Society early in 1917 did Masefield's innovatory re-working of Greek tragedy for a world of warring imperial powers, *Good Friday*. And three years later came Barrie's wild formal experiment *The Truth about the Russian Dancers*. The story of the Great War as brutal punctuation point has the effect of concealing the experimental work and handily presenting a fresh start for Modernism (again appropriately capitalised, in every sense) with another 'right', oh all too right, man, Eliot.

My own narrative has followed the writers in their development. Their post-war ideas connect to their pre-war ones, with war-time engagement as part of a continuing development. The war was hideous enough in itself without its being used as a punctuation device that effectively shores up the literary canon and silences the rest. I suggest that those canonical figures, to whom we might add another self-produced person, Shaw, be put to one side and the rest be retrieved from silence. That then offers a picture of an avant-garde that doesn't centre itself on belligerent individualist poses but is instead 'non-phallic'.

But it also offers a picture of something larger. Through the chapter I have described various interconnected networks and avantist discourses which form the environment for several avant-garde practices. If that description is not wholly misinformed, then it implies that London was not different from other imperial cities in that it indeed saw rich avant-garde activity. And from there it follows that, while of course London may have been different in its governance and class structure and social arrangements, these did not inhibit avant-garde formations. In other words, the causality, the enabling conditions, of the avant-garde aren't quite what they're supposed to be. Which is an oddly, though not perhaps inappropriately, queer place to end up.

But it makes a good starting place from which to begin exploration of the ideas and stagings of this non-phallic avant-garde as it meditated, characteristically, on sex and sexuality, pierrots, fairies and children all gathered up in what they called, and we've of course learnt to dismiss as, fantasy plays.

References

Unpublished

88957: The British Library; Gordon Bottomley papers
978: Senate House Library, University of London; Thomas Sturge Moore papers

Published

Anderson, Perry 1984 'Modernity and Revolution' *New Left Review* volume 144: 96–113
Armstrong, Tim 2008 *Modernism: A Cultural History* Cambridge: Polity
Bottomley, Gordon and Nash, Paul 1990 *Poet and Painter: Letters between Gordon Bottomley and Paul Nash 1910–1946*, introduced by Andrew Causey Bristol: Redcliffe Press
Boughton, Rutland and Buckley, Reginald R. 1911 *Music Drama of the Future: Uther and Igraine: Choral Drama, with Essays by the Collaborators* London: William Reeve
Buckley, Reginald R. 1911 *The Shakespeare Revival and the Stratford-upon-Avon Movement* London: George Allen & Sons
Bürger, Peter 2007 *Theory of the Avant-Garde*, translated by Michael Shaw Minneapolis: University of Minnesota Press
Carter, Huntly 1912 *The New Spirit in Drama and Art* London: Frank Palmer
Carter, Huntly 1914a 'The House That the Set-Backs Built' *The Egoist* volume 1, number 6: 114–15
Carter, Huntly 1914b 'Theatricalising the Drama and "Pygmalion' *The Egoist* volume 1, number 15: 297–98
Carter, Huntly 1914c 'The Impersonal Note of England, Russia and Japan' *The Egoist* volume 1, number 24: 461–62
Chapman, Don 2008 *Oxford Playhouse: High and Low Drama in a University City* Hatfield: The University of Hertfordshire Press
Clark, T.J. 1982 'On the Social History of Art' in Francis Frascina and Charles Harrison (eds) *Modern Art and Modernism: A Critical Anthology* London: Paul Chapman Publishing
Colls, Robert 1987 'Englishness and Political Culture' in Robert Colls and Philip Dodd (eds) *Englishness: Politics and Culture 1880–1920* London: Croom Helm
Cook, Matt 2008 *London and the Culture of Homosexuality, 1885–1914* Cambridge: Cambridge University Press
Cooper, John Xiros 2004 *Modernism and the Culture of Market Society* Cambridge: Cambridge University Press
Craig, E. Gordon 1913 *Towards a New Theatre* London: J.M. Dent & Sons
Fenollosa, Ernest and Pound, Ezra 1916 *'Noh' or Accomplishment: A Study of the Classical Stage of Japan* London: Macmillan & Co.
Hassall, Christopher 1959 *Edward Marsh: Patron of the Arts: A Biography* London: Longmans
Hatcher, John 1995 *Laurence Binyon: Poet, Scholar of East and West* Oxford: Clarendon Press
Hobson, J.A. 1909 'The Task of Realism' *The English Review* volume 3: 543–54
Hobson, J.A. 1988 *A Reader*, edited by Michael Freeden London: Unwin Hyman
Housman, Laurence 1910 'A King's Proctor for Plays' *The Fortnightly Review* volume 88: 852–56
Hynes, Samuel 1990 *A War Imagined: The First World War and English Culture* London: The Bodley Head
Innes, Christopher 1993 *Avant Garde Theatre 1892–1992* London: Routledge
Jackson, Holbrook 1909 *Bernard Shaw* London: Grant Richards

Jackson, Holbrook 1988 *The Eighteen Nineties: A Review of Art and Ideas at the Close of the Nineteenth Century* London: The Cresset Library

Kennedy, Dennis 2009 *The Spectator and the Spectacle: Audiences in Modernity and Postmodernity* Cambridge: Cambridge University Press

Levitas, Ben 2016 'The Theatre of Modernity' in Vincent Sherry (ed.) *The Cambridge History of Modernism* Cambridge: Cambridge University Press

MacFall, Haldance 1913 *The Splendid Wayfaring* London: Simpkin, Marshall & Co

Nairn, Tom 1981 *The Break-Up of Britain* London: Verso

Nicholls, Peter 1995 *Modernisms: A Literary Guide* Basingstoke: Macmillan

Orton, Fred and Pollock, Griselda 1985 '*Avant-Gardes* and Partisans Reviewed' in Francis Frascina (ed.) *Pollock and After: The Critical Debate* London: Paul Chapman Publishing: 167–83

Peppis, Paul 2000 *Literature, Politics, and the English Avant-garde: Nation and Empire, 1901–1918* Cambridge: Cambridge University Press

Peters, Margot 1984 *Mrs Pat: The Life of Mrs Patrick Campbell* London: The Bodley Head

Postlewait, Thomas 2004 'The London Stage, 1895–1918' in Baz Kershaw (ed.) *The Cambridge History of British Theatre*, volume 3 Cambridge: Cambridge University Press

Rodker, John 1996 *Poems & Adolphe 1920*, edited with introduction by Andrew Crozier Manchester: Carcanet

Samuel, Horace B. 1913 *Modernities* London: Kegan Paul, Trench, Trubner & Co

Schuchard, Ronald 2010 *The Last Minstrels: Yeats and the Revival of the Bardic Arts* Oxford: Oxford University Press

Sell, Mike 1998 'The Avant-Garde of Absorption: Happenings, Fluxus, and the Performance Economies of the American Sixties' *Rethinking Marxism* volume 10, number 2: 1–26

Shepherd, Simon (ed.) 2021 *The Unknown Granville Barker: Letters to Helen and Other Texts 1915–18* London: Society for Theatre Research

Stephenson, Andrew 2000 'Refashioning Modern Masculinity: Whistler, Aestheticism and National Identity' in David Peters Corbett and Lara Perry (eds) *English Art 1860–1914: Modern Artists and Identity* Manchester: Manchester University Press: 133–49

Strychacz, Thomas 1993 *Modernism, Mass Culture, and Professionalism* Cambridge: Cambridge University Press

Thatcher, David S. 1970 *Nietzsche in England, 1880–1914: The Growth of a Reputation* Toronto: University of Toronto Press

Watson, Steven 1991 *Strange Bedfellows: The First American Avant-Garde* New York: Abbeville Press

Williams, Raymond 1996 *The Politics of Modernism: Against the New Conformists*, edited by Tony Pinkney London: Verso

Yeats, W.B. 1989 *Essays & Introductions* London: Macmillan

5
FANTASY PLAY

It is Friday 23 December 1904. We are sitting in that progressive arts experiment, the Court Theatre under its Vedrenne-Barker management. Their Christmas show has just started. Gardeners are trimming hedges while an unseen boy scares away birds. A statue of Love stands over a fountain. This orderly garden and its house are run by three women, Prim, Prude and Privacy, guardians to a young girl, daughter of a former inhabitant who had run away with a man. Their gardeners' attempts to discipline nature into straight lines, the boy's efforts to drive off hungry birds: together they make a loaded image. On the morning the play opens the three women are attempting to fortify their house against their proximity to, and young Prunella's interest in, the 'rabble' and their mummers passing in the street. As the mummers' music comes closer, the women rush inside, leaving Prunella to find the key that locks the garden gate. Suddenly a head pushes through the not quite thoroughly disciplined hedge. This, all in white, is Pierrot. He summons Scaramel, they trick Prunella into giving them the key, and the whole company presses through the now symbolically unlocked gate. They circle round the girl, encouraging her to kiss Pierrot. When she does so 'He meets the kiss passionately, holding her fast. She is overwhelmed, breaks from him, and runs into the house' (Housman and Barker 1906: 34). Pierrot and Scaramel are left on their own, but in possession of the key.

So ended the first act of *Prunella*, co-written by Laurence Housman (1865–1959) and the Court's manager, Granville Barker, who also played Pierrot. In the next act we shall see him convincing Prunella to overcome her fears and run away with the troupe. With his companions keeping watch, he puts a ladder up to her window and carries her out of the house. He takes her to the statue of Love, who wakes and speaks and strums his viol, an enchanted moment from which Pierrot stands detached. The rest of the company dance and Prunella is then revealed in the costume of Pierrette. She surrenders herself to Pierrot.

DOI: 10.4324/9781003033295-5

Rational asceticism

This fictional abduction of a young woman is taking us into a chapter rather different from its predecessors. Previously we have investigated the forms of drama. Now, however, the interest must move to its stories, and specifically the sorts of stories associated with so-called fantasy plays. Such plays were a characteristic and distinctive product of the Edwardian theatre and to structure our consideration of them this chapter is divided into three parts. The first deals with fictions about sexual experience, narratives which work to define a particular way of doing sex. The second is principally engaged with supernatural beings and in particular fairies. And the third with children. But as we go on these topics start – what shall we say – leaking into one another. For sex, fairies and children are all part of the ideological project whereby the new drama of this period breaks with its past and challenges its present. Whatever we may now think of fairies and such, for a consciously modern, indeed avant-garde, commentator such as Huntly Carter as an attempt to 'redramatise the drama' (1912: 225) the fantasy play sat alongside Chekhov. Fairy spangle can have rather sharp edges.

To begin to explore the modernising potency of the fantasy play let's return to that young woman who has run off with mummers. In the final act the garden is overgrown and the house emptied of all but Privacy and her servant Quaint. Pierrot enters, now a prospective purchaser, but still upset, despite appearances, that after two years Prunella had walked out. After he goes into the house Prunella enters. Looking like a beggar she is recognised by nobody. She falls at the feet of the statue by the now moss-covered fountain. It speaks. Love says he will watch over her, so when Pierrot enters Love interrogates him but refuses to reveal where Prunella is. Pierrot must find her for himself. He puts a ladder to her window, in vain. She then rises from the fountain, he kneels, she remains motionless. She asks if he will give up his life for her. He drops his head on her breast and sobs.

As a vehicle for a Christmas show the story of a mummers troupe liberating a trapped young woman should have been ideal. But audiences didn't find it appropriately comfortable. Among other things, as Housman tells (1937: 243), Barker's performance of Pierrot 'had too much bite in it […] audiences preferred a Pierrot whom they could like – and forgive – more easily'. Barker's way of playing it stemmed from his intentions for the whole project. In his initial approach to Housman, who had already published 'fairy' stories, he asked: 'Have you or do you know of any "Fairy" plays (That epithet only explains what I mean if you don't tie it to its strict meaning) which would appeal to the more "refined" section of the Public (there again you must judge my meaning)' (Bryn Mawr Sep. 27). Housman sent him a draft of a text with the working title *Cupid*. For its music Barker suggested a score like Debussy's cantata *L'Enfant Prodigue* played on the piano: 'It should I feel be illustrative – practically continuous', with other music for lyrics to be spoken over. The cantata had become the basis for a wordless pierrot play done in London in 1891 (and parodied in *Ibsen's Ghost*).

This gives one sense of the texture of the piece. Another, rather different, comes from Barker's discussion of Act 3: 'I got as far as Tannhauser's pilgrimage – I mean Pierrot's history of himself'. But he found Housman's treatment too tame, proposing instead a version in which Pierrot returns 'not poor and ragged but well-to-do – a plutocrat's Pierrot'. He grieves over parting from Pierrette 'but it's a sentimental grief upon which he rather plumes himself. He has bought the old house and garden that it may enshrine her memory. He arrives – and turns out the old aunt'. When Pierrette (Prunella) arrives, appearing through the hedge, she is ragged but still beautiful. Her treatment by Sganarelle is unsympathetic. He tells her to 'start sweeping up the dead leaves', an underline that shows Barker making symbolic use of the setting. When Pierrette discovers the statue of Cupid, she curses it, wanting to change places and become stone - which happens. Cupid then resolves to bring the couple together. Of his version Barker explains that 'I feel the end of the play mustn't be quite an "As you were" There must be something more to it – a rounding off of the moral' (Bryn Mawr Oct. 22).

Although it altered during discussions – Prunella for example doesn't become stone – the ending retained this quality. In an exhausted untamed place two characters discover the terms on which they can, with caution, restraint, free choice, connect again with each other. One sort of fairy tale might have ended with the liberation of the young woman from a repressive household. Another might have had the young couple still innocently, youthfully, seeking for, then finding, one another. The inclusion of *Tannhaüser* alongside the grown-up proprietorial masculinity of Pierrot, and a scenography which is part symbolic and part musical pierrot play, indicate the unsettling complexity of the portrayal of sexuality that *Prunella* was intended to contain.

This was never going to be a straightforward Christmas romance with supposedly normal expectations around sex and gender safely intact. Both its authors were suffragists, with strong views on women's rights and competences. Barker's first solo play tells the story of a woman who walks out of a materially comfortable country house to marry the family gardener. Just over a decade after *Prunella* he told a suffrage meeting: 'When the women voters get into the stride I think they will surprise you. I do not think they will show much sentimentality. I think they will be rather ruthless' (*New York Times* 9 May 1915). His co-author Housman was one of the founders in 1907 of the Men's League for Women's Suffrage. Other founders included the radical journalist Henry Woodd Nevinson and the activist and journalist H.N. Brailsford, a member of the Independent Labour Party and the Union of Democratic Control, and a supporter of the 1917 Russian Revolution.

Housman's own analyses of the social problems related to gender were set out in a series of speeches and pamphlets. On 18 October 1911 in Essex Hall, a regular venue for left-wing meetings, he lectured on 'The Immoral Effects of Ignorance in Sex Relations'. In his analysis 'girl nature' is more vulnerable because of ignorance than is 'boy nature', for in girls sex 'remains far more dormant than with the average of our male youth'. Two examples of the effects of ignorance are the girl who dreads that any contact with men will lead to motherhood and the girl who doesn't understand that it might. Such girls have to be given knowledge about the discourses and problems of sex, even if in doing so 'you have to give up a certain amount of modest reticence'. But there is a problem. The 'untrained virginal mind' has to be educated 'without making it unduly introspective' and self-conscious. But its ignorance is kept in place by social institution. Housman relates how he was told by a mother that a girl's ignorance is 'too valuable an addition to the virginal charm of womanhood in the marriage market'. Thus as an alternative to this way of organising sex relationships Housman proposes 'The only real surrender of love from woman to man that is worth having is the free and conscious surrender which knows the meaning and the value of what it is giving; and to her the man, in turn, should freely and gladly render back, as an inalienable right, the freedom to give herself again or to refrain from giving' ([1911b]: 32, 39, 41, 35, 41).

This is the basic shape of the Prunella narrative. The only learning she does is the recitation of passages of verse. Consequently she is actually in a state of 'ignorance'. She physically recoils from Pierrot, who forces an embrace on her, but then runs away with him literally not knowing where it may lead, as if combining in her person both effects of ignorance. By the end, however, Pierrot has to wait on her agreeing to take him back. When she allows him to sob on her breast it is as it were a 'free and conscious surrender', for Pierrot has already had to acknowledge that she might refrain from giving herself.

For Housman problems for girls related to, and derived from, wider problems with how both gender and sexuality were thought about and handled. In a later pamphlet, 'The Relation of Fellow-Feeling to Sex', he explored the tense relationship between sexuality and the assumed gender system. Written for the British Society for the Study of Sex Psychology it argues that 'fellow-feeling' is an 'amative instinct' which operates without regard to gender or procreative function. A child or child-like adult does not wish to copulate but will display toward 'the object of affection conduct very closely resembling the secondary and attendant demonstrations, which take place between lovers in the full sense of the word'; 'it will lavish its demonstrations of affection quite irrespective of sex'. To follow his logic where it is radically going Housman moves, for illustration, to the superficially more comfortable territory of the plant world. A vine tendril chooses 'quite blindly as regards utilitarian benefit'. Nature indeed allows for 'a certain amount of unselectiveness or promiscuity', for 'a selectiveness too prudential and utilitarian in character might impair a quality much more important – its vitality'. Thus, in the safely nonhuman world, 'a certain proportion of sterile embraces, and the will or the capacity to indulge in them, seem necessary to the establishment of certain species of plant life' (Housman [1917]: 5, 6).

Pause here and note that Housman was writing in a society where, as Tosh (1999) explains, a couple of decades before anxieties about male sexuality led not only to Social Purity campaigns that regarded extra-marital sex, homosexuality and masturbation as aberrant but also to pressure within at least the middle-class household to restrict the only legitimate form of sexual activity, uxorious sexuality – sex with a wife – and reduce the number of births. As for children, 'The late Victorians were even less prepared than their grandparents to recognize childhood sexuality' (Tosh 1999: 150). With that noted, let's return to Housman's argument about an amative instinct that flourishes, like exuberantly sprouting vegetation, beyond the tidy well-clipped lines of supposedly normal ideas about sex and gender. Since fellow-feeling is tangled up with sex feeling, 'sympathetic natures have a certain tendency to carry sex-feeling across the utilitarian border-line into the domain where ordinarily we should expect to find fellow-feeling only'. That border-line, always snipped ruthlessly straight, is of course the one that segregates legitimate procreative sex from any other version of it. But what it tries to police, the sex instinct, is itself 'unfixed' with no regard for norms. Indeed 'it is not out of the accentuation of sex-differences, and their segregation into absolute male and absolute female, that understanding and sympathy and fellow-feeling have arisen in social life, and sensitiveness and creativeness in art; but rather a gradual approximation and drawing the one into the other of what were once two extremes'. To get to the 'full degree of fellow-feeling', says Housman, 'there must be interplay of a more subtle kind than we have hitherto been able to see our way to' (Housman [1917]: 11, 14). In that simple word 'interplay' writhe a whole set of prospective horrors for a society where masculinity only retained its social status, and power, by drawing very firm lines between what was proper and what improper, between marriage and non-marriage, use and waste, employment and unemployment, production and play, and then maintaining those lines with very sharp shears.

Housman's proposition that fellow-feeling is engendered by de-emphasising, mixing up, sex differences has implications that were difficult, risky, to stage. For an example of how it might be dramatically imagined take Henry Bryan Binns' *The Adventure*. It was it seems his only published play, and perhaps never intended to be staged. Binns (1873–1923) was a member of the Fellowship of New Life and a Quaker committed to initiatives such as the establishment of a collectivist church in London and a scheme for Rural Fellowship Settlements (Armytage 1968: 339). He lived in and was a champion of the first Garden City, Letchworth (the subject of mockery by Shaw). Biographer of Whitman the influence is clear in his first volumes of poems, *For the Fellowship* (1905–1906), but in *The Great Companions* he also paid tribute to the importance in his life of Edward Carpenter (1911b: 56–57). As with Carpenter, the actual practice of fellowship was crucial. 'There is a continence in fellowship', he said, 'we will draw together of free will, chastely. Personality is sacred as sex' (in Charlton 1985: xvi).

That chaste drawing together is imaged in *The Adventure*. Its story, from Homer, is of Ulysses on the island ruled by Circe, whose magic takes men prisoner and transforms them to beasts. Ulysses resists her temptations, and as a result she recognises him as the man of real truth and fortitude for whom she has been waiting. In this version Binns' decision to write it as a play becomes highly significant. His prose poems of the same date had invoked the figure of the 'divine

Companion', the 'Lord of Life', the 'Friend', or indeed, the lover: 'With a knife my lover comes, through every barrier he cuts his way, to where within, in an enchanted slumber, I await his lips. He comes. All, all of mine he asks and takes and crushes under his feet, my lover. All, all, till there is nought' (1911b: 75). This is feasible in mystical prose, but a play – whether staged or not – has to be imagined as physically enacted. So it offers an opportunity for an embodied exemplification of chaste fellowship.

Ulysses tells Circe that he wants her magic to 'enfranchise' him to 'Waken up manhood howso wrapt about/In dreams'. His resistance to her is to be understood as rejection of both debasing fleshly passion and ideological mystifications. She recognises the 'clear flame' burning in him, and he feels the fire from her. Touching her 'wakes in me/Some godhood of immortal potency'. He offers her his sword. Holding it she 'kisses him on the mouth'. With her cup of 'the god's ecstasy' in one hand and his sword in the other, she demands of him 'Divine adventure'. To which, taking her by the hands, he looks forward. In the next act she advises that in the underworld his way will be shown by one who on earth was 'Twi-sexed, man-woman'. Opposition to this adventure comes from the Captain, who warns they go to perdition. But Ulysses' fellows gather round him. Telling them to forget the Captain's 'vain prudence' he resolves to follow his recently dead piper, 'the lad of dreams'. Circe promises that her magic 'taken/Into his frame' will enable him to defy death. In front of them all she embraces him, and he announces: 'out of your embraces are my flesh/And soul and spirit wrought together anew'. The men, speaking in unison, resolve to descend with Ulysses, 'Seeking for Freedom' (Binns 1911: 79–103). At the very last even the Captain joins them. The fellowship is complete. In its formation there is, clearly, both spiritual purpose and corporeal union. The kiss on the lips and the necessarily public embrace are essential to the spiritual mission. And, whereas it's the woman who kisses, the presence of male comradeship is staged in the unison speaking, the Captain's joining of the group, and the return, at the end, of the sound of the loved piper. This seems to be a version of chaste drawing together in which there is a place for physicality and in which 'personality' – both female and male – is as 'sacred as sex'.

Ulysses, the man of immortal potency, is nonetheless central. A rather less physically intact masculinity was imagined by Housman's co-author Barker. In *The Madras House*, as we've seen, he invites distaste and contempt for the Madras father's predatory heterosexuality but also for the 'man-milliner' Mr Windlesham, with his inhuman hair and complexion and 'gait of a water-wagtail', who organises the objectification of the female models (Barker 1977: 73). In the privacy of an intimate letter Barker went much further. To Helen Huntington in July 1916 he wrote: 'The woman inspiring the man – we've had much of it – But why not the man inspiring the woman – if he has enough of "womanhood" in him to give that unselfish love. Please God I have – I try to have' (Barker BL: 71897/92). By this time he had just written an extended story called *Souls on Fifth*, published spring 1916. Its ruse is that the narrator, on a regular night-time walk on

New York's Fifth Avenue, becomes aware that the space around him is populated by the souls of its deceased inhabitants. Early on he encounters a preacher whose congregation was rich and luxurious but who had no romantic vision of the future, whose imaginations were only 'a stimulus to erotic frivolities'. The preacher does nothing to interfere with or upset their complacent attitudes. But among all these souls there is one who is different, who belonged, she says, not on Fifth Avenue but in the 'wild places'. The narrator calls her the 'Little Soul'. In their conversations, the story moves from social satire to sex, gender and emotional fulfilment. She starts to develop an affection which the narrator does not return. He claims he has never been in love: 'I am a practical man. I have no use for these fantastic exercises of imagination'. She regards this dismissal of his need for tenderness as conceited and a pretence. By the end of the story she has persuaded him to take her away from Fifth Avenue. They arrange to say goodbye to each other out on the prairie. He kneels and waits for the wind to rise before letting her go from his hand. When it strikes, he flings himself to the ground to protect her. He feels her fluttering close to his bare neck, then suddenly shakes and chokes. Turning on his side for air, he 'crushed her soul between my hands. I ground it to my breast'. He cries out. 'And the ice within me broke and the tears sprang.' His hands are empty and the Little Soul has vanished. 'But my soul was full of joy' (Barker 1916: 13, 40, 54, 60–61). Barker's narrator, the practical man with no use for love or imagination, has his ice broken for him. The implication is that, as he experiences physical and emotional trauma, where the female soul has vanished is into him.

In his biography of Barker Eric Salmon argues (1983: 247) that *Souls* was strongly autobiographical. Barker's lover Helen Huntington lived on Fifth Avenue, under the vigilant eye of her husband, and in autumn 1915, having returned to America, with no means of legitimately contacting her Barker walked Fifth Avenue hoping to bump into her. His plan was to take her away, for her own good, from that 'damned' house and the social 'machine' of New York. But when the story was written and published she was still in the house, and he was first in France and then in Williamstown. Neither knew how things would – or could – end. Huntington, with a copy of the story hidden at the back of her book-shelves, strongly identified with the Little Soul, and asked her lover to take her away in his pocket. All of which close biographical correspondence makes the ending more astonishing. For, insofar as he is the narrator, Barker is volunteering to be a man who has, so to speak, had his ice broken by a female soul.

This biographical correspondence suggests something different from what is usually assumed about Barker and sex. Famously in *The Madras House* the hero Philip rages against the 'farmyard world of sex', a sentiment taken to be Barker's own. Philip's view is explicable both as reaction to his father's promiscuity and a business that needed to objectify women. But it's made difficult to sympathise with Philip because of the critique from his wife Jessica. Instead of hearing Barker's own view here we are looking at a constructed staging of attitudes to sex. On the one hand there is the abusive physicality, on the other a rejection of physicality. Somewhere between the two comes the description of what Housman might call 'interplay' between the male narrator and the Little Soul. It seems to offer a physically felt union between one entity and another which is not anchored, so to speak, in genital-based practice. Of course one of those entities has no body as such. But it can be felt as it flutters and moves, which makes it different from a state of spiritual ecstasy. What's imagined is an interaction between two different entities that could be described both as non-standard and 'amative'. In its relationship to the love-affair with Huntington it could also be described as sexual. To understand more fully the way in which it could be sexual, and the sort of sex involved, we can use a model created by somebody who was famous, indeed notorious, for his writings on sex and gender, Havelock Ellis (1859–1939). His 1897 volume *Sexual Inversion* had been banned. When its bookseller George Bedborough was prosecuted in 1898 Barker's close friend Bernard Shaw publicly protested, in the journal *The Adult*, though he also disliked this 'sex nonsense' being associated with socialism (Brady 2009: 144, 206).

Ellis argued, in an essay on 'Modesty' (1898), that its fundamental element is negative, 'the social fear of evoking disgust'. The socio-historical function of modesty was to protect from attack the female body which was owned by a male. This system persists most strongly among the least educated and least wealthy but 'civilization tends to subordinate, if not to minimize, modesty'. Nonetheless modesty remains fundamental to the 'art of love'. Without modesty we could not properly value 'that bold and pure candor which is at once the final revelation of love and the seal of its sincerity' (Ellis 1931: 51, 82). Lust, at the other pole, as it were, from modesty, has also to be distinguished from love. While lust is 'adequate to the end of reproduction [...] it is not until lust is expanded and irradiated that it develops into the exquisite and enthralling flower of love' (Ellis 1945: 86). This observation comes from 'The Valuation of Sexual Love'. It begins by addressing those who reject or despise the body and sexual love, one of the types, we'll remember, of Housman's 'ignorance'. Sexual love, it argues, is a positive quality, generating social feelings, morality, religion, poetry and art. Moreover, as Crozier (2008: 30–31) says, 'Ellis's model of the sexual impulse is [...] an undifferentiated model which can be used to explain *all* sexual phenomena', and the political implications of this, as Housman with his similar model surely realised, is that 'no sexual practices should be outlawed'.

But the positive value of sexual love itself depends on another quality: 'Without chastity it is impossible to maintain the dignity of sexual love'. That this doesn't require rejection of the body and sexual love Ellis illustrates from early Christians, who adopted a form of chastity that was not ascetic but 'possessed the charm of a new sensation, of a delicious freedom, of an unknown adventure'. This in turn had impact on heterosexual gender relations. He tells the story of Thekla whose chastity 'represents the assertion of women's rights'. In general, indeed, 'This early Christian movement of romantic chastity was clearly, in large measure, the result of women against men and marriage'. On its own this might sound like the anti-sexual Social Purity movement but crucially Ellis, always radical and indeed political (Nottingham 1999), emphasises the potential pleasures and varieties of sex. The early Christian chastity enabled access to 'more refined forms of sexual intimacy' (Ellis 1945: 95, 103, 105–106). Here is an instance of what Cocks observes as religion providing a 'location for the expression of unconventional sexuality' and, more specifically in the examples through this section, of 'the language of chivalry, [sic] and spiritual comradeship' in turn-of-the-century writing 'turning tentatively into an explicit vocabulary of sexual desire' (2006: 158, 170).

The language Ellis uses to describe romantic chastity may help explain an aspect of *Prunella* which we have not yet noted. The narrative moves from initial recoil from the body through to conscious choice: 'If you but touch me', she says, 'all I am, you share/For life, or death!' (Housman and Barker 1906: 88). The ensuing embrace is an image neither of 'modesty' nor of lust. And at this moment the dramaturgy requires the light to brighten and birds to sing. The sensual transformation of the environment can be said to have the 'charm of a new sensation'. Rather than easy-going mobilisation of the usual effects to make a happy ending glisten, this seems to be carefully calculated to maintain the precision of focus on a chastity that is romantic. But, as in Ellis' essay, this sexual contact only happens in a mixed gender liaison. While Ellis talked of gaining access to more 'refined' forms of intimacy, Housman felt that the desired expansion of fellow-feeling into 'interplay' of a more 'subtle' kind between people had not yet got there. His difference from Ellis may derive from his thinking about forms of interplay which were as much single as mixed sex. A decade or so after *Prunella* he was planning plays which showed a form of romantic chastity between men.

In late July 1916 he read Barker a new one-act play. Since *Prunella* he'd written *The Chinese Lantern*, based on his fairy story about the relationship between an aspirant young artist and a revered, now dead, painter, to which the dramatisation added a heterosexual love interest. This was followed by a re-working of Aristophanes' comedy about women who go on sexual strike, in *Lysistrata*, and an historical drama about George IV's divorce of Queen Caroline, *Pains and Penalties*, with the sympathy much focussed on a monarch who was not only female but also foreign and hence subject to the hostility of an English state that was both sexist and racist. In the new play which Barker heard that evening in 1916 the focus was now on a man, St Francis. This was an early part of what became *Little Plays of St. Francis*, a series telling the life of the saint from secular hedonist to monk.

Housman was not alone in his interest in this saint. A couple of years before, in an exploration of philanthropy in his book *The Great Society* (1914), Graham Wallas (1858–1932) included in his account the particular love for mankind exhibited by St Francis. It's one moment within a book-length description of the social effects of the industrial and financial order called by economists 'The Great Industry'. Wallas approached his subject as a socialist who had fallen out with the arid and authoritarian technocracy of the Fabians under the influence of the Webbs. For him the prospects of Great Society were dark because it encouraged individualism: 'Men whom we are compelled to trust will continue to prefer the smaller to the larger good'. From this flows an inequitable system the effects of which are seen 'in the slum and the sweating shop, the barracks and the base-hospital'. This made urgent the question of how a proper public spirit can be engendered. It begins with temperament: 'a man conspicuous for Public Spirit will normally start with an unusually sensitive disposition of Love'. That love, in the case of St Francis, 'clearly extended itself into love for non-human forms of life'. And it was a mistake made by the philosopher Comte that he did not realise 'that for one, and perhaps the highest type of religious genius, man as part of a living universe may excite more Love and Reverence than Man as an isolated species' (Wallas 1914: 14–15, 155–56). This could be seen as a variant on Housman's 'fellow-feeling' that is not bound by ideological distinctions between either gender or genus.

Several years before Wallas set St Francis' undiscriminating love as a corrective to the individualism of Great Society another socialist, Ellis, positioned Francis as 'in a very real sense antagonistic to the Church', 'resisting fiercely any attempt of the Church to encroach on the free activity of his personality'. The saint's life-style was a form of 'rational asceticism'. This encompasses love for all sorts of other beings, expressiveness, sexuality and physical enjoyment. For Ellis it was important that Francis' career began as a young man about town immersed in secular pleasures. Rather than deny or repress them, Francis assimilates them to holiness. His 'delight in natural things', his 'profound contempt for luxury and superfluity' were the outcome of 'a beautifully free and excessive life'. 'We can only', argues Ellis, 'attain a fine temperance through a fine freedom, even a fine excess'. Unlike religious asceticism, which is like investing pleasure 'in a heavenly bank which will pay large dividends in another world', 'rational asceticism' is 'sweet' for its own sake and for 'its immediate and visible results in human joy'. Written in the late 1880s Ellis' essay coincided with the Social Purity movement. In that context he used Francis to delineate a form of purity which is not to do with sensual or sexual denial: 'He brings us to a point at which we are enabled to go beyond his own insight, a point at which we may not only see that asceticism is a simple and natural instinct, not alone recognize the beauty of sex in flowers and birds, but in human creatures also, and learn at last that the finest secrets of purity are known only to the man and woman who have mingled the scent of their sweat with the wild thyme' (1940: 86–87, 89, 90, 100). By 1921 he was blunter: 'The functions of sex on the psychic and erotic side are of far greater extension than any act of procreation, they may even exclude it altogether' (1921: 1).

As against denial, rational asceticism is like the love which opposes both modesty and lust. They both belong to a gender system which treats women as property to be used for procreation. That system discounts the enjoyment of bodies for their own sake or for sexual pleasures not dedicated to the job of procreation. Thus modesty and lust each devalue and hate the body. And both play a part in the way that the Great Society privatises and individualises. By contrast rational asceticism has the charm of 'a delicious freedom'. On the one hand, then, in the opposition sketched by these three socialists there is the oppressive, inequitable, individualising system which allows only uxorious sex. On the other hand there is the interplay between human beings which can be described, in its various forms, as fellow-feeling, rational asceticism and sexual love.

All the positives here are gathered up in the figure and meaning of St Francis. In ideological terms this mediaeval saint provided an alternative to contemporary dominant norms, an alternative made vivid in a 1912 dramatic poem by Reginald Buckley. His preface aligns Francis with Arthurian legend which for Buckley had political overtones of race and nation. Francis, he says, regarded his followers as successors to the Apostles and as Grail knights. The image gives campaigning force to Francis' commitment to 'a return to absolute simplicity and poverty, made not only bearable, but delightful, by the sunlight and birdsong'. That effect again… The keynotes of the Franciscan ideal are 'social work and the power of song', and in Francis' song one hears that 'sense of unity of all things, still or moving'. Which is important, 'because all philosophies seem to separate men and women – and even Christianity, through divisions and dissensions, has failed so far to bring to the world a spirit of joy'. So we turn to Francis 'with a new hope'. Buckley here repeats the familiar features of the Franciscan ideal – a sensual or 'rational' asceticism, a fellow-feeling that unites irrespective of differences. But it's his characterisation of that ideal that gives the edge to his argument. 'One might apply to the Franciscan philosophy', he says, 'the Nietzschean term, "a transvaluation of all values." Indeed, I believe that the Nietzschean is often nearer to the ideal of Christian strength than are those who have built upon the sayings of Christ a tyranny of weakness' (1912: 17–22). Francis at this point slides into identity with Wagner's Siegfried, as understood by Buckley, and as such makes heroic challenge to the norms of commercial bourgeois society.

With this set of associations Francis may have appealed to a homosexual socialist who supported the rights of women. The added advantage, much like *Prunella*, was that it bracketed off reference to contemporary society and in particular the city. A range of specifically urban spaces were associated with sex which was improper and criminal. Barns and haylofts presumably escaped scrutiny. Intimacy between men in night-time parks and public toilets was figured as physically sexual in a way which was negative whereas intimacy between a community of artists or monks barely seemed physical, let alone sexual. But here the Francis story becomes interesting. As Ellis insisted it begins with a conventional pleasure-seeking young man. Housman's opening scenes show Francesco revelling, joking, taking bets with friends albeit while developing the consciousness particular to Francis.

After rejecting secular life Francis founds a monastic order. But he nevertheless remains, as Ellis says, outside the Church as institution. In *Brother Elias* the new leader of the order, Elias, scolds Francis for subverting discipline. Juniper, the lovable incompetent 'fool', is ticked off for creating disorder and for giving everything, including the order's treasures, to charity. We have already learnt that he has disobeyed Mother Church by not being afraid of women. In *Sister Death* Elias sequesters the dying Francis within a fortified precinct. The local townspeople gather at the gate, wanting to see Francis and take him home with them. As Francis is dying he asks that the gates be opened. In his final moments the Brothers enter, with the crowd, singing 'De Profundis'. The filling of the stage, and then the expectant silence, recapitulate the dominant attitude in Francis' life, a constant opening of himself to all beings, human or animal, and all objects, even to sin and death. Persistent through these scenes is a contrast between a levelling religion and a hierarchical Church, a contrast that makes the disorderly both legitimate and deeply humane.

The medieval religious story, the brotherhood outside secular society, outside formal institution, allow Housman to portray loving relations between men. In some episodes this simply amounts to therapeutic intimacy where Francis encourages his brothers to speak about their troubles. The supposed 'fool' Juniper, for example, is led to overcome humiliation and brought to a state of bliss by Francis singing with him. More importantly for us here the plays also show men making loving physical contact. In *The Chapter* Leo sits and holds Francis' hand. In *Brother Sin* Juniper asks him if he doesn't love Francis. Leo replies: 'Would God I did not love him so well! For when we worship the creature, then is the Creator not in us!' In his commentary on the plays Barker seems to have thought Housman was chickening out of this one: 'I wish it had been a little clearer in the beginning about Leo's sin' (Bryn Mawr: H.G.B.'s criticisms: 6). Perhaps it is too cagey but there does seem a clear sequence. Francis asks Leo: 'is it not strange that we, children of Love, look upon each other thus through eyes of flesh?' Leo mortified asks: 'where from my heart has gone the love of Christ?' To which Francis: 'Unto mine, Brother'. He then asks Leo to give him his pen and his hand, and, holding both, Francis writes a blessing, 'as thou has blest me' (Housman 1931: 260–61, 265–66). It is very intimate, close physical touching, yet kept within the purpose of the activity. Neither lust nor repressed asceticism this seems to be 'rational asceticism', what Housman called 'fellow-feeling'. Driven by 'amative instinct' fellow-feeling is barely distinguishable from love which is sexual but not necessarily genital. In Barker's image of the repressed male seemingly entered by a female soul and Housman's images of monks holding hands the key element is not the difference between mixed sex and same sex relations as between non-procreative amative instinct and procreative lust.

Here as in *Prunella* and *The Adventure* the staging of ideas about sexual interplay was facilitated by a setting placed well outside social drama. But monks, pierrots and even Homeric heroes are quite straightforward topics compared with one that was both more frequent and potentially more unsettling: fairies. And it is with the assistance of fairies in particular that fantasy plays made their impact on the theatre. So to these we now turn.

Seeing fairies

And find ourselves back again in the Court Theatre. It is Tuesday 27 February 1906. On the stage in front of us a young shepherd called Neanias stands on a heath. He speaks of his embarrassment about being treated as a boy rather than a man because he has never been to town and 'never courted a maid, nor spoken with one of such things as men and maids speak of when they are alone'. His only knowledge of them comes from his female friend Merla, 'a country girl'. But tonight he is on a quest to catch sight of the ladies of the wood.

They will, he says, be sitting in a ring. He will ask them to explain his encounter with a frightened girl who had an open soundless mouth, and then ask them to take him to their dwelling and 'touch me here and there that I may become wise, kiss me and seal my knowledge into me'. He expects that after his courtly eloquence he will be kissed 'lightly on the cheek' and then led into their dance. Afterwards, he doesn't yet know how, he will 'become initiate'. Suddenly at this moment we hear voices from offstage, shouts in the night, coming closer. Earth's Daughters enter, five of them dancing and singing with joined hands, at their centre the frightened dumb girl that shocked Neanias earlier. They sing of the pleasures of the woodland, of the hunt and the dying deer, of washing in the beams of sunlight. After dancing more, they notice Neanias, and drag away the fearful boy.

Things now turn out very different from what he imagined. They sit around him, inspecting his body, noting his blushes. One kisses his cheek, another fondles his smock. A third, Erotion, takes his hand and asks him if he is afraid. She is, she says, 'Warmth of the Earth, and must love furiously'. And specifically 'You I marked out as you tended your master's herds, and desired your young blood to enrich and deepen the dye of it. [...] I would take you between my breasts and teach you understanding'. Rather than courteously kissing his cheek she embraces him full on the lips (Hewlett 1898: 14–32).

This is *Pan and the Young Shepherd*, originally published in 1898. Its author, Maurice Hewlett (1861–1923), was famous for his historical, often medieval, romances. The first of these, *The Forest Lovers*, appeared the same year as *Pan*, and told of the adventures of another young, but more knightly, man, Prosper le Gai, in another strange forest, Morgraunt. But alongside his imagined landscapes Hewlett had an interest in the real countryside of England, and in particular the grim history and conditions of its labourers. His anger about the class system drives a speech delivered to the working men of Leicester on 15 January 1910. He begins by asking them to use their vote to abolish the House of Lords: 'you are being governed by an antiquated, mediaeval, feudal kind of system which every other nation but ours in Europe has discarded'. He then tells them that they have in their hands 'a terrific, paralysing weapon' to win their cause, General Strike. This could be used by the Labour parties of Europe to prevent war. The objective is 'to prevent any money-lender, newspaper owner, or interested politician from sending the flower of our manhood to shameful death or shameful death-dealing' (Hewlett 1910: 302–4). This combination of contemporary politics with an interest in medieval culture is familiar, most famously, from William Morris, and like Morris Hewlett, at least at this point, was a socialist. He also was a regular of the self-consciously modern literary circle around Harold Monro's Poetry Bookshop and a friend of Ezra Pound. In this respect he resembled those that Saler (2001: 15) calls 'medieval modernists', who 'welcomed the new styles in art and associated them with their idealized vision of the Middle Ages'. This range of interests shadows the story of the rural lad we see before us.

After his meeting with Earth's Daughters, Neanias resolves to rescue the dumb frightened girl, Aglaë. He is warned that she is the property of Pan, who has made her dumb. Undeterred Neanias decides to marry her and take her back to his village. One night a sudden ferocious storm threatens the sheep, and Neanias goes out to see to them. In his absence, Aglaë, 'looking out fixedly', herself departs (Hewlett 1898: 87). Both are taken prisoner by Pan. But Neanias' sexually knowledgeable friend Merla, who had really wanted to marry him herself, resolves to find and rescue him. Meeting an old man, who is actually Pan, she shows no fear and stands by her village values. Pan finds the defiant girl attractive. So in return for offering herself as his partner, Merla negotiates the release of both Neanias and Aglaë.

Pan's physical manifestation as old man, together with his power and lechery, provoke a very obvious contrast with the boyish inexperience and idealism of Neanias. The play's title, with its adjective Young, suggests a story of sexual growing up. But in telling this story it asks questions about the nature of the eventual sexual relationship. As against Pan, for whom the song of the world is 'couple, and couple, and couple', Neanias and Aglaë observe a careful restraint with regard to each other's bodies. Early on in their marriage Neanias tells her 'I, your sworn master, scarce dare touch you. There is some sacred solemn thing comes beaming from your quiet eyes'. Recognising that as a shepherd he is a foster-child of mother Earth, he says that 'We were as brother and sister before her, Aglaë, or ever we were man and wife' (Hewlett 1898: 118, 80–81). There are similarities here to the sort of sexual relationship modelled in a previous play co-written and directed by the director of this one, Granville Barker. This time, however, it uses the vocabulary of an explicitly 'fairy' play.

Or, rather, of one variant of the several that might be meant by 'fairy'. Bown (2001: 166–67) says that at this period folklorists were arguing that the decline of belief in fairies was symptomatic of dissolution and alienation of rural community: 'the fairy stands both for the past modernity has lost, and for what that loss means to modernity'. This doesn't really capture what is going on in Hewlett's play. And Hewlett's Daughters are in turn a long way from the fairies who inhabit the garden of young Pinkie and Tony, the main characters in Graham Robertson's *Pinkie and the Fairies*, a musical comedy performed at His Majesty's theatre for the Christmas season 1908. On May Eve, as we discover, Pinkie and Tony and their adolescent guest Molly are invited to attend a ball hosted by the Fairy Queen. This will be an opportunity for much delightful dancing and singing, with star appearances by such persons as Sleeping Beauty. Molly is allowed to go because she can still see fairies even though she is both a town-dweller and on the verge of being adult. This ruse enables the show to shape and purvey its particular sort of pleasure.

Robertson says he conceived the idea of a 'Fairy Play' in order to keep amused a young child in his care, and if *Pinkie* had any aim it was 'to put upon the stage the passing of a day and a night in the life of an imaginative child'. His fairies were those of a child's imagination, derived from picture books and dreams, separate from 'the ballet ladies of pantomime', and no more, and no less, real than the rest of a child's dream world (1945: 310, 314). This unfixable quality is of regular interest, and might have led to interesting results. But Robertson put his goods in the wrong shop. His Majesty's, run by the actor-manager Herbert Beerbohm Tree, specialised in the sale of scenic spectacle, elaborating Shakespearean settings with actually babbling brooks and live rabbits. A play offering a day in the life of a child has entertainment possibilities for all ages, particularly adults, since what it offers is the inhabitable illusion of watching from the supposed position of a child. Within that it includes some distinctly adult experiences and attitudes. The fairies dismiss Molly's interest in shops. Spurning 'Bond Street' and 'St. James's', they sing that 'despite its fascination,/Half the stock is imitation'. The only object that remains consistent is 'the Purse of Fortunatus,/Always full of gold'. Later the Fairy Queen tells Molly that she is 'Too old for a Free Pass to Fairy Land'. These money jokes are surely for an adult audience that knows how to spend its money. So too for an adult audience the fairy songs and dances follow the format of a genre that specialised in the exhibition of attractive bodies, of all sexes. But here there is one crucial difference. Several of the fairies were played by child actors, with the fairy-tale characters played by young women in their early twenties. So adults in the audience were not only able, like children, to see fairies, but the fairies they saw were also children put on display as miniature versions of themselves. The vehicle facilitating that display is often an arch campness. When Pinkie and Tommy appear in fairy clothing Pinkie is of course, being female, of course, delighted. Tommy replies: 'Silly rot, I call it. Men don't care for this sort of thing'; then says to an elf: 'You haven't got a looking-glass anywhere, have you?' (Robertson 1920: 27–28, 66, 61) This isn't just a joke about hidden vanity. It's a joke that invites us to imagine Tommy showing off his body. Tommy was played by a boy of 10. There's a lot of potentially murky desire leaking into those upholstered seats in the stalls. But none of it comes to the surface, for on the surface the fairies, in a wholly different idiom from Hewlett's Pan, have been entrained into musical comedy routines, their gossamer laundered and radiance ironed.

Pinkie's fairies inhabit a world which is marked as consistent with that of the audience while being apparently fanciful and enchanted. Because any sexual pleasure they offer is unacknowledged normative ideas about sex remain in place. By contrast while Hewlett's *Pan* didn't stray too far from assumed norms it worked to make explicit the desires that operate around a vulnerable boy.

The female physical desire, the heroic cynicism of the country girl, the cruelty of phallic power: insofar as the fairy play is a way of staging what might be called sexological discourse, it is a force for the modernising of culture as well as the stage. The *Pinkie* version of fairies works to tidy that force into, so to speak, its closet.

It needs putting that way round, with *Pinkie* as an active intervention, because Hewlett's *Pan* is continuous with a pre-existing use of the fairy tale to speak about relationships and sex. Contemporary with the writing of *Pan* Laurence Housman's 'A Chinese Fairy Tale' tells of a boy who loves art but must only sweep the studio floor. By night he teaches himself to paint. Copying a masterpiece on the wall he wishes its painter could coach him. The elderly painter then appears in his painting and beckons him in for a lesson. Over time the boy's master notices a change in him and resolves to spy on him to find the cause. Seeing the artist come out of a door in the painting he paints bricks over it so that the boy cannot return. But after five years the boy, now grown tall and strong, appears in the painting with his tutor. They make a handsome pair. The master is killed. The boy steps out of the painting, and the painter disappears into it for ever. It's a fulfilment found through a male relationship that cannot be accommodated in the real world. In the hands of another contemporary, 'Prince Alberic and the Snake Lady' (1902) depicted an adolescent boy discovering a sexual attraction that did not fit with, and refused, the model on which his libidinous heterosexual grandfather insisted. At the age of 11 Alberic becomes fixated on an image seen in a tapestry, a snake woman. When it is destroyed because it's old, it's replaced by another, which the boy in rage shreds. His furious grandfather exiles him. In his new dwelling the snake woman appears, materialising at night-fall. The boy falls in love, and, continuing to reject all plans for marriage, is taken back to the court and imprisoned. As in Housman's story the suspect young male is spied on, the snake is destroyed, and he dies. It's a grim narrative about the domination of lustful masculinity and the brutality of enforced sexuality. That sexuality was one which the author, Vernon Lee (1856–1935), herself defied, living openly with her female partner. Against such defiance the job of work done by texts like *Pinkie* is to see to it that snake-women and such are elbowed out of the frame by Sleeping Beauty and Cinderella, whose prettiness and youth are safely secure from melting into something else and thus reliably supply an appropriate object for satisfactorily heterosexual princes of all ages to rescue.

That rescue, unlike the one done by Neanias, is secure enough because, although Cinderella and her mates may be fairy-tale characters, they are themselves safely human. The problems – or indeed pleasures – happen when the interaction is between human and non-human – that's to say, fairy – person. Vernon Lee's story centres on an adolescent boy whose pleasurable fixation on the snake-woman leads him to deviate, fatally, from his grandfather's world. Another version of this model centres, significantly enough, on a young woman. In Yeats' *The Land of Heart's Desire* (1894), dedicated to Florence Farr, a newly married bride sees fairy figures from the mysterious wood outside and defiantly says in front of her mother-in-law: 'Come, faeries, and take me out of this dull house!/Let me have all the freedom I have lost' (Yeats 1969: 61). Later the family bring a fairy child into the house and entertain her. The child invites Mary to go with her to the woods, where we discern dancing figures. Mary volunteers to go, and dies. In a similar way a dramatist influenced by Yeats, Gordon Bottomley, tells in his first play, *The Crier by Night*, of a bond-woman who loves her married master. He doesn't return her love and she imagines persuading the magical Crier to draw him to his death in the storm, after which she will follow. Going out of the house she says: 'I stand outside my keen body, yearning into you as I cry' (Bottomley 1920: 67). Back inside an old man enters. Thereafter the husband is drawn to his death, the bond-woman collapses at the feet of the wife who brutalises her and the old man returns, inviting her to go with him, offering her rest for evermore. It ends with her running out into the night, followed by a scream.

While Lee imagines a young male sexuality finding its pleasures outside lustful normative masculinity Bottomley's play, like Yeats', stages an anxiety about the patriarchal compliance of young women who are amenable to being drawn to somewhere beyond, their domesticity disrupted by desire. Generating an anxiety, rather than pleasure, about deviance, this trope could be said to be normative. But here the staging does its unsettling work. These supernatural entities are the reverse of *Pinkie*'s song and dance fairies. Yeats' fairy girl only dances when the crucifix is removed, with Mary thinking she also hears other feet and pipes. These are not made available for visual consumption. The Crier by Night cannot be conceived hosting a ball at which Sleeping Beauty arrives. These fairy creatures, far from miniaturised humans, operate in a world outside human motivations and logics. The young woman drawn out into the night is not going off to become a prostitute or suffragette. She's going somewhere inscrutably beyond. It's this aspect of the supernatural which is its defining feature, as one of the period's fairy specialists saw it.

In *Lore of Proserpine*, published in 1913, Maurice Hewlett gathered his previous writings on fairies. In relating various stories he raises a question so lightly passed over in *Pinkie*: what is it to see fairies? He himself first sees a fairy when he is 12. It seemed to be a boy his age, and it was slowly killing a rabbit for pleasure. In later life he repeatedly sees an Oread. On the final occasion she has a child with her. Her body is 'sanguine brown', her half-revealed breast 'snowy white', the breast of a maiden not a mother. Her clothing seems to stick to her body. Her eyes, of which he got full sight 'for one throbbing moment', had lashes that were 'long, curving and very dark'. It is noon on a sunny day in the countryside. Other people are at work and only he seems to see the Oread. 'Who knows what his neighbour sees? [...] Every species of us walks separate from the others'. As he watches her he is conscious of being 'blundering, trampling, make-shift man [...] tempted to gauge her by my man-taught balances of right and wrong, and use and wont'. These balances are inapplicable because in the fairy world 'anarchy is the rule', they have no leaders 'and certainly no royal houses'. And they have no sense of Right and Wrong (Hewlett 1913: 116, 123).

Most noticeable of all is that they do not have the human – English late-Victorian – sense of family. A fairy boy at puberty can begin to pair, motivated by liking rather than respect for parents, to whom from this point he has no allegiance. Fairy love 'is a wild and wonderful rapture in all its manifestations, and without regard necessarily to sex'. Hewlett recalls as an example two fair women he saw greet and embrace on Parliament Hill. They look at each other, touch cheeks, then take hands, and then one nestles into the side of the other and rests her head. The 'elder and taller' of the two has face and lips 'like a man's'; the younger is 'a beautiful little creature'. We are dealing here 'with an order of Nature which knows nothing of our shames and qualms', and that has none of the self-consciousness of humans. If, says Hewlett, he were to enlarge on this aspect of his subject, 'I should make my readers call fairies shameful' but for them the concept has no meaning (Hewlett 1913: 44, 125). Invoking the idea of shame in relation to this picture of apparent lesbian sexuality, he simultaneously dismisses it, arguing it is merely a different order of that which is natural.

Humans call fairy activity shameful because humans have been taught a particular sort of morality. As a schoolboy Hewlett says he discovered love was shameful, though he had crushes on other boys. 'Every one of us lives in a guarded house'. Human adults are less likely to see fairies than children or pets, who not only communicate with fairies but do so wordlessly. For the different order of fairies is one to which humans are susceptible where their own moral order is incomplete, beyond formal education, beyond verbal language, beyond uxorious sex. What the 12-year-old Hewlett saw in a wood at dusk was the rabbit's captor repeatedly, rhythmically, squeezing the rabbit's throat: 'I saw its tongue like a pale pink petal of a flower dart out as the pressure drove it. Revolting sight as that would have been to me, witnessed in the world, here, in this dark wood, in this outland presence, it was nothing but curious'. This surely is like seeing another boy masturbating (how dear Reader does one know such things?). And with the sight comes a contract. The rabbit's captor watches the effect on the rabbit, and then, as his 'cruel fingers' do their work, 'he continued to look at me' (Hewlett 1913: 36, 12). The fairy looking at his display being watched. It's in part a story of sexual awakening but also in part a story of an engagement that, despite its moral status, has irresistible fascination. Fairy – or what constitutes fairy – is a way of doing unapproved sex.

Among the various sexual possibilities there is even the most taboo. Hewlett describes seeing a fairy who manifests as a telegraph boy, and walking through various London parks at night. Both the profession and the spaces had associations with male homosexual encounters, but these remain just associations, available only for certain readers. We're not here invited to contemplate male homosexual activity. A more productive opportunity was, however, offered by a rather different fiction. Hewlett's Introduction to *Twelfth Night* (1907: xiii) says it presents 'Shakespeare's favourite notion of having a young woman dress like a young man, and of letting her go far into the logical consequences of the adventure. There is no doubt at all but that the Elizabethans considered that highly romantic; and as perversion is strange, and strangeness pleasurable, very likely it is romantic'. As to our response to it, 'If the notion of maid wooing maid please us, stir us pleasurably, all is said; but I may add that the opposite notion, unless treated with an almost impossible tact, would not please us at all'. Instead of fairies we've got here something equally unreal, and equally present, theatrical fiction. If the fairy world provides an alternate reality in which other sexual possibilities can be imagined, if not wholly named, then so perhaps does a certain sort of theatre. This is the theatre that does its work by embodying romances, creating fantasy.

To exemplify it, let's take our seats again in the theatre, but as we do so having in our head thoughts about fairies and that which lies 'beyond', landscapes which are ideologically outside dominant urban life, beings that demonstrate ways of doing sexuality that are possible only, as yet, in a supposedly unreal world.

It is October 1917 and we're in Wyndham's theatre, a regular commercial venue. As the show opens we find ourselves looking into a dark room at the back of which are French windows. Beyond, the moonlight glimmers on the garden. All is comfortably familiar, except for the quality of that light, and indeed the garden. In his direction for it, as prepared for the printed text, the author says the moonshine has 'left a smile' upon the flowers in the garden, 'but it is a smile with a menace in it for the dwellers in the darkness' (Barrie 1948: 995). This instruction for scenic arrangements works also as a suggestion for a mode of playing. As if not quite centred in the space, as if uncomfortably observed.

It's the opening of J.M. Barrie's *Dear Brutus*. We shall discover that all the characters have been gathered together in a country house for the occasion of Midsummer Eve, but they don't know why they have been selected. Two of the married couples seem to be on the verge of breaking up. Their host is an enigmatic little man called Lob. He has invited them, for their evening's entertainment, to go for a walk in a wood that appears in random places at this time of year. By the end of Act 1 it has materialised in that malign garden just outside the French windows. And one by one they walk out into it.

Act 2 opens with two characters whom we know, Lady Caroline and the butler Matey, but now transformed. They are in different clothes, married and Matey is no longer a butler but a very affluent man. What is strange about this transformation is that in Act 1 we learnt that Matey was once a failed bank clerk and particularly despised by Lady Caroline. Things remain strange with the entry of an unhappy woman, Joanna, looking for her husband, and then an elderly gentleman whistling on a twig and pirouetting as he does so. Caroline and Matey dance off after him, Joanna hides, and Purdie, checking the coast is clear, dances from tree to tree with Mabel. In Act 1, by contrast, Purdie had been unhappily married to Mabel while conducting a secret affair with Joanna. What's going on is that the characters are experiencing the world as they wished it might have been. But this is not necessarily a recipe for happiness. Although the roles of Purdie and his women have changed, the emotional dynamic remains constant. For other characters, the experience in the wood is joyful and fantastical, but all return to their previous selves as, one by one, they step out of the wood into the familiar drawing-room of Act 3.

This fable has been interpreted as proposing that second chances in life are illusory, because in the shaping of a person's life their psychological constitution, their human 'nature', will dictate their mode of behaviour irrespective of circumstances and opportunities. This analysis doesn't quite work for all the characters and it tends to play down the fable's more consistent critique, which is directed at conventional forms of sexual relationship and, in particular, the behaviour of men. The implication is that men will repeat the same behaviour because they have been born, and treated as, men. It's not human nature so much as socially ascribed gender, and its expectations, that are the determinant on behaviour.

This argument is not unusual for Barrie, nor indeed very different from that proposed by much social drama. The particular Barrie touch, initially, is that among these characters who could have walked out of social drama their host, Lob, is much harder to categorise. Physically he is gnome-like, and his age is uncertain. His butler reports him saying that he is all that is left of Merry England, and villagers claim he looked just the same seventy years ago. The guests compare him to Puck, but he is more like Pan, not perhaps as violent as Hewlett's Pan but certainly given to leery laughter. And as host he presides over a world which is potentially as unsettling as a fairy landscape.

The play that begins looking like social drama moves into a magic wood. The dramaturgic slippage between the two is seamless. The characters in the wood speak and dress within the same conventions as they do outside it. They remain recognisable as social types. But the drawing-room is not necessarily more real than the wood, for of course it belongs to Lob, a person of uncertain humanity. So since the play refuses to establish any distinction in authenticity, or importance, between drawing-room and wood what we're faced with is two simultaneously existing alternative realities. This impression is strengthened during the final act. Characters begin to emerge from the wood, now again wearing their formal evening-dress but behaving as they did in the wood. Lob appears to be asleep in his chair, with a leery grin which seems to move around his face. One by one characters experience what feels like a tap on the forehead and start to recognise their surroundings. Lob twitches periodically. Barrie's dramaturgy keeps the dialogue in balance with the silent mime, never quite fixing their relationship, keeping it unsettled. At the very end Lob mysteriously vanishes from the chair and reappears outside the windows cultivating that garden that looks back at the characters, and us. It is now made possible to think that everything we have seen was simply dreamt by Lob.

Potentially ancient and therefore not securely human, what's also interesting about Lob is his name. Within the contemporary process of reappraising the status of rural work and society Lob was created as a positively charged image of the country labourer (Howkins 1996), an alternative to the anciently down-trodden Hodge, whose history Hewlett had published as verse epic the year before (Hewlett 1916). In Barrie's hands, however, any sentimental positivity is subverted. Using the skills of the comic actor Arthur Hatherton, his Lob is the wrong class, hard to categorise, his intentions enigmatic, his gaze at the characters – and possibly us – leery. Not so much the countryman as Pan. Or indeed a playwright.

In the opening speech in the wood, Caroline says that she feels like Rosalind to Matey's Orlando and suggests they pin poems on trees. When Joanna appears she asks whether Matey has seen her husband whom she has lost in the wood. Lob's magic wood is thus put into relationship with the Forest of Arden and the wood outside Athens. It's another place of enchantment but one now self-consciously theatrical. That connection between wood and theatre is underlined in the character of Dearth. In Act 1 he was the drunken and irresponsible husband of an alienated wife. In the wood he becomes the sober, charming, artistic father of Margaret. The role was played by Gerald du Maurier. He came to fame initially in *The Admirable Crichton*, playing Ernest – he of the epigram. By 1917 he was famous for a performance mode which was elegant, light-touch and glamorous. His daughter says people went to his theatre attracted not by the plays but by 'his charm and personality' (Du Maurier 1934: 147). These are not, however, the dominant qualities of the character we meet in Act 1, who enters drunk, bleary-eyed and shaky, in his own word a 'waster'. By contrast in the wood du Maurier was required to play more closely to his expected image at that date. That image then fades away again after he has stepped out of the wood. It is as if it's only in the wood that du Maurier can achieve his properly theatrical presence. This use of the casting, linked to the quotation of Shakespearean mode, implies both the theatrical dimension and the potency of the wood. And in doing so it places in parallel Lob's relation to the wood and Barrie's relation to the play, just as, at a different level – so to speak – Lob's shortness of stature might be seen to mimic Barrie's, dramatist as fairy.

Certainly a theatre that deals in alternate realities functions like fairy land in that it does its work precisely by not imitating social reality. For, as Hewlett said, the distinctive feature of fairies is their resistance to human systems of categorisation, a resistance that questions the operation and viability of assumed beliefs. In this respect, fairies are a bit like children.

Child's play

Now, as Pinkie and Tony would claim, it's only children that can see fairies. This makes them different from grown-ups, who are, of course, constitutionally boring. The pleasure for grown-ups, the show suggests, is not so much seeing fairies as watching children see fairies, producing innocent spectacle, or perhaps spectacular innocence, into which their gazes were indeed boring. But the mechanism only works, only becomes possible, by fetishising the difference between child and adult. It is the production of this difference as a site of pleasure which is the commodity sold by the show.

But in a culture restlessly interested in the mechanics of theatre this pleasure becomes problematised. One instance is a slightly unlikely collaboration between Granville Barker and the artist and writer Dion Calthrop (1878–1937). In 'The Passing of Pierrot' in 1910 Calthrop lamented the loss of the romance of traditional pierrot plays in the face of a depressing 'ultra-modern' realism that deals in social problems. He argued that contemporary drama was bound so tightly by conventions that the only way to reform it was 'to write about children', for 'We need to reinstate Pierrot' (Calthrop 1910: 906). When in 1913 he attempted that reinstatement he did it, oddly enough, with Barker, often regarded as a leading 'ultra-modern'. What they produced, *Harlequinade*, is largely a sentimental history of theatre showing its origins in Greek deities that metamorphose into members of a pierrot troupe which transforms through the centuries to modernity. More interesting is the meta-theatrical frame for which Barker was probably responsible. In front of the curtain sit Alice played by the 25-year-old Cathleen Nesbitt and Uncle Edward. Alice narrates between episodes and during the silent pierrot pantomime. Her Uncle manages the show, not only cueing the start of episodes but also correcting Alice in the delivery of her narrative. Both are part of the show but Alice, despite repeated watchings, still gets engaged by the action and takes delight in the jokes. Her responses enact a regular version of the child. She comments that one character cannot see another 'because he doesn't believe in him' and the epilogue speaks of children seeing pierrots and fairies. Her Uncle, by contrast, remains sufficiently detached to ask for, and get, a beer during the show. Thus far, thus standard. But after one episode Alice wonders if the audience understood it. Her Uncle replies that any child could. 'But', she replies, 'that's the trouble'. They are not children. 'Don't we only wish they were'. Her Uncle looks them over, seems to say 'You take your public as you find 'em', but actually only says 'Alice, get on with your bit' (Calthrop and Barker 1918: 12, 69). This frame seems to allow Barker to rehearse his customary scepticism about audiences, but simultaneously it produces a complex position for the staged child. Alice's childish enthusiasm, as part of a rehearsed entertainment, offers the commodified pleasure of Pinkie seeing fairies. But the energy of her delight breaks the discipline of her rehearsed role. The play makes us conscious of what it's doing while not undervaluing the 'childish' delight that all audiences should acquire.

Harlequinade begins to suggest to us why children were important to the otherwise adult medium of the fantasy play. The child was a dramaturgic device that elaborated and intensified the fantasy-play work which we've already noted. Thus the device might, first, frame and foreground the discourse around sexuality (we watch Alice, for example, commenting on Columbine's relation to the rather slimy Man of the World); second, add an enlarged discourse around play (see Alice's pleasure in that which exceeds the discipline of her role); and, third, catalyse formal innovation (where Alice is a meta-theatrical entity). These three functions of the fantasy play child will be taken in turn.

The importance of children for discussion of sexuality has already been seen in Housman's remarks that a child or child-like adult 'does not wish to copulate'. It is perhaps in this sense that Granville Barker and his lover Helen Huntington described themselves as children (in Shepherd 2021: 255). But the child's sexuality calls into question more than mode of sexual practice. It 'will lavish its demonstrations of affection quite irrespective of sex' (Housman [1917]: 5). This point would be taken up by Eden Paul in *The Sexual Life of the Child* from 1921. The characteristic of the 'undifferentiated stage' of sexuality, he says, is 'the desire which may be indifferently directed towards a homosexual or a heterosexual object'. This was the indifference displayed by Hewlett's fairies. If knowledge concerning this stage were, says Paul, 'more widely diffused' it would contribute to 'breaking down the prevalent cruel attitude towards homosexuality' (Paul 1921: 9). Child sexuality becomes a model for challenging received prejudices about how sex was done and between whom. The staged child's gaze back at the audience is, in this respect, inscrutable.

It's not just their undifferentiated sexuality which supposedly made children different from adults. It was also their capacity for imagination. In 'The Fairy Tale in Education' Greville MacDonald (1856–1944) argued that the fairy tale should be read in school 'if we would have our children saner and happier than ordinary teaching makes them'. Its educational importance is that it communicates 'the individual sense of unity with the world beyond', which in turn is the 'well-spring of imagination'. MacDonald, a doctor who wrote fairy tales as well as books both about children and about medicine, argued that while intellectual training was of course important for 'enterprise' it had to incorporate this sense of a world beyond. If we want to understand the 'true importance of the fairy tale, we must believe that the child', he said, 'has native rights and mysteries'. Born with freedom and contact with the elements these, along with imagination, are educated out of children as they are submitted to 'rule and routine' (1913: 491–93).

A theatrical enactment of this argument became the project of the writing team which made *Prunella*. All that remains of *The Pied Piper* is a scripted first act and scenarios for the other two, but this is enough to show that it tells the familiar story with a new emphasis, marked by its subtitle, *A Municipal Drama*. Hamelin is financially tight-fisted, bureaucratic, internally competitive, harsh on beggars and pleasurably excited by public hangings. Barker told Housman it was a parable: 'Burghers who live too selfishly and luxuriously always attract scavenging parasites'. The only real solution is 'clean plain houses and food' (Bryn Mawr: Tirol 13 May).

In his gaol cell Hans sees a vision of his beloved Geyna surrounded by children in the Happy Land where the Piper has taken them. They sing of building a new Hamelin, 'The song of a new race' (Bryn Mawr PP: Act 3, p. 4). But Hans discovers he can only join them there if he carries with him the disabled boy Nickie. When he arrives, to a stage full of children, he says 'the Piper called him to leave his pride and selfishness and begin again like a little child'. To Geyna's statement that they are not children – for they are of marriageable age – the Piper tells them they are. Barker here advised Housman that the 'business about the spirit of childhood' should be sharpened up (Bryn Mawr: Tirol 13 May). For these children, of all ages, the Piper builds a new town, easily done he says where all are brothers and sisters, or, as Bryan Binns might say, in fellowship. Nickie will be their Councillor and bring 'peace and righteousness'. Having done this the Piper will depart for his major task, 'the cleansing of Great Babylon'. The children begin to enter their new town. The solitary Piper hears 'the clang of factories, the call of newsboys', and leaves. Geyna and Hans wonder where he has gone. But Nickie knows. Pointing into the auditorium he says to the audience: 'It's you he's gone to, you're going to catch it now – hot!' (Bryn Mawr PP: Act 3, pp. 9–12).

In old Hamelin adults discipline and dragoon children, while Geyna secretly tells them stories. This is the opening image of the play and crucial to the authors' politics. The imagination of children is to be encouraged, especially through play. In a piece written for *The Manchester Guardian* in 1917 Barker reflected on the efficacy of play in a story about Cain and Abel. Seeing a cat seize and eat a squirrel they decide to imitate the event themselves, with the eventual upshot that Cain pounces so heavily that Abel bangs his head and cries. Which, as from nowhere, Eve describes as a tragedy (in Shepherd 2021: 22–24). In this parable Barker deviated from the dominant hypothesis that classical Greek drama emerged from sacred rite and dance. But his position was consistent with that of his close friend Barrie, who in his autobiographical novel *Sentimental Tommy* (1897) describes his hero at play. Tommy fully inhabits his role as a Jacobite rebel 'Stroke', among other roles, also fully inhabited, while at the same time stage-managing the game, prompting the cues and lines of his friends: Sir Joseph pauses, forgetting his words, '"Go on," says someone in a whisper. It cannot be Stroke, for his head is brooding on his breast. This mysterious voice haunted all the doings in the Den' (Barrie n.d.: 252). Later, the sympathetic adult Mr McLean realises that to engage Tommy, and break down his hostility, he too has to invent a persona and enter the game. To enter is to agree to the reality of what is played and thereby to allow the play to do real work beyond the play. Which is, of course, not unlike theatre.

Redramatising drama

What we are shown in Tommy's game is that play can – perhaps must – sustain two different realities at once. Tommy is inhabiting it and he critically watches and manages it. It is rather like the presence alongside Alice of her Uncle. Neither is in the pierrot story. The dramatic work they do is to suggest different ways of watching that story. To create space for the notional child's view Barker has used a framing device. He had already tried it out in a collaboration with Elizabeth Robins based on her experiences in Alaska. In the scenario for *The Bowarra—An Artic* [sic] *Fairytale as told by Cecilia*, Cecilia is 22. Her younger siblings are bored with her usual stories so she will tell one in the best way, as theatre, so it begins with them in front of the curtain. The story has as its central character Kaviak, a boy with abilities to speak to the animals around him, which incidentally opens the way for a wonderful dance with up to 22 polar bears. For Barrie, Kaviak's ability is characteristic of a fairy play, where, confronted with impossibilities, 'you conceive yourself in a world in which they are ordinary occurrences, and act accordingly' (Green 1954: 105). Woods move, statues speak. What to me seems crucial about the fantasy play, as opposed to the fairy play as musical comedy, are the shifts between ways of looking and the formal devices that produce such shifts. Both the realistic play and the fairy musical comedy had coherence of form which gave the audience a secure position. That coherence could be unsettled by framing devices, by Hewlett's combinations of lengthy speeches, music and sensuously physical activity, by Housman's saint's life done as a series of gested scenes with large scenic effects, by pierrots who behave as recognisable adults while remaining pierrots, or by the permeability between a recognisable drawing-room and a magic wood. The main proposition about 'fairy', as put explicitly by Hewlett and implied by others, is that there is always something beyond the apparent completeness of human knowledge and experience. The proposed existence of alternative realities, neither superior to the other, requires the production of dramatic devices and dramaturgies that work to relativise assumed norms and dominant values and in doing so redramatise the drama.

Of all these plays one of the most fantastically and formally extreme is also one of the most famous in the English language. An account of it can provide a summary of the various points we have noted, hopefully, through this chapter.

And to that end we find ourselves for positively the last time sitting in a theatre, now December 1904. We are in Charles Frohman's Duke of York's theatre. It is late in the proceedings. A child on stage suddenly turns to us and asks us to clap our hands if we believe in fairies. This is the most famous moment in *Peter Pan*. And as happens with famous texts it is now calcified under layers of interpretation that have sedimented out of a process of almost constant re-stagings. From this state we have to try and recover the effect of that first emergence. As before I shall use the text of the Definitive Edition, being even more aware this time of the number of versions beneath its surface. Symptomatically, its Dedication begins with a confession 'that I have no recollection of having written it' (Barrie 1948: 490).

To begin somewhere simple in a complicated exercise, the story presents three children from a professional-class family being taken to a magical place called the Never Land and then returning. It's the basic dramaturgical structure of Barrie's previous two plays, *Quality Street* and *Crichton*. In the latter an aristocratic household is shipwrecked on an island where a new social order is established among them, only for the original order to resume at their return. In *Peter Pan*, more pessimistically, the alternative setting has only partial transformative effect on the children. They begin the story playing at being parents and in Never Land the boys can enact the part of adventure heroes and patriots, albeit ineffectual ones, in a way very different from their bossy, deceitful, city-clerk father. Their sister, Wendy, on the other hand, assumes the same role that she played in the nursery, mother. Not for her the adventuring of Lady Mary in *Crichton*. While all three children can be seen to be shaped by grown-up ideologies, the gender difference is deeply inscribed. It's a cynical view of children as young adults.

But here's a first complication. Barrie supposedly doesn't do cynical. His contemporary reputation, and since, associated him with sentimentality. Even a critic who admired his craft and inventiveness, Beerbohm, repeatedly castigated Barrie for sentiment. But he's clear about its target: 'Barrie's view of children [...] is very dear to us adults'. It's not accidental, we might observe, that Barrie surnamed the family Darling. Children themselves, Beerbohm says, are highly resistant to sentiment. What is sentimental about children is unattractive to children. Two years later, although still maintaining it was directed at adults, Beerbohm said the play was 'Written ostensibly to amuse children' (1970: 118, 335). This claim was based not so much on anything Barrie said – he didn't – but on the way the marketing machine was positioning it. The theatre box-office, for example, had been turned into Wendy's house. And thus a hare was set running.

The association of *Peter Pan* with children's literature grew steadily stronger and the hare was finally cooked into a literary critical stew, spiced with psychoanalysis, by Jaqueline Rose in 1984. Reminding her readers that it was not written for children she set about analysing it as 'a play for children' (1985: 38; also 99), thereby making a diligent – perhaps appropriately psychoanalytic – account of the very thing it wasn't. Like Beerbohm she couldn't evidence her claim that it was written for children. But she could have shown that it was very unlike the 'fairy' play staged by Barrie's producer Charles Frohman for Christmas 1901, *Bluebell in Fairyland*. Written by Seymour Hicks (1871–1949) it's a musical comedy, with scenic spectacle and dreadful puns. Bluebell, a flower girl – not a young child – is chosen by the fairies to go on a mission to awaken the Sleepy King (played by Hicks). The good fairy summons her by suddenly appearing, courtesy of the stage trap, in her poverty-stricken, and now presumably draughty, room and then leading her out, as one does, through the fireplace to the magic land, accompanied, naturally, by a talking cat. In *Pan* there are no fairies with such powers, no regular dance routines.

Nor is there much of the apparatus of the other genre with which it has become associated, pantomime. Certainly it was done in pantomime season, and it's reasonable to expect, given Barrie's interest in form, that there are connections. But as Tracy Davis (2005) shows the central roles are all perverted away from type. Peter was played by a woman but there is none of the sexuality associated with Principal Boy, instead of the Dame there is Mr Darling's humiliation and the Good Fairy is somewhat bad-tempered and possessive. Indeed back in the day Beerbohm had warned pantomime makers not to be lured into taking *Pan* as a model, because they would forfeit the excitements that children really enjoy.

Barrie's own sense of it was that it was so unlike anything else that he thought it would be a flop. Certainly it wasn't *Bluebell*. But he was nevertheless committed to going ahead with the risky experiment so he offered Frohman a second text on which he could recoup his probable losses. For the producer its challenge was that it was very expensive, requiring a cast of over fifty and complicated scenic effects. Among these the play's signature effect, the flying of the children, depended on technology patented by George Kirby just four years before and now specially adapted. It also required an extensive variety of modes and skills in performance, including competence in unspoken activity. A different challenge came from the play's wilder extension of a characteristic Barrie feature, tonal uncertainty. The Darling household is furnished with customary features of social realism, except that the children's nanny is a dog, a circumstance naturally treated as entirely normal. In the Never Land there are adventures with 'redskins' and pirates, but delivered in language that declares itself as pastiche of boys' fiction. The pirate leader is indeed based on Stevenson's Long John Silver. And the dancing and singing fairy is deconstructed, literally. Tinker Bell is, as Purkiss (2000) rightly says, the only character with anything near adult sexuality. Given a foul mouth, which lives up to her name, her physical fairy body, neither child nor ballet lady, is totally eviscerated. Tinker Bell is light and mirrors, flashing around the stage with all the thrill of a specially created new effect.

These theatrical inventions are doing the work of the narrative voice which Barrie used in the printed version designed for reading. A 'stage direction' tells us that in her exquisitely decorated room Tinker Bell, who lights the space herself, 'has a chandelier for the look of the thing', that last phrase plugging into adult social snobbery. This of course is entirely pointless as a stage direction, since Tinker Bell is merely an effect. Arguably more functional, but still double-edged, is the prescribed tone of voice for Peter's dismissal of the 'redskin' Tiger Lily, which has in it 'a note of finality [...] which is never far from the courteous reception of well-meaning inferiors by born leaders of men' (Barrie 1948: 547, 549), which this time is a more pointed satiric swipe. With this tonal quality *Pan* addresses itself not to children but to social attitudes, especially about children. In one of the most astute – and mercifully witty – analyses, Diane Purkiss suggests that buried in the play is a 'contemporary anxiety about who is minding the children' (2000: 268). By analogy with the preceding play, this useful insight could be taken further. If *Crichton* depicts the household unit and ideas about social order, *Pan* depicts the family unit and ideas about gender order. These, as we shall see, get pretty disorderly.

At the start of the play the Darling children play games about having babies. John notes that after his sister Wendy has been given a baby she has failed to ask the most important question: 'boy or girl'. 'I am so glad to have one at all, I don't care which it is'. 'That is just the difference', he says, 'between gentlemen and ladies'. At the end, at home again, Wendy tells her mother the baby fairies are dropped into the birds' nests and 'all the mauve fairies are boys and the white ones are girls, and there are some colours who don't know what they are' (Barrie

1948: 506, 574). In between these conversations the experience of Never Land has wobbled any simplified binary of gender.

For Wendy things are initially clear. When she gets to the Never Land, she is rapidly constructed into the role of mother to Peter's companions, the Lost Boys. As in *Crichton* the space outside everyday norms produces a new order. This is a family with a mother but not necessarily a father. Although Wendy puts him in the role of father, Peter talks of himself as the boy who won't grow up and certainly can't relate to a woman as a sexual rather than mothering person. When Wendy develops affection for him he claims she is behaving like Tiger Lily: 'there is something or other she wants to be to me, but she says it is not my mother' (Barrie 1948: 550). We should note, in passing, that the name Wendy was invented by Barrie from the mispronunciation of the daughter of a friend, who called him her 'fwendy'. In other words, Wendy is Barrie.

Peter, impervious to female advances, is basically asocial, with little sense of emotional bonds. When Wendy's brothers arrive on the island Peter 'has already forgotten them, as soon maybe he will forget Wendy' (Barrie 1948: 533). He likes killing pirates but will change sides in a conflict for the fun of it. That children were insensitive to, and cynical about, emotion was a view shared by contemporaries such as Beerbohm, who said Barrie was more sentimental than the average child (1970: 335). But that sentiment had invented a child who is partly Pan. Pan, whom we met in Hewlett's play, was one of the most popular mythic figures in contemporary arts (Merivale 1969), including an essay by Barrie's favourite author Stevenson. One of Pan's many versions included a notorious – and sometimes deleted – appearance among Rat and Mole and other fluffy animals of the riverbank, with 'hooked nose between the kindly eyes' 'rippling muscles on the arm' 'the splendid curves of the shaggy limbs', and nestling between his hooves the lost baby otter (Grahame 1983: 245–46). Peter is Pan-like in that he is wilful, potentially violent, and desired by three of the females in the play, but very unPanlike in that he has no notion of them as sexual beings. He himself must never be physically touched by anyone. In these respects Barrie has made him not easy to like, a response compounded by the way he was played by the actress who created the role, Nina Boucicault, which Beerbohm described as 'eerie and emotional' (1970: 337). Wullschläger's claim – not wholly evidenced – that Barrie was cashing in on a fashion for romantic accounts of childhood (1995: 120) has to concede that he does so by evacuating that fashion.

While the household of the Lost Boys was run by a mother and the ambivalent Peter, the adult males on the island are the violent figures of the pirates, whom Barrie wanted costumed in a way which wasn't Gilbert-and-Sullivan comical (Green 1954: 78). Their leader is Captain Hook, named after the claw he has for a hand. If the late Victorian male was still fundamental to the social structure, like a well-bedded concrete slab, this role in particular Barrie destabilised. Hook slides in and out of pastiche. He's a boys' adventure pirate, but also given to Latin phrases and lines with a Shakespearean echo: 'I'll show you now the road to dusty death', and then before throwing himself off the boat declaiming 'Floreat

Etona'. In the first production Barrie gave him a routine, quoting *Bluebell*, where Hook did a set of imitations of star male actors of the time. This conscious theatricality of manner is given a sexual frisson when Barrie has him characterised as foppish. With a 'courtliness' which 'impresses even his victims', 'In dress he apes the dandiacal associated with Charles II'. In short, 'There is a touch of the feminine in Hook, as in all the greatest pirates' (Barrie 1948: 568, 526–27, 541). This element was picked up in the flamboyant costume, designed by the artist William Rothenstein, with its lace cuffs. The actor was Gerald du Maurier, recently famous as the well-meaning inept Ernest in *Crichton*. But Hook was very different: 'That ashen face, those blood-red lips, the long, dank, greasy curls; the sardonic laugh, the maniacal scream, the appalling courtesy of his gestures'. The effect of this foppish feminine pirate was that 'children were sent screaming from the stalls' (Du Maurier 1934: 110). And what made it so shocking was that the very same actor had begun the play as the ineffectual Mr Darling, as it were good father to Hook's bad father, and in each case, both being men, unattractive.

Hook's performance suggests that in formal terms *Pan* is less pantomime and fairy play than melodrama and burlesque, a combination which takes us somewhere different from either. In the boys' fiction world boys fight aggressive adult males and win. In the world of family roles it is more complex, as it were. Barrie brings Hook and Peter physically close when Hook penetrates Peter's hidden house. Peter is asleep, in a posture for which the stage direction is explicit. Peter is lying with one arm out of bed, an arched leg, and the mouth open just enough to show his teeth, 'the little pearls' which he gnashes when angry. He is dreaming of pursuing 'a boy who was never here, nor anywhere: the only boy who could beat him', and the expression on his face 'implies that something heavenly is going on'. Hook's face 'goes green as he glares at the sleeping child' (Barrie 1948: 556–57). The boy's required pose may seem to offer him for visual consumption. The play, says Rose (1985: 98), gives us 'the right to look at the child'. But at what are we looking? In the play-text Barrie's remark about the dream reminds us (and the performer) of Peter's self-absorption and egotism. The on-stage look of Hook is not of curiosity let alone desire. But, perhaps most unsettling of all, was the careful casting. We're not simply looking at a boy here, we're looking at a woman, in middle age. Nina Boucicault was 37. This meant that Peter's body was ten years older than Wendy, eight years older than Mrs Darling, and six years older than the pirate who was glaring at him. Mimesis can sometimes be so convincing that bodily actuality is concealed, but that's not the mode here. Barrie, so careful about casting, could have had a boy play Peter, as for *Pinkie*'s Tony, but chose not.

The complexity of the Peter-Hook relationship is summarised in a stage picture that follows Hook's demise. At the first production, the curtain rose again to reveal a tableau. The freezing of action into pictures, and sometimes imitation of specific paintings, was an old melodrama trick. Here they imitated Orchardson's famous painting of Napoleon. Thus Nina Boucicault as Pan as an oil painting as an old-fashioned stage-effect represents the ancient national arch-enemy

Napoleon. The effect is joyously mimetic, the layers highly ambivalent. To ram it home, after this tableau the curtain must not rise again, says Barrie (1948: 568), 'lest we see him on the poop in Hook's hat and cigars'. Beneath the conflict between boy and adult there is the persistence of what unites them, an always potentially violent masculinity.

The importance of these tonal uncertainties is evidenced by Barrie's efforts to stop the play-text hardening into predictability. Jack (1991) testifies to there being at least twenty different endings. So too there were cuts and additions. The scene of Hook imitating actors went, as did a surely ironic scene of Mothers being auditioned for the Lost Boys, and so too a scene in a park where a man removes a baby from a pram so that he may use it to transport his toy sailing-boat, the baby thereafter being swept up with the rubbish. These were not just changes responding to what worked best. New material such as the scene in the Mermaids' Lagoon shows Barrie carefully managing the new tonal possibilities. Peter and Wendy have been left by the pirates to die on a rock in the lagoon. He says his famous line about dying being 'an awfully big adventure' and Barrie directs 'His eyes glisten – she covers her face, but both are simple – no passion' (LCP/1905/32). Overall then Barrie viewed *Pan* as a work continually being produced, never achieving final shape.

It is in this context that the audience are invited to clap their hands if they believe in fairies. This moment was yet another innovation. Direct address may have been common enough in music halls or in Shakespeare's epilogues, perhaps pantomimes, but not in so to speak straight plays. Jack (1991: 222) quotes Frohman's biographers saying the scene 'registered a whole new and intimate relationship between actress and audience', this alone making the play distinctive. So new was it that the band was primed to lead the clapping. But its problem is not that it was a novelty. Its real problem is that it is a dramaturgic trap. The only way the audience can have a satisfactory happy ending is by displaying their willingness to claim they believe in the palpable fiction of fairies, which, remember, is made particularly difficult in this play by having the fairy both contrary to type and reduced to a mechanical effect. In a way even more brutal than Hankin's provisional endings this device reveals the ideological mechanism of the form. The audience are asked knowingly to participate in a pleasurable deceit. Put another way, they are invited to play.

It has been assumed, from early on, that those who do the clapping are children. For Barrie, as for some of his contemporaries, this category could also include adults. The division between child and adult fetishised in *Pinkie* is, as Barrie saw it, fluid. The adult can participate in child's play. This is clear in his notes on a 'Fairy Play' as summarised by Green (1954: 105): 'The difference between a Fairy Play and a realistic one is that in the former all the characters are really children with a child's outlook on life. This applies to the so-called adults of the story as well'; 'The actors in a fairy play should feel that it is written by a child in deadly earnestness and that they are children playing it in the same spirit'. This is what Beerbohm got wrong when he said that sentiment about children was relatively recent: 'Twenty years ago [...] Children were not regarded as specimens of a race apart' (1970: 119). But it was not about age difference. For Barker, Barrie, Housman among others, 'child' was a subjective and ideological position. An adult who behaves as a child is an adult with imagination. As Jackson put it, 'The people who play are the creators'. To the extent that it gives significance to 'the childlike spirit of the universe', *Peter Pan* is a 'mystery play'. Pan himself is 'the emblem of the mystery of vitality, the thing that is always growing, but never grown'. To be grown-up is to lose 'the impulse to play' (Jackson 1914: 94, 89, 91). Willingly to say in public that you believe in fairies is to agree to play. This doesn't just position you against repression and utilitarian values. It also lines you up with something that is outside the current gender system, beyond human order.

Having arrived again at this point we can look back at *Peter Pan* stripped of the labels of children's play or pantomime and see instead, I think, an early example of one of those texts that came to be recognised as distinctly Modern. Alongside the ideological disruptions we have noted how it presses against and reveals the material constituents and operation of its form, the incorporation of elements from popular and high culture, the texture of pastiche and tonal fragmentation, the efforts to refuse fixity and finality. True it is that children – of all ages – loved it, possibly because what it did was to create children. It did so by drawing them into play. Barrie might well have been worried about it not so much because it was Modern but because it was, in almost every sense, very queer.

That we have lost sight of this Modern, indeed queer, play is symptomatic of the fate of so much of the material with which we have been dealing. A preferred version of the literary canon and cultural history, combined with the operation of the cultural market-place, have effectively buried these diverse attempts at what we might attempt to label with that always mucky term an English theatrical avant-garde.

References

Unpublished

Barker BL: The British Library. Barker, Harley Granville, letters to Helen Huntington. Harley Granville Barker papers

Barker, H. Granville and Robins, Elizabeth *The Bowarra—An Artic Fairytale as Told by Cecilia* The Theatre Museum THM 147/4

Bryn Mawr: Bryn Mawr College Libraries, Laurence Housman papers, Box 2, folders 3.1–2

Bryn Mawr PP: Bryn Mawr College Libraries, Laurence Housman papers, *The Pied Piper: A Municipal Drama*

LCP: The British Library, The Lord Chamberlain's Plays

Published

Armytage, W.H.G. 1968 *Heavens Below: Utopian Experiments in England 1560–1960* London: Routledge

Barker, H. Granville 1916 *Souls on Fifth* Boston: Little, Brown, and Company
Barker, H. Granville 1977 *The Madras House* London: Eyre Methuen
Barrie, J.M. 1948 *The Plays of J.M. Barrie [The Definitive Edition]*, ed. A.E. Wilson London: Hodder and Stoughton
Barrie, J.M. n.d *Sentimental Tommy: The Story of His Boyhood* London: Cassell & Company
Beerbohm, Max 1970 *Last Theatres 1904–1910*, introduced by Rupert Hart-Davis London: Rupert Hart-Davis
Binns, Henry Bryan 1905–1906 *For the Fellowship: A Bundle of Free Rhythms* London: Headley Bros.
Binns, Henry Bryan 1911a *The Adventure: A Romantic Variation on a Homeric Theme* London: A.C. Fifield
Binns, Henry Bryan 1911b *The Great Companions* New York: B.W. Huebsch
Bottomley, Gordon 1920 *King Lear's Wife and Other Plays* London: Constable & Company
Bown, Nicola 2001 *Fairies in Nineteenth-Century Art and Literature* Cambridge: Cambridge University Press
Brady, Sean 2009 *Masculinity and Male Homosexuality in Britain, 1861–1913* Basingstoke: Palgrave Macmillan
Buckley, Reginald R. 1912 *St. Francis: A Troubadour of the Spirit* London: David Nutt
Calthrop, Dion Clayton 1910 'The Passing of Pierrot' *The Fortnightly Review* volume 88: 903–11
Calthrop, Dion Clayton and Barker, H. Granville 1918 *The Harlequinade: An Excursion* Boston: Little, Brown, and Company
Carter, Huntly 1912 *The New Spirit in Drama and Art* London: Frank Palmer
Charlton, Christopher 1985 'Introduction' in Wilhelm J. Rowntree and Henry Bryan Binns (eds) *A History of the Adult School Movement* Nottingham: University of Nottingham Department of Adult Education
Cocks, H.G. 2006 'Religion and Spirituality' in H.G. Cocks and Matt Houlbrook (eds) *Palgrave Advances in the Modern History of Sexuality* Basingstoke: Palgrave Macmillan
Crozier, Ivan 2008 'Introduction' in Havelock Ellis and John Addington Symonds *Sexual Inversion: A Critical Edition* Basingstoke: Palgrave Macmillan
Davis, Tracy C. 2005 '"Do You Believe in Fairies?": The Hiss of Dramatic License' *Theatre Journal* volume 57, number 1: 57–81
Du Maurier, Daphne 1934 *Gerald: A Portrait* London: Victor Gollancz
Ellis, Havelock 1921 *The Play-Function of Sex* London: British Society for the Study of Sex Psychology
Ellis, Havelock 1931 *Studies in the Psychology of Sex: Volume 1* Philadelphia: F.A. Davis
Ellis, Havelock 1940 'St Francis and Others' in *Selected Essays* London: J.M. Dent & Sons
Ellis, Havelock 1945 *Sex in Relation to Society* London: William Heinemann Medical Books
Grahame, Kenneth 1983 *The Wind in the Willows* in *The Penguin Kenneth Grahame* Harmondsworth: Penguin Books
Green, Roger Lancelyn 1954 *Fifty Years of Peter Pan* London: Peter Davies
Hewlett, Maurice 1898 *Pan and the Young Shepherd: A Pastoral* London: John Lane, The Bodley Head:
Hewlett, Maurice 1907 'Introduction' *Twelfth Night: or What You Will* in *The Complete Works of William Shakespeare*, volume 11 New York: George D. Sproul

Hewlett, Maurice 1910 'The Labour Party and the Future' *The Fortnightly Review* volume 87: 299–304
Hewlett, Maurice 1913 *Lore of Proserpine* London: Macmillan & Co.
Hewlett, Maurice 1916 *Song of the Plow: Being the English Chronicle* London: William Heinemann
Hewlett, Maurice 1945 *The Forest Lovers* Harmondsworth: Penguin Books
Hicks, Seymour 1927 *Bluebell in Fairyland: A Musical Dream Play in Two Acts* London: Samuel French
Housman, Laurence 1904 'A Chinese Fairy Tale' in *The Blue Moon* London: John Murray
Housman, Laurence 1908 *The Chinese Lantern* London: Samuel French
Housman, Laurence 1911a *Pains and Penalties: The Defence of Queen Caroline* London: Sidgwick & Jackson
Housman, Laurence [1911b] *The Immoral Effects of Ignorance in Sex Relations* London: Women's Freedom League
Housman, Laurence 1911c *Lysistrata: A Modern Paraphrase from the Greek of Aristophanes* London: The Woman's Press
Housman, Laurence [1917] *The Relation of Fellow-Feeling to Sex* London: British Society for the Study of Sex Psychology
Housman, Laurence 1931 *Little Plays of St. Francis First Series*, with a Preface by H. Granville-Barker London: Sidgwick & Jackson
Housman, Laurence 1937 *The Unexpected Years* London: Jonathan Cape
Housman, Laurence and Barker, H. Granville 1906 *Prunella: Or Love in a Dutch Garden* London: A.H. Bullen
Howkins, Alun 1996 'From Hodge to Lob: Reconstructing the English Farm Labourer, 1870–1914' in Malcolm M. Chase and Ian Dyck (eds) *Living and Learning* Aldershot: Scolar Press
Jack, R.D.S. 1991 *The Road to the Never Land: A Reassessment of J M Barrie's Dramatic Art* Aberdeen: Aberdeen University Press
Jackson, Holbrook 1914 *Southward Ho! And Other Essays* London: J.M. Dent & Sons
Lee, Vernon 2004 *Supernatural Tales: Excursions into Fantasy* London: Peter Owen
MacDonald, Greville 1913 'The Fairy Tale in Education' *The Contemporary Review* volume 103: 492–99
Merivale, Patricia 1969 *Pan the Goat-God: His Myth in Modern Times* Cambridge, MA: Harvard University Press
Nottingham, Chris 1999 *The Pursuit of Serenity: Havelock Ellis and the New Politics* Amsterdam: Amsterdam University Press
Paul, Eden 1921 *The Sexual Life of the Child* London: British Society for the Study of Sex Psychology
Purkiss, Diane 2000 *Troublesome Things: A History of Fairies and Fairy Stories* London: Allen Lane
Robertson, W. Graham 1920 *Pinkie and the Fairies* London: William Heinemann
Robertson, W. Graham 1945 *Time Was* London: Hamish Hamilton
Rose, Jacqueline 1985 *The Case of Peter Pan or The Impossibility of Children's Fiction* Basingstoke: Macmillan
Saler, Michael T. 2001 *The Avant-Garde in Interwar England: Medieval Modernism and the London Underground* Oxford: Oxford University Press
Salmon, Eric 1983 *Granville Barker: A Secret Life* London: Heinemann Educational Books
Shepherd, Simon (ed.) 2021 *The Unknown Granville Barker: Letters to Helen and Other Texts 1915–18* London: Society for Theatre Research

Tosh, John 1999 *A Man's Place: Masculinity and the Middle-Class Home in Victorian England* New Haven: Yale University Press

Wallas, Graham 1914 *The Great Society: A Psychological Analysis* London: Macmillan and Co.

Wullschläger, Jackie 1995 *Inventing Wonderland: The Lives and Fantasies of Lewis Carroll, Edward Lear, J.M. Barrie, Kenneth Grahame and A.A. Milne* London: Methuen

Yeats, W.B. 1969 *The Collected Plays* London: Macmillan

INDEX

Abercrombie, Lascelles 75; *Adder* 74, 75; *Poetry and Contemporary Speech* 80; 'Poetry in Drama' 79–80; on professional actors 81
Achurch, Janet 5
Alexander, George 65
Alma-Tadema, Laurence 36
Anderson, Perry 107–110
Appia, Adolphe 41, 67
Archer, William 9, 13, 33, 113; 'Cinema Supper' 16; on Moore's *Aphrodite* 65
Armstrong, Tim 105
Asche, Oscar 62
Asquith, Cynthia 5, 109
Atkinson, Madge 90–91

Barker, Harley Granville: *Bowarra* 153–154; 'Cinema Supper' 16–18; on drama as communal art 121–122; on everyday acting 16, 18; and Greek plays 49; *Harlequinade* 151; influence on Masefield 84; *Madras House* 13–16, 114, 135, 136; *Marrying of Ann Leete* 1–2, 8–10; *Miracle* 63; and modern European theatre makers 34, 36–38, 40, 117; on origins of theatre 153; *Pied Piper* 152–153; *Prunella* 130–132, 138; Savoy Shakespeares 43, 45, 52; *Secret Life* 18–21; and simple writing 121; *Souls on Fifth* 135–136; on women's suffrage 132

Barrie, J.M.: *Admirable Crichton* 3–4, 10–12; *Alice-Sit-by-the-Fire* 12–13; and Charles Frohman 119; 'Cinema Supper' 16–17, 108; *Dear Brutus* 148–150; *Ibsen's Ghost* 30; *Little Mary* 21; *Pantaloon* 23; *Peter Pan* 12, 154–160; *Punch* 22–23, 33; *Sentimental Tommy* 153; textual revisions 12; *Truth about the Russian Dancers* 24–25; *Wedding Guest* 31
Bax, Arnold 25
Beerbohm, Max 7, 15, 48; on *Peter Pan* 155–158
Binns, Henry Bryan 134; *Adventure* 134–135
Binyon, Laurence 45, 60, 62, 116–117; *Attila* 62, 69; *Ayuli* 88; *Bombastes* 73; on Bridges' *Prometheus* 60–61; *Flight of the Dragon* 88–89; and Oriental art 87; and Pound 87, 90, 119; *Sakuntala* 88
Bishop, Gwendolen 62–63
Bottomley, Gordon 74–76, 121; on *Blast* 117; *Crier by Night* 146; critique of Yeats 92; on *Festspielhaus* 124; *King Lear's Wife* 77–79; on Maeterlinck 36; *Midsummer Eve* 75; on Moore's 'Platonic Marriage' 68; and Oriental art 87–88, 90; on 'personality' performers 82; *Riding to Lithend* 76–77; on sound of verse 83; Theatre of Poetry 79; theory of character 77; on T.S. Eliot 120–121; on verse and music 70, 80–81; on Wilde 126
Boucicault, Nina 157, 158

Boughton, Rutland 41, 70–71, 124
Buckley, Reginald 41, 70–71, 125; *Arthur of Britain* 70, 72; on Nō 92; on St Francis 140; on Temple Theatre 124
Bürger, Peter 25, 44, 105–106, 125

Cabaret 30, 38, 39, 125
Calthrop, Dion 151
Campbell, Mrs Patrick 125
Carr, Comyns 64
Carter, Huntly: as avant-garde 124–125; critique of Shaw 32, 33; on fantasy play 131; on Ibsen 113–114; on the nature of drama 122–123; *New Spirit in Drama and Art* 50, 103–104
censorship, attacks on 5–6, 66, 105, 110, 117, 118
Charrington, Charles 5
Corbin, John 14–15
Court Theatre 37, 40, 63, 130, 142; as avant-garde 110, 126; Barrie and 119; critique by Carter 103, 113
Craig, Edith 61
Craig, Edward Gordon 28–29, 40, 42, 61; and Fascist Party 53; influence on Bottomley 76; influence on designers 43–44, 46, 52; on Poel 48; and Theatre Exhibition 51–52; use of curtain 49
Crane, Walter 5, 61
curtain 49, 91; Moore's use of 68, 82, 92, 94; in Savoy Shakespeares 43, 45

Darrell, Maudi 6
Dramatists' Club 117
Drinkwater, John 66, 74–75; critique of Hankin 7; poetic theatre versus capitalism 83; on rhythm in verse 81
Duke of York's Theatre 5, 119
Du Maurier, Gerald 150, 158

Edwards, Osman 90
Egoist, The 33, 103, 105, 118, 123
Eliot, T.S. 20, 105, 120–121, 124, 126, 127
Ellis, Havelock 137–138, 139–140
Ellis, T.E. 71
Elvey, Maurice 38

Fabian Society 29, 32, 109, 138
Farr, Florence 62–63, 81–82
Field, Michael 126
Fogerty, Elsie 82
Fraser, Claud Lovat 46–48, 50, 106

Frohman, Charles 3, 119, 155–156
Fry, Roger 44–45

George, W.L. 14
Gibson, Wilfrid 74–75
Gray, Terence 52, 79
Greet, Clare 6
Grein, J.T. 1, 14
Guilbert, Yvette 38, 39
Gullan, Marjorie 82

Hagedorn, Karl 90–91
Hankin, St. John 5–8, 11, 29
Hewlett, Maurice 142–143, 146–147, 149, 152, 154
Hicks, Seymour 155
Hobson, J.A. 95, 102–103, 108, 118, 121–122
Housman, Laurence 126, 132; *Bethlehem* 49, 62; on censorship 118; 'Chinese Fairy Tale' 145; 'Immoral Effects of Ignorance in Sex Relations' 132–133, 137; *Little Plays of St Francis* 140–141; *Pied Piper* 152–153; *Prunella* 130–132, 138; 'Relation of Fellow-Feeling to Sex' 133–134, 138, 152
Howard de Walden, Lord 16, 40, 52, 62, 71
Howe, Percy 3–4, 13, 15–16, 32–34
Hynes, Samuel 127

Ibsen, Henrik 22, 28–33, 113
Imagism 89, 105, 107, 108, 110, 119
Independent Theatre 1, 29, 61, 103
Innes, Christopher 111–112, 115
International Theatre Exhibition 50–53

Jackson, Holbrook 13, 21, 63, 106, 109
Jast, Stanley 90–91, 94, 116

Kennedy, Dennis 9, 13, 110, 114, 120, 125
Kingston, Gertrude 125
Komisarjevsky, Theodore 52, 79

Lee, Vernon 145
Levitas, Ben 34, 63, 111
Levy, Oscar 117
Lewis, Wyndham 105, 106, 117–120
Literary Theatre Club/Society 42, 59–63, 64, 66, 69, 111

MacCarthy, Desmond 7, 14, 45, 110
MacDonald, Greville 152
MacGowan, Kenneth 50–51

Maeterlinck, Maurice 34–37, 76
Marsh, Edward 119–120, 125, 126
Masefield, John 83–84, 121; *Faithful* 88–89; *Good Friday* 85–86, 93, 127; and Hill Players 94, 124; *King's Daughter* 94–95; *Nan* 83–84; Oxford Recitations 82; *Philip the King* 84–85, 93; *Pompey* 84; theory of verse drama 86
Masquers, The 61–62
McCarthy, Lillah 37, 84, 125
Meyerhold, Vsevolod 23
Monro, Harold 48, 126, 143
Moore, T. Sturge 60–62, 76, 117, 121, 126; *Aphrodite* 59–60, 61, 65–66; and Appia 67; on biblical drama 66; critique of Yeats 92; *Judith* 67–68; *Marianne* 67; on Masefield's *Good Friday* 93; *Medea* 92–93; *Niobe* 94; and Oriental art 87; 'Platonic Marriage' 68; 'Renovation of the Theatre' 39–40, 60; theory of verse drama 66–67, 70, 80–81, 82
Murray, Gilbert 48, 61, 69, 72, 118

Nairn, Tom 108–9
Nash, Paul 24, 52
Nietzsche, Friedrich 28, 38, 62–63, 72, 140
Nō drama 90–93
Noguchi, Yone 87, 90

Okakura, Kakuzo 88–89
one-act play 36, 76, 77
Orton, Fred 104–105
Ould, Hermon 51–53
Oxford Recitations 79, 82

Paul, Eden 152
Phillips, Stephen 64, 65
Phoenix Society 46
Pilgrim Players 74
Poel, William 48, 50, 74
Pollock, Griselda 104–105
Pound, Ezra 87, 105–106, 124–125, 127, 143; and *Egoist* 103, 105, 118–119; and Nō drama 90, 91
Pye, Sibyl 61, 81
Pye, William Arthur 61, 62, 88

Ransome, Arthur 80
Reburn, Lilian 91
Richards, Grant 5
Ricketts, Charles 41, 60, 62, 118, 125–126; design for *Tintagiles* 37, 49; influence of 43–44, 67; and Literary Theatre Society 42, 46, 62–63; and Oriental art 87–88; 'Stage Decoration' 41–42
Robertson, Graham 143–144
Rodker, John 123
Rothenstein, William 42, 158
Rutherston, Albert 42–44, 45–46, 52

Samuel, Horace 28–29, 37, 38
Schnitzler, Arthur 36–40, 44
Shannon, Charles 41, 60, 87, 118, 125
Sharp, William 6
Shaw, G. Bernard: 'Cinema Supper' 16–17; critiqued by contemporaries 13, 32–33, 113; as Fabian 109; *Heartbreak House* 32; *Misalliance* 13; *Quintessence of Ibsenism* 29, 31–32; in theatre history 33–34, 113–114; *You Never Can Tell* 2
Shaw, Martin 40
Shelving, Paul 47
Sladen-Smith, Frank 90, 116
Stage Society 1–2, 31, 40, 127; as avant-garde 110, 116; critiqued by Carter 103, 113; and Freie Bühne 5; and Literary Theatre Society 63, 93
Stopes, Marie 92
Strindberg, Madame 125
Symbolism 34, 35–36, 39, 61, 91
Symons, Arthur 10, 49, 61

Toole, J.L. 29–30
Tovey, Donald 70
Trevelyan, Robert Calverley 69, 73, 82, 109; *Bride of Dionysus* 69–70; *New Parsifal* 71–73; and Oriental art 88; *Pterodamozels* 73–74

Unicorn Press 116
Unnamed Society, The 90, 116

Verhaeren, Émile 37, 90
Vienna Café 87, 116, 119
Vorticism 105, 118, 119, 120

Wade, Allan 10
Wagner, Richard: Bottomley and 79, 124; in Buckley and Boughton 70–71, 92, 124, 140; Ricketts on 41; in *Secret Life* 20; in Trevelyan's work 70, 71
Waley, Arthur 91
Walkley, A.B. 9, 45, 102
Wallas, Graham 138–139
Wheeler, Christopher 38
Wheeler, Penelope 38, 63, 94

Whelen, Frederick 6
Whitworth, Geoffrey 53
Wijdeveld, Hendrikus Theodorus 51
Wilde, Oscar 3, 41, 63, 116; Bottomley and 75, 126; *Salome* 62, 63, 111, 126
Wilkinson, Norman 44–45, 51, 53, 107; Savoy Shakespeares 45–46, 49
Williams, Raymond: 33–34, 112–117

Williams, Vaughan 37
Wolzogen, Ernst von 38

Yeats, W.B. 61; on Craig 50; on decoration 43; influence on dramatists 76, 84; *Land of Heart's Desire* 145–146; and Nō drama 49, 90–92, 124–125; on representation 61, 64

For Product Safety Concerns and Information please contact our EU representative GPSR@taylorandfrancis.com
Taylor & Francis Verlag GmbH, Kaufingerstraße 24, 80331 München, Germany

www.ingramcontent.com/pod-product-compliance
Lightning Source LLC
Chambersburg PA
CBHW051400290426
44108CB00015B/2095